More Praise for *Getting Ready for College, Careers, and the Common Core*

"This book confirms David Conley's place as America's foremost expert on college and career readiness. It will serve as an invaluable guide to parents, public officials, and educators at all levels who are struggling with these issues. It is a timely and invaluable resource for practitioners."

—Jim Nelson, executive director, AVID

"David Conley provides a comprehensive view of what it takes for the youth of America to be college- and career-ready and relates it to the Common Core State Standards, so educators can easily see how the efforts support each other. Conley not only provides a road map of what will it take to align instruction and assessment to improve college and career readiness for all students in this new era of Common Core, he also addresses important issues of student motivation and ownership of their learning and makes clear that college and career readiness is a long process, which starts in elementary school and involves educators at all levels. The book provides both a high-level understanding of the key issues and also practical, time-tested strategies and tools to help students succeed."

—Betsy Brand, executive director, American Youth Policy Forum

"David Conley's passionate, relentless, and lifelong commitment to college and career readiness is the basis of this thoughtful and actionable book for educators and policymakers who are serious about giving every child a shot at the American dream."

—Barbara Chow, program director, Education Program, The William and Flora Hewlett Foundation

Other Books by David T. Conley

College Knowledge: What It Really Takes for Students to Succeed and What We Can Do to Get Them Ready

College and Career Ready: Helping All Students Succeed Beyond High School

GETTING READY FOR COLLEGE, CAREERS, AND THE COMMON CORE

What Every Educator Needs to Know

David T. Conley

A Wiley Brand

Cover design: JPuda
Cover image © Christopher Futcher/Getty

Published by Jossey-Bass™
A Wiley Brand
One Montgomery Street, Suite 1200, San Francisco, CA 94104-4594—www.josseybass.com

Jossey-Bass books and products are available through most bookstores. To contact Jossey-Bass directly call our Customer Care Department within the U.S. at 800-956-7739, outside the U.S. at 317-572-3986, or fax 317-572-4002.

Wiley publishes in a variety of print and electronic formats and by print-on-demand. Some material included with standard print versions of this book may not be included in e-books or in print-on-demand. If this book refers to media such as a CD or DVD that is not included in the version you purchased, you may download this material at http://booksupport.wiley.com. For more information about Wiley products, visit www.wiley.com.

Library of Congress Cataloging-in-Publication Data

Conley, David T., date
    Getting ready for college, careers, and the common core : what every educator needs to know/David T. Conley. — First edition.
        pages cm
        ISBN 978-1-118-55114-1 (hardback); ISBN 978-1-118-58496-5 (pdf); ISBN 978-1-118-58500-9 (epub)
        Includes index.
        1. Education, Secondary—United States. 2. Education—Curricula—Standards—United States. I. Title.
    LA222.C57   2013
    378.1'610973—dc23

                                                                                2013022219

Printed in the United States of America
FIRST EDITION
HB Printing   10 9 8 7 6 5 4 3 2 1

CONTENTS

Responsibility to Teach the Common Core State Standards? • Understanding Key Areas Related to College and Career Readiness • A Key Role for Elementary School Teachers • The Challenge of the Common Core and College and Career Ready

The Goals of the Consortia Assessments • Characteristics of Each Consortium's Assessment • Preparing for the Consortia Assessments • The Challenge Remaining

Performance Tasks: Key Element in a System of Assessments • How a System of Assessments Addresses a Wider Range of Standards • Moving toward Student Profiles

What Will "Ready" Mean? • A Blurring of the Line between High School and College • The Future of the Common Core State Standards and Consortia Assessments • The Overall Outlook

To Judy. You've been there all along this journey, and I wouldn't be where I am today if you hadn't accompanied me the whole way. Thanks.

PREFACE

Many of you who are students of the topic of college and career readiness or who simply wonder about these sorts of things have asked me what caused me to get into this line of research so long ago and to pursue it over such an extended period of time. It's a fair question, particularly in light of the fact that when I started to think about this in 1991, pretty much no one else was doing so. That was just after the 1989 announcement in Charlottesville, Virginia, by President George H. W. Bush of National Educational Goals, the first call for US schools to adopt high standards for all students. How did I get from that to the notion of college and career readiness, an idea that didn't mature fully as a policy topic until the latter part of the first decade of the twenty-first century? What drives someone to persist with an idea when most others are nowhere near as willing to take it up seriously or to act on it?

The Social Justice Imperative

I'll spare you a psychological profile. Instead, I'll describe some of my thought processes and experiences along the way that caused me to sustain my efforts and activities in this field and take you on a brief tour of the route I followed, how it led me to take up the topic of college and career readiness in the first place, and why I persisted with it.

As those of you who read the foreword to my previous book, *College and Career Ready*, already know, I was first in my family to attend college, partly the result of luck and partly the result of the California Master Plan for Higher Education, which enabled me, after not taking high school seriously enough, to spend two years in a community college transfer program and be accepted at the University of California, Berkeley. I arrived at Berkeley in the late 1960s, a time on that campus of tremendous tumult. A common saying is that if you can remember the sixties, you weren't there. And I must admit that much of the time at Berkeley is a blur, punctuated by memories of political protests, campus unrest, and searing self-examination. I came out the other side of the experience with a deep commitment to social justice, but with an equally deep cynicism about the value of radical political action as the primary means to achieve genuine social change. Education, I came to believe, was the engine and vehicle by which we might address issues of social justice toward the goal of all citizens having the opportunity to fulfill their potential in a society that treats them with dignity and respect.

I spent seven years cofounding, codirecting, teaching in, and administering two public alternative schools dedicated to this proposition. Multicultural and multiracial in nature, with great variation in student socioeconomic status, these two schools had wide latitude to experiment. We engaged in the type of radical redesign and rethinking of education that two decades later policymakers would look to charter schools, academies, and boutique experiments to accomplish. We obviously never completely uncovered the secret formula by which all students from all backgrounds succeed, but I do think we made a positive difference in the lives of the students we served.

Putting Ideas into Practice: Easier Said Than Done

In the process, I learned a tremendous amount about schools and schooling. These were students who had given up on the public schools or, in many cases, vice versa. Most were categorized as failures of one type or another. What was amazing to me was that once I got to know them well, I realized that almost all of them had a talent or interest that was not immediately apparent but could serve as a hook to making them successful. Not all of them were ever going to top out on conventional academic measures, but I came to see that even the most challenged of them had the potential to succeed in life.

We did our best to make that happen, but these young people who faced so many obstacles in their lives needed to be part of the solution as well. The ones who had the greatest success were those who were willing to take some modicum of ownership of their learning and responsibility for their behavior. Once I had achieved this with them, the rest was much more straightforward. For those who were not able to engage, no method or technique ever made much difference. This lesson about the importance of ownership of learning never completely left me. Interestingly and unexpectedly, I had reached the conclusion that the social contract was a two-way street: society has a responsibility to create a level playing field, and individuals have a responsibility to take advantage of it.

 This lesson about the importance of ownership of learning never completely left me.

The next fifteen years were a time for me to cement my professional identity and skills and to transition to teaching adults primarily. Oddly enough, the lessons I learned working with challenging young people paid off with dividends when I started to offer professional development to teachers. No group of students can really hold a candle to a bunch of restless teachers assembled involuntarily for an in-service training.

I recall a class early in my tenure as district staff development coordinator on the topic of Madeline Hunter's essential elements of effective instruction. (Does that name ring a bell for some of you? Her model of effective instruction was ubiquitous throughout the 1980s.) After diligent preparation, including making the coffee for them, I faced thirty or so teachers who were mandated to be there at 4:00 p.m. on a Thursday, intent on getting them excited about teaching to objectives, checking for understanding, and a host of other instructional techniques and strategies.

Predictably, one veteran who sat in the back of the room proceeded to pull out a newspaper and begin reading it, positioning it prominently between me and him (the equivalent of the current practice of texting while someone else is speaking as a way of showing disdain). Having dealt with some pretty tough kids, I knew I needed not to let this challenge go unanswered. But one has to be particularly careful with the feelings of adults, so I continued my presentation without missing a beat while slowly moving across the room until I had placed myself prominently and directly behind the gentleman with the newspaper. Luckily, he got the hint and put the paper away, and I also got to model the classroom management technique of proximity at the same time.

Having some understanding at this point of difficult students and difficult adults, I turned my attention to the exponentially more difficult issue of the educational system while spending two years on special assignment to a state education department, implementing legislation that school superintendents weren't wild about, and then two years as an assistant superintendent in a midsized school district, where I learned the politics of the central office and that I wasn't very interested in them.

The Fork in the Road

At this point, I had twenty years of experience in education and had become restless. I decided to make a career change of sorts. Many of my colleagues had told me in what was ostensibly meant to be a compliment that I didn't exactly fit the typical mold of a school administrator. Knowing I didn't want to be a superintendent, I realized I didn't have much of a career path open to me in school administration. I resolved to take a shot at being a faculty member at a research university. I was determined not to be the kind of educator who enters higher education to tell war stories to neophytes about what it was like to be a teacher or principal. I wanted to be judged by the standards of the university. I was fortunate enough to find a university that shared this vision for my appointment—sort of.

It's very difficult not to be typecast when coming from public schools into almost any college or university that prepares teachers and administrators. Initially I did teach my share of courses in the licensure program and in the process got to work with some outstanding future administrators and just plain great educators. My passion, however, was (and is) the notion that educational policy is a potential tool to promote social justice. This connected me back to my roots in those alternative schools and my time spent on the Berkeley campus.

My passion, however, was the notion that educational policy is a potential tool to promote social justice.

The one thing I have always liked about being a professor is that I can decide how to spend my time on things I deem important, something I couldn't do always as a teacher and certainly not as an administrator. One day soon after my appointment, I made the sixty-mile drive up the road to Salem, the capital of Oregon, to meet with key leaders in the department of education. Timing being everything, it turned out that the legislature was just taking up a sweeping educational reform initiative. Being a professor who had real interests in educational policy and some experience in educational practice put me in a unique category. I was able to contribute to legislation designed to create standards-based education that had the goal of getting the state's students to become the highest achievers in the nation and best-prepared workers in the world. Heady stuff, this.

An Unexpected Turn into College Readiness

Needless to say, implementing a policy is much more challenging than making up something to implement, and a reform of this complexity was certainly no exception. After assisting the state education department with its initial and largely chaotic efforts to translate all of this into practice, I decided to step back a bit and think about where all this was leading. Professors get to ask questions like: If students were expected to meet standards to demonstrate what they know, wouldn't it make sense to start thinking about what they would be doing after high school so that all this demonstrating could be tied to some tangible goal, such as college or careers? Can we really expect students to perform at higher levels without their taking greater ownership of their learning? Those implementing policy often don't have the luxury of stepping back to contemplate the broader implications and unintended consequences of a complex policy.

Life turns on seemingly small events. Soon after, the chancellor's office of the state's higher education system office asked me to take a leave from my faculty role in order to serve as its liaison to the state department of education on matters related to K–12 school reform issues. Initially this meant attending a lot of meetings in the state capital while all those affected by the reform struggled to figure out what to do with its multiple mandates and requirements.

In the forefront was a pressing issue: What would be the purpose of the two new certificates, the certificate of initial mastery and certificate of advanced mastery? Mastery of what? Toward what end? Everyone was far more absorbed with implementing these certificates than to giving much thought to what would happen after students received them. Would they just be ignored by college admissions officers who would continue to look at high school courses taken, grades received, and scores on college admissions tests? It didn't make much sense to me that students would expend tremendous energy to demonstrate higher levels of learning and then not be rewarded for it in any visible way. Where was the incentive to take any ownership?

All the time, it was becoming clearer to me that the two educational systems, K–12 and postsecondary, were not connected in any of the ways necessary for K–12 students to develop the skills they would need in the postsecondary system. The fact that some students did so was perhaps more a testament to their perseverance (and parental support) than it was to systems that support such an outcome.

In this new and relatively unique position as liaison between systems, I had considerable leeway to define how higher education could support certificate-based school reform focused on dramatically improving educational attainment for all students. It was readily apparent to me that if more students reached higher levels of achievement, more would be ready to move on to postsecondary learning and would be more likely to do so. In other words, higher education should be a key constituent and stakeholder in this certificate enterprise. But what could higher education do to support and encourage such a potential outcome? My thought was to start by defining the knowledge and skills students would need to be ready for college and then figure out how to use performance data from their certificates in combination with other sources to determine readiness for admission.

In retrospect, taking this on was a little like Gilligan going on his three-hour cruise. It took seven years to develop and fully field-test a proficiency-based college admission system. It's described in chapter 2. Although the state board of higher education adopted the system, the K–12 department of education never fully integrated it into the certificates, and so it was left for individual school districts to take on that work, which a number did.

Taking Readiness to the National Level

What does one do next after seven years identifying the proficiencies for college success at the state level? Try something like it on the national level, of course. My university president nominated me for a task force being assembled in 2000 by the Association of American Universities. One of its charges was to determine how its members should react to and perhaps support standards-based school reform. Armed with this charge, I organized a work group within the chancellor's office, and we created Standards for Success, also described in more detail later, which led to the first set of comprehensive standards describing what students need to know and be able to do to succeed in US universities. Four years devoted to this work culminated in the publication of the standards, a copy of which was distributed to every high school in the United States.

At this point, I had a clear sense of the enormity of the next step: reshaping the relationship between high schools and colleges to something more like a partnership than that of two neighbors with a high wall between them who communicate only by tossing things over the wall, a particularly unfortunate metaphor if we're talking about students. That quest has continued for a decade, during which time I founded the Educational Policy Improvement Center (with the modest, unassuming acronym of EPIC), which is devoted to achieving the goal of a more rational, seamless educational system designed to enable more students to be ready for successful learning beyond high school.

> At this point, I had a clear sense of the enormity of the next step: reshaping the relationship between high schools and colleges.

How Far Have We Come toward Readiness?

As I prepare to make the transition from my role as CEO of EPIC into the role of chief strategy officer, and also to relinquish my tenure as a professor at the University of Oregon after a twenty-five-year stint in that role, I look back now to see how far we have come. The notion of college and career readiness, while not exactly a household phrase, is nevertheless a prominent and important educational policy issue that has, I believe, developed some amount of staying power. While we are far from resolving all the systems issues needed to create an aligned educational experience for students, we nevertheless have made great strides, first defining better what we mean by "college ready" and then "career ready" (although a healthy debate about precise meanings continues), then by launching an array of programs and strategies to get more students ready for college and careers, and, finally, addressing the policy context within which college and career readiness occurs.

I am not through studying this issue or contributing to solving this complex, multifaceted problem. I am heartened, though, to realize that I am not quite so alone anymore. It is gratifying to see the emergence of a whole new class of researchers, positions in educational agencies, and new groups and organizations focused on the issue and its many components. I hope my initial contributions to the understanding of college and career readiness have helped move along the discussion and improve to some degree educational outcomes for all students, and particularly those in whom I was so invested earlier in my career.

I plan to be contributing to this field for some time to come, and I look forward to continued colleagueship and inspiration from those who now share the challenge with me. We are a long way from refashioning the US educational system into one designed to get all students ready for college and careers, but we have taken a significant step down that road. Let us ensure we do so in a way that is just and fair for all students. Let us celebrate our accomplishments along the way and rededicate ourselves to the challenges that still lie ahead.

This concludes the story of my journey to date. I look forward to hearing the stories of those taking up the torch now and to continue to witness and participate in the evolution of college and career readiness in the United States.

DAVID T. CONLEY
AUGUST 2013
PORTLAND, OREGON

The website accompaniment to this book can be found at www.collegecareerready.org.

ACKNOWLEDGMENTS

It is not possible for me to identify every person who has contributed to the research I conducted at the Educational Policy Improvement Center (EPIC) over the past eleven years and that I summarize at various points in this book. Therefore, I offer a blanket thank-you to all of my colleagues there who have helped develop the body of research that underlies much of what is contained in this book.

Although it's always risky to call out specific people by name when so many have been instrumental in helping to make this book happen, several folks did contribute directly at a level that warrants individual recognition. Lizzie Dunklee has ridden herd on this process and on me in ways that were critical to the completion of the manuscript. She managed the EPIC side of the external review process and also ensured that all of the figures, tables, and the appendix were in order, no small tasks. Brandi Kujala-Peterson contributed in many of these areas as well and offered assistance as needed all along the way. Robyn Conley Downs lent support in numerous ways, including reading an early version of the manuscript and offering suggestions. Mary Seburn was the first to read several early chapters and provided me with encouragement and positive feedback when I was still unsure where the book was headed. Whitney Davis-Molin and Sarah Collins also reviewed an early draft of the manuscript and contributed resources for the Action and Awareness tasks at the end of each chapter, and Karin Klinger prepared many of the illustrations for publication.

I also acknowledge the two anonymous reviewers commissioned by Jossey-Bass and the ten reviewers recruited by EPIC. All offered excellent suggestions, and I have worked diligently to incorporate them. I hope that I have been responsive to their recommendations and ideas. The book is much stronger as a result of the time they took to provide thoughtful critiques.

As always, I extend my gratitude to the professional staff at Jossey-Bass. Although I did not have the pleasure of working directly with Lesley Iura as much on this book as on the two previous books of mine that Jossey-Bass has published, she was nevertheless instrumental in getting me to write this in the first place. Marjorie McAneny has done a stellar job of nudging me along and offering just enough of the kinds of support, encouragement, and communication I needed to keep going.

And, finally, I acknowledge my wife, Judy. I have dedicated the book to her for her unstinting support of me over the entire span of my career. Her unselfishness has allowed me to focus on preparing this manuscript over an extended period of time, and I am truly grateful for her unequivocally positive comments as she read early versions of chapters. I needed both of these kinds of support to be able to stay on this project and see it through to its completion.

THE AUTHOR

David T. Conley is professor of educational policy and leadership and founder and director of the Center for Educational Policy Research at the University of Oregon in Eugene, Oregon. He is also the founder and, for ten years, chief executive officer of the Educational Policy Improvement Center, known more commonly as EPIC. In 2011, he founded CCR Consulting Group, where he serves as president. Both EPIC and CCR Consulting Group are located in Eugene and Portland, Oregon. Through these organizations, Conley conducts research on a range of topics related to college readiness and other key policy issues, with funding provided by grants and contracts from a range of national organizations, states, school districts, and school networks. His line of inquiry focuses on what it takes for students to succeed in postsecondary education.

His previous books on these topics include *College and Career Ready: Helping All Students Succeed Beyond High School* and *College Knowledge: What It Really Takes for Students to Succeed and What We Can Do to Get Them Ready.* He received his BA from the University of California, Berkeley, and master's and doctoral degrees from the University of Colorado, Boulder.

Before joining the University of Oregon faculty, he spent twenty years in public education as a teacher, building-level and central office administrator, and state education department executive. He has authored numerous journal articles, book chapters, and monographs. He regularly serves on technical and advisory panels, including as cochair the Common Core State Standards Validation Committee and as a member of the Smarter Balanced Assessment Consortium Technical Advisory Committee. He is the recipient of both the Innovation in Research Award and the Faculty Excellence Award from the University of Oregon.

GETTING READY FOR COLLEGE, CAREERS, AND THE COMMON CORE

INTRODUCTION

Teachers want students to learn. It's one of the most basic reasons people go into teaching, and it's certainly one of the basic expectations society has of teachers. However, supporting students to learn requires more than presenting information to them. Learning occurs more often, and more deeply, when students understand, retain, and are able to apply and use what they are taught, not just routinely, but in new and novel ways. Getting students to these deeper levels of learning is a key goal of current educational reforms and one toward which most teachers strive, but the path to achieve that end may not always be clear. When students are motivated to learn, when they know that what they are being taught is important, when they can apply what they are learning to their interests and aspirations so that they value what they are being taught, they do a much better job. Under such circumstances, teaching can be a most rewarding undertaking. Absent these conditions, it can be alienating for students, a battle of wills, or worse.

I raise this issue at the beginning of this book because over the past twenty-five years, states and the federal government have worked to define more clearly and explicitly the expectations teachers should have for students by implementing academic content standards. Such standard-setting activities took place in all states between 1990 and 2002. As of spring 2013, forty-five states and the District of Columbia had signed on to the Common Core State Standards, requiring an overhaul of their standards and assessment systems and related supports for districts and schools. Educators are seeking methods, techniques, tools, and materials—in short, solutions—to get students to meet the higher and deeper expectations of the Common Core State Standards. As I illustrate throughout this book, higher student achievement of the type envisioned by the Common Core State Standards is unlikely to occur without students' taking greater ownership of their learning. Even if student test scores go up, such improvements alone are not likely to result in significantly more students being ready for college and careers, because readiness is far more multifaceted than what is captured by a few test scores, a point that I explore in depth throughout this book.

Many young people have accepted the idea that they need to do what they are told if they are to succeed in school and beyond in life. Their parents and other supportive adults have emphasized the importance of academic success, perhaps even obsessed over it. These students affiliate with peer groups in which everyone seems willing to do what they are expected to do to succeed. But in the process of complying with the wishes of adults, many of these young people lose their enthusiasm for learning. They produce just enough work at just a high enough quality level to meet the expectations of their teachers and parents. But they do not necessarily do so with enthusiasm or joy.

Others refuse to comply beyond showing up and following directions as literally as possible. They may not create any problems, but they are clearly marking time toward the day they receive a diploma that in the end may not have much meaning, significance, or value to them. They may not be giving much thought, if any, to what they will do with their lives except in the broadest of terms. It is not that they lack ambition or interests; they simply don't make connections between what they are learning and where they are going beyond high school.

A final group presents its own unique challenges and opportunities. It consists of students who have special needs or face special challenges, particularly those with disabilities and those who are developing their English proficiency. These students are rarely given the chance to show what they can do in the first place and have few, if any, opportunities to shape or own their learning. Interestingly, colleges are witnessing a steady increase in students from these groups, an indication of the latent potential present in these students, as well as a harbinger of the challenges that colleges will face in the future as their numbers grow. Viewing these students as capable of aspiring to postsecondary readiness and success has been the missing first step in getting them to engage more deeply with learning.

I am increasingly convinced that educators are never going to see the types of improvement in student learning that they desire and that policymakers seek if students are not able to take more ownership of their learning and to connect their schooling to their goals and ambitions. The key to achieving this, in my estimation, is for college and career readiness to become the universal focal point for all students. I present a full definition of what I mean by *college and career ready* in chapter 2, but the key concept is that all students need to be ready to succeed in a postsecondary setting in which they can be successful as they pursue their aspirations.

Getting students ready to do so begins by encouraging them from an early age not just to think about college, but also to think about what they want to do with their lives and then make connections between what they are being taught and what they need to do to be ready to pursue any of a range of options after high school. Throughout elementary and secondary school, students will need many more opportunities to learn about the possibilities for their futures—the career pathways, the topics, and the interest areas that can excite and motivate them to take on greater academic challenges. They need to make connections between the academic content they are learning and their goals and aspirations.

The Common Core State Standards, Student Ownership of Learning, and College and Career Readiness

The Common Core State Standards and the assessments being developed by two consortia of states, the Partnership for the Assessment of Readiness for College and Careers (PARCC) and the Smarter Balanced Assessment Consortium, pose a new challenge for US students and their teachers. The key question is whether students can reach the deeper levels of learning and demonstrate mastery on these new, potentially more demanding assessments. More important, if more students achieve the fundamental goal of the Common Core State Standards, will they be ready for college and careers? This is the path down which the states that have adopted the Common Core State Standards now venture. The states outside the Common Core have their own demanding expectations, and most of the content of this book is relevant and useful to educators in those states as well.

The Common Core State Standards and the assessments being developed by PARCC and Smarter Balanced are important focal points and organizers, and a substantial portion of the book is devoted to helping educators think about how to enable students to learn the Common Core State Standards in ways the result in high performance on the consortia assessments. But that is not a book about preparing for those assessments. Its larger purpose is to present and explain a framework around which classrooms, schools, and systems can be organized that enables full alignment with the goal of college and career readiness for all students within a Common Core world.

The Role of Elementary and Secondary Schools

This book is not just about secondary schools or students on the verge of attending college or starting a career. The process of being ready to learn begins much earlier—in preschool, ideally. Many of the principles explored in this book apply to elementary school students and teachers as much as or more than they do to students in secondary school. Attending to the needs of younger students is particularly important because they have the advantage of still being programmed to learn, with a drive to understand the world for the simple joy of doing so. As students mature, they demand more reasons to learn. They need more than an explanation; they need an internal force that reaffirms that what they are doing is important and valuable to them.

The Elementary School as Frame Setter

For elementary school students, most of the content they learn is not necessarily specific to college and career readiness, and it shouldn't be. However, a great deal can be done in the early grades to help students acquire and develop the foundational content knowledge, essential learning skills and strategies, and the frame of mind necessary for success after high school. The following are examples of learning skills and mind-sets that contribute to readiness later on. They are the ability to

- Set goals
- Manage time
- Be aware of personal strengths and weaknesses
- Self-monitoring the quality of their work
- Recognize when help is needed, and then be able to ask for help
- Persist with challenging tasks
- Achieve through effort and not rely solely on aptitude
- Identify and develop personal interests
- Have aspirations that require education beyond high school

In terms of foundational content knowledge, elementary school students can strengthen their literacy skills early so that they can quickly transition from learning to read to reading to learn. They do this in part by mastering academic vocabulary, the language used in the learning process at the secondary and postsecondary levels. Achieving and consolidating fluency in key foundational areas in mathematics is also necessary, along with a deep understanding of scientific principles, the scientific method, and techniques used to collect and analyze information systematically. Grasping the notion of social systems and how they operate, and the general outline and flow of historical events and themes, gives students context for the detailed and specific information to which they will be exposed in their studies of history and social sciences. Cultivating the visual and performing arts encourages creativity, principles of design and expression, the ability to persist with a challenging task, experience with self-assessment, and a greater openness to having one's work or performance critiqued.

In short, elementary school can and should be a time when students are gaining insight into the structure of academic disciplines and ways of knowing that are important in today's knowledge economy. Students should also be developing an appreciation of how other cultures experience and interpret the world so that they understand that learning occurs in many different ways. These general understandings are buttressed by solid content in areas specified in the Common Core State Standards and other core knowledge, which creates a solid foundation on which more advanced studies can be undertaken. These understandings also frame and mediate student identification of potential future interests, one of the keys to increased ownership of learning.

> Elementary school can and should be a time when students are gaining insight into the structure of academic disciplines and ways of knowing that are important in today's knowledge economy.

Secondary School, a Time for Students to Set Aspirations and Define Interests

Secondary school is the time and place where students begin to examine in greater detail areas of interest and where they start to think about their future in more concrete ways. Using the Common Core as a framework, students can conceivably begin to make connections between their interests and aspirations and the specific knowledge and skills they need to be ready for postsecondary programs aligned with their goals. Getting them to make a connection between what they are learning and what they want to do or become is the key to generating greater student ownership of learning and getting them to put in the time, effort, and energy necessary to do the demanding work that the Common Core State Standards require.

Secondary school is also a time when educators can find out a lot more about their students' postsecondary readiness. Students take tests that gauge their content knowledge. However, a lot more information is needed. To get a better sense of their cognitive development, students need challenging assignments and classroom assessments that require deeper engagement and more sophisticated information processing skills. In addition, students can learn to use a variety of learning strategies and techniques effectively and develop attitudes toward learning that enable them to succeed in difficult situations. Finally, schools can gather information on how well students understand and are prepared for the complex process of applying to college, garnering necessary financial aid, coping with the culture of college, and advocating for themselves within large, complex institutional settings.

All of this information needs to be actionable by school site staff, students, and parents. Students need to be able to change their behaviors, add new skills, and eliminate ineffective ones. They need to be able to influence their own destiny by taking affirmative steps to be better prepared for the future they want to create. They need to use available data to internalize a cause-and-effect view of the world, one in which their efforts lead directly to achievement of their goals. And the adults in their lives must use the information to reinforce this behavior and solidify causal notions for students who would otherwise not invest the time and energy necessary to succeed as learners.

Not many school systems or individual schools teach all of this or develop all of these skills. Neither do they gather information on how well students are doing in most of these areas. Furthermore, few elementary and secondary schools have instructional programs that would enable students to use this type of information to become college and career ready more efficiently. While the Common Core State Standards can be a catalyst for better alignment with postsecondary expectations, the challenge remains for schools to design instructional program that directly address the expectations those standards contain in order to improve college and career readiness for all students. This book is about what it will take to do this.

Overview of the Chapters

Chapter 1 begins with a discussion of why college and career readiness for all is now a goal for education and how challenging this goal is. The US economy continues to reinvent itself at a rapid pace. This process is driving changes in the very nature and organization of work that will require new skills but also a new definition of what it means to be ready to succeed in this dynamic environment. Education has a significant impact on economic opportunity and financial well-being for most people. Being career ready is not the same as having a vocational skill or getting a job right out of high school. Schools need to move beyond job training models that have been in place for the past hundred years. The traditional academic core is also being challenged to change and evolve to better meet the needs of all students, not just those going to the most competitive colleges and universities.

Chapter 2 examines the similarities and differences between college readiness and career readiness. The Common Core State Standards say they address both. Some studies suggest that college readiness and career readiness are one and the same, but others point to a more complicated relationship. Understanding student interests is one of the key factors in determining what readiness means for each student. Profiles that connect student performance to student aspirations offer a strategy for thinking about how college ready and career ready individual students are. Readiness exists along a continuum from work ready to life ready, and chapter 2 presents a model for considering various levels of readiness.

Chapter 2 concludes with a comprehensive definition of *college and career readiness* and suggests how this definition can be used to enable more students to focus their high school studies and continue beyond to the postsecondary level.

 Understanding student interests is one of the key factors in determining what readiness means for each student.

Chapter 3 begins with an overview of the four keys to college and career readiness. The four keys offer a larger, more comprehensive framework within which the Common Core's role in helping students become college and career ready can be better understood. The chapter then presents an in-depth description of the first two, key cognitive strategies and key content knowledge, and explores the role they play in helping students master the Common Core State Standards. Key cognitive strategies are the ways in which students approach complex problems or challenging tasks. They are how students process information to gain greater meaning and value from it. They are critical to postsecondary readiness and, increasingly, to success in the workplace. Key content knowledge explores the importance of the mind-set students bring to learning and the ways in which they explain their successes and failures. Rather than presenting additional content, this key assumes that the Common Core is a useful framework for specifying what students need to know.

Chapter 4 continues the exposition of the four keys by introducing the second two factors, key learning skills and techniques and key transition knowledge and skills. The first explains all the important ways of learning students must master to be college and career ready. The second outlines all the privileged knowledge that some groups of people have and use to help their students go to college but that most students lack. These two keys are complex and multidimensional. The key learning skills and techniques reintroduce the notion of student ownership of learning and explore it in more depth in a section devoted to this topic and to all of the subskills that contribute to student ownership. The key techniques are what students need to know how to do as learners if they are to become college and career ready and if they are to do well with the Common Core State Standards—skills such as note taking, time management, and studying. The second half of the chapter is devoted to the key transition knowledge and skills, and it organizes them into five categories:

contextual, procedural, financial, cultural, and personal. These include making the right college choice, applying, financing a postsecondary education, coping with the differences between high school and college, and managing the personal identity issues associated with becoming an independent learner and person.

Chapter 5 introduces the notion of deeper learning. It begins by explaining the knowledge complexity progression continuum, a model of how students use and express the knowledge they are learning. Beginning with declarative knowledge, where students simply state what they know, the continuum proceeds through procedural knowledge, where students apply knowledge in a step-by-step fashion; conditional knowledge, which necessitates students' making decisions about when and where to use specific knowledge and skills; to conceptual knowledge, which is predicated on a deeper understanding of the organization of a subject area. Next, the chapter explores the history and background of deeper learning and offers a definition and rationale for why it is needed now. Four models of deeper learning developed by leading groups in this area describe the similarities and differences in the way each conceives of deeper learning. The chapter offers a definition, explanation, and examples of what it means to teach for deeper learning and identifies specific standards from among the Common Core State Standards that require deeper learning.

Chapter 6 shifts to considering how deeper learning takes place at the classroom level. The deeper learning instructional approach considers learning progressions across grade levels (vertical progressions) and across courses of varying cognitive challenge level at a grade level (horizontal progression). Key knowledge and skills are learned and then repeated and applied in a variety of settings over time to maximize comprehension and recall. Key cognitive strategies need to be practiced at each grade level and across subject areas, leading to the development of the strategic thinking skills necessary in most postsecondary settings and increasingly in the workplace. The challenges of getting deeper learning to take root in classrooms include ensuring that teachers understand how to teach subject matter for deeper learning, developing and implementing the wider range of instructional strategies necessary to support deeper learning, creating a culture in the school that supports deeper learning, and knowing how to assess it. The chapter presents and discusses an example of a scoring guide that illustrates how to do so, and then concludes with a discussion of the relationship between and among deeper learning, the Common Core State Standards, and college and career readiness.

Chapter 7 offers a closer look at the Common Core State Standards in order to get a deeper understanding of where they came from, how they were developed, and how they are different from previous sets of content standards in math and English language arts. While the chapter explores the rationale for and organization of the standards, it pays particular attention to the college- and career-ready level of the Common Core. The structure and organization of the Common Core State Standards are analyzed to ensure that readers truly understand how these standards seek to represent expectations for student learning. The chapter continues with a consideration of what the Common Core State Standards do not do. While the standards do address many key priority areas, they do not contain everything needed for college and career readiness.

Chapter 8 considers the current state of evidence on how well the Common Core State Standards represent the knowledge and skills for college and career readiness. The chapter summarizes research connecting the Common Core State Standards to college and career readiness to establish the validity of the standards as measures of and markers for college and career readiness. Beyond the research lies a series of issues associated with their implementation, including who is responsible to teach them, how current standards and practices should be mapped onto the standards, the balance of informational texts versus literature, the challenge of more writing that the standards pose, the importance of research skills, the role of the speaking and listening standards, the integration of mathematics skills into other subject areas, and the role elementary school teachers can play.

The consortia assessments, PARCC and Smarter Balanced, are the focus of chapter 9, which describes how these assessments differ from one another and the strengths and potential limitations of each. Some of the key issues of which educators should be aware include the level of cognitive challenge to which the assessments will be pitched, the types of items that will be used and how these may be different from what students are used to seeing, the mix between formative and summative components and how these relate to each other, and the types of score reports each test will produce for students and for schools. States need to set performance levels properly so that they are not discouraging students from pursuing postsecondary education. This is a choice between a conjunctive approach, where students are expected to meet all standards at the same level, and a compensatory approach, where higher performance on some standards can compensate to a degree for lower performance on others. Teachers need to know how best to use the formative and interim assessment resources available to them.

Chapter 10 contrasts the idea of a dynamic system of assessments with conventional notions of a static assessment system. Although the consortia assessments may be an important step beyond current state tests, they cannot capture all the information that is necessary or useful to determine college and career readiness completely, nor can they sufficiently inform students on where they stand at any given moment in relation to this large and complex goal. What is needed is a variety of types of assessments that can be arrayed along a continuum that extends from short items that are easy and inexpensive to administer and measure basic and discrete knowledge and skills, to tasks that are completed in class and capture information on more complex uses of acquired knowledge but take more time and are potentially more costly to score, to tasks that are really more like projects and may extend over most of an academic term. This continuum is likely to yield greater insight into knowledge acquired and create an opportunity to apply that knowledge in ways that demonstrate in greater depth readiness for college and careers. The ultimate result of a system of assessments is more like a profile of student knowledge, skills, attitudes, and strategies rather than a single score. A profile approach can combine scores from Common Core assessments, grade point average, college admissions tests, and other evidence such as student papers and projects, teacher and student reports on student behavior, and other accomplishments. Such a profile can help students know better what they need to do next because the profile can be linked to the aspirations and futures these students are pursuing. Profiles of this nature hold the key to revolutionizing teaching and learning, particularly when tied to competency-based education.

Chapter 11 offers a glimpse into what may lie ahead for the Common Core State Standards and for college and career readiness, which is likely to look different in the future. Increasing amounts and types of data will transform what is known about readiness, and competency models of learning and assessment will allow more valid and complex demonstrations of readiness. Online learning will offer opportunities and pose challenges to demonstrating competency and will advantage learners who know how to take ownership of their learning. Students will be earning more college credit in high school, which will continue to blur the line between high school and college. The future of the Common Core State Standards and consortia assessments is unclear at present. The amount of support they are able to garner for their implementation and institutionalization over the next few years will be critical and may come from an unlikely combination of people and organizations. Many issues remain unresolved regarding where the Common Core State Standards will reside and how and when the standards will first be revised. A similar but more complex set of issues exists for the consortia assessments as well. Thoughts on these are tendered without necessarily offering complete solutions.

The conclusion of the book lays out some of the challenges of raising standards for all students and setting postsecondary readiness as the goal for more students. The changing demographics of the US student population will become an increasingly significant factor that schools will need to address. This phenomenon will also heighten the need to get more students college and career ready and the challenge in doing so. The book concludes with a reminder of the importance of quality instruction that engages students and how the reforms of the Common Core State Standards can help reinvigorate teaching and teachers.

The appendix outlines a readiness system that schools can use to improve alignment with college and career readiness. Organized into three groupings, the system can help educators collect more and better information about readiness, align instruction to focus on key readiness factors, and improve understanding and communication between secondary and postsecondary faculty. Most of these will already have been referenced in the body of the text and are included here for easy access. More information is available on the website that accompanies the book, found at www .collegecareerready.org.

Using This Book to Support Implementation of the Common Core State Standards

The measure of success for this book is the degree to which readers will be able to act as a result of what they have read. The book suggests actions that educators can take individually in the classroom, collectively at the school level, and systemically at the district, state, and national levels to implement the Common Core State Standards and use the consortia assessments in ways that lead to more students ready for college and careers. Although this is the stated goal of the Common Core State Standards, it will be very easy for schools to become distracted from this goal and end up focused on test scores and whatever accountability measures that states or the federal government enact. The book is designed to be a reminder that there is more to it than just doing well on tests of the Common Core State Standards. College and career readiness is complex and multifaceted and will require schools to go well beyond the Common Core State Standards and consortia assessments to achieve this goal for most students. This book is designed to help educators to achieve this larger goal and to use the Common Core State Standards as an important means to do so.

> The book is designed to be a reminder that there is more to it than just doing well on tests of the Common Core State Standards.

Design of the Book

This book is written with elementary and secondary school practitioners in mind, although much of what is covered will be of interest as well to those who shape, make, implement, and critique educational policy, along with a range of postsecondary faculty and administrators. The emphasis is on readability and usability. For that reason, I have chosen not to use in-text citations or footnotes. I will provide on the accompanying website fuller information about research and evidence that is referenced in the book. For the most part, the intent is not for this book to be a review of the literature but to draw on well-established findings, including research my colleagues and I have conducted on this subject over the past fifteen years, along with evidence from practice in order to frame a specific set of issues around college and career readiness and the Common Core State Standards.

Many of the observations I make and conclusions I offer have far-reaching implications for schooling. It is not therefore possible to present and explore recommendations or offer detailed specifications for every aspect of practice that might be affected or in need of change. Some illustrations and examples are included within the body of the text.

I have also avoided listing exemplary school sites, although I did so in my previous book. I do this now for a variety of reasons. The phenomena of Common Core implementation and of college and career readiness are multidimensional and require attention to a wide range of learning variables and numerous educational practices and programs. Few schools have yet reached the point where they are addressing all of these successfully, and it can be misleading to label a school as being a model for achieving college and career readiness for its students when it is doing only some of what is necessary, and doing it for only some of its students. Visitors to such schools often leave with the observation that the school has as many problems as their own school, and they can miss some of the key differences for which lessons can be learned. Just as often, a school that is listed in a book as exemplary sees a change in leadership at the building or district level and soon no longer demonstrates the exemplary characteristics for which it received accolades even very recently. And while it is useful to see an interesting or innovative program in action, this is not a substitute for a deeper understanding of the full set of issues that must be addressed to make the changes necessary for the Common Core State Standards to have a transformative effect in a school. For these reasons and others, I do not identify individual schools or programs. I will, however, list information about exemplary sites and programs on the website while repeating the caveats I note here and encouraging educators to use exemplary sites as resources, not solutions.

I have included at the conclusion of each chapter a section entitled "Awareness and Action Steps." These are largely suggested activities and useful resources to help deepen understanding of the issues laid out in this book. They are not intended to substitute for a detailed plan to improve college and career readiness or the Common Core. Some schools may wish to begin with awareness activities before plunging into action steps; others may be ready to move forward to improve college and career readiness by taking action now.

These awareness and action steps are included without a specific recommended sequence of use based on the principle, validated by the research on innovation implementation, that every change occurs within the unique context of a school, and even a classroom, and that some actions will make more sense in some schools than in others. Getting to action often requires passing through awareness, and I include many strategies for thoughtful reflection, understanding, and planning, all necessary prerequisites to action. The suggestions and resources are designed to help schools undertake the manifold actions necessary to help more students become ready for college and careers in the context of the Common Core State Standards and their attendant assessments.

Similarly, when it comes to specific resources for implementing the Common Core State Standards, numerous organizations and vendors have moved to fill the breach. Information on these resources changes rapidly. Therefore, I will offer regularly updated links to key sites on the website that accompanies this book. I am also confident that diligent readers will likely already have begun the process of seeking resources relevant to local efforts to implement the standards and that what I offer here will, I hope, be supplemental.

I do offer some suggestions about specific tools and techniques in the appendix, but I consider these to be illustrative examples more than definitive solutions. I include these materials to demonstrate how a more systems-type approach to college and career readiness in the context of the Common Core State Standards will be more effective than simply adopting new curriculum materials and conducting training on how to implement the standards.

What the Book Is Not About

Although I want this book to inform action at all levels of the educational system, and I include many examples and illustrations throughout the text in addition to those provided in the Awareness and Action Steps, and I have described some specific tools in the appendix, this is for the most part not a how-to book. I have grappled with this because I'm well aware that teachers and administrators want to know what to do and not just what the issues are. I ask for your patience and for you to keep an open mind as you read the book. Although I do not present a one-size-fits-all set of solutions for improving college and career readiness, implementing the Common Core State Standards, and doing well on the consortia assessments, I do offer many ideas and suggestions that can be adapted to specific educational contexts and environments. I also plan to identify more resources on the website that accompanies the book. The goal is to help you gain greater insight into the big-picture issues surrounding college and career readiness and the Common Core State Standards so that any decisions you make and actions you take will be informed by this deeper understanding of what you are trying to accomplish, and why.

This is not a book about postsecondary reform or reinvention generally, although chapter 11 touches briefly on some of these issues in their broadest form. It's important to emphasize that the thesis presented here about aligning secondary schools to postsecondary education is not that college teaching is all good and high school teaching is all bad, or that high school teaching just needs to be more like college teaching. Quite the contrary. Each level has its own driving prerogatives, in no small measure influenced by the nature of the students served and student willingness to own their learning. Each level can and must learn from the other, even as each engages in what promises to be tectonic shifts in how education is delivered. This book is about how the changes that will and must occur at the K–12 and postsecondary levels can lead to greater student ownership of learning and control over their lives and futures. In the final analysis, little is certain about the future except that young people will need to be far more active participants in creating their own destinies.

> Little is certain about the future except that young people will need to be far more active participants in creating their own destinies.

While this book does mention at various points the needs of special groups of learners, it does not substitute for a full exposition of the programs and strategies that best serve these students toward the goal of more of them being college and career ready. This is not out of lack of concern or interest, but largely due to issues of space combined with the fact that I believe that much of what is discussed in this book applies to all students. On this topic as well, I offer resources online that may help readers with interests in specific groups of students find help, ideas, and strategies that address specific types of special learning needs.

Finally, this book does not touch on the larger question of teacher preparation even though I have been encouraged by some of the reviewers to do so. My reason, once again, is that this topic deserves a volume in its own right. I cannot address this sprawling systemic issue sufficiently within the confines of this book, nor do I necessarily consider myself sufficiently expert in this area to offer much in the way of solutions. It is a critically important issue and one to which others with greater experience and more dedication are sure to make better contributions than could I.

What This Book Is About

This is the third book I've written on the topic of readiness for college and careers. The first two, *College Knowledge: What It Really Takes for Students to Succeed and What We Can Do to Get Them Ready*, and *College and Career Ready: Helping All Students Succeed Beyond High School*, set the stage for this publication. During the past twenty years, I've researched and written a lot about this topic, but I consider this book to be a culmination of sorts of my studies in this area. In it, I present not just research findings and conceptual models that I have derived from my research, but also suggestions for techniques and strategies to get more students ready to make a successful transition to learning and life after high school.

I include more of my own voice in this book than I have in previous works. By this I do not mean my opinions necessarily, but my interpretation of what readers might want to take away from the book. Those of you who have worked with me or heard me speak know that I have a tendency to challenge conventional wisdom. I do that from time to time in this book, which will no doubt cause some to find it provocative and others to find it wrongheaded or just annoying, which I think is entirely healthy. It's fine with me if you don't agree with all I have to say as long as it causes you to think and reflect on your knowledge and assumptions about the topics I explore here. I'm hoping you'll find an insight, idea, or observation that perhaps causes you to question some of what you think and believe currently. For those of you who find yourself in substantial agreement with my point of view, I hope you find the models, frameworks, definitions, concepts, and ideas I present to be useful as you pursue the goal of improved college and career readiness for all students, particularly in the context of the Common Core State Standards.

While I believe the Common Core State Standards are a step in the right direction, they are not without their faults and issues, and I critique elements of them at various points. This hardly means I believe they should be rejected, but it does mean that clear thinking about how to improve them will be necessary if they are to be the guiding light for schools in the states that have adopted them, especially if they are identified as the standards that specify college and career readiness in these states. At points, I am descriptive, while in other places I adopt a more analytical tone. This can be troubling to those looking for unadulterated support or unstinting criticism. I seek for the most part to avoid telling anyone how to think while still laying out my own perspective.

Is this book about college and career readiness or about the Common Core State Standards? It's about both, at least to the degree that the Common Core is a potential means to improve student readiness for college and careers. I don't intend to duplicate or compete with any of the high-quality resources available to describe the Common Core State Standards and how to teach to specific standards or topics contained in those standards.

Who, then, is the ideal reader for this book? Really, it's anyone who wants to understand better what it is going to take to make more students college and career ready in the era of the Common Core State Standards. I intend for a wide range of educators, policymakers, and perhaps even interested parents and others to be able to take a lot away from this book. I hope school administrators gain insight into how their school can be organized to promote the Common Core as a means to college and career readiness. I hope policymakers are able to see how they need to nurture the Common Core and not use it for inappropriate purposes or expect it to be more than it is. I hope teachers and everyone else working on the front lines of education are able to take away some ideas about what to change in the classroom tomorrow, next semester, and next school year. I hope this helps put the Common Core in perspective and maybe even create some excitement about what is possible if and when the Common Core is implemented.

In the final analysis, the Common Core State Standards are not merely about content knowledge acquisition, or at least they shouldn't be. They are about students' acquiring a set of skills that enable them to be successful learners beyond high school and to take progressively greater charge of their learning as they move through the educational system. Self-motivated, self-managing students equipped with solid academic skills are going to be the best prepared for the uncertain and turbulent world in which they will spend their adult lives. The education system, K–12 and postsecondary, must be designed to enable them to achieve this goal. The Common Core is an important step in that direction, but it should be implemented not as an end in and of itself, but with its broader goal of getting students college and career ready always in mind.

CHAPTER 1

THE NEW CHALLENGE: ALL STUDENTS COLLEGE AND CAREER READY

The Common Core State Standards are designed to culminate at the level of college and career readiness, a lofty expectation given that as recently as the mid-1970s, fewer than half of high school graduates went on to college directly from high school, and many of them did not last long once there. Since then, the percentage of high school graduates making an immediate transition to community college has increased by 9 percentage points, from 18 to 27 percent, while the percent going to a four-year institution has gone up by 8 points, from 33 to 41 percent. This represents a 50 percent increase in students going directly to community college and a 25 percent increase for those going to four-year colleges.

Taken together, these figures tell us that high school graduates increasingly view a postsecondary education as their best option after high school, whether they wish to pursue a career or a college degree. However, among those who attend, a significant proportion, in the range of 40 percent or more, must take remedial courses initially. Many still drop out during the first year or don't continue to a second year. More students may be going to college, but this does not necessarily mean that more students are *ready* for college. This represents a new challenge to high schools, which were never designed to prepare the vast majority of students to be ready for postsecondary success.

This chapter seeks to address these challenges by asking what it means in the era of the Common Core State Standards to expect all students to be college and career ready. Why is this a worthwhile goal, and how will this goal affect high schools that have historically sorted students? And how has the development of college readiness standards over the past decade set the stage for a better understanding of college readiness?

Why College and Career Readiness for All?

The answers to these and related questions posed and discussed in this chapter have far-reaching implications for how US secondary schools are organized and how they educate students. The ways in which schools respond to them will have a profound effect not only on students, but on the economic and social future of the nation as a whole. Increasingly education is the key to social mobility and economic survival in a rapidly and continuously changing economy, particularly for young people who are not born into backgrounds of privilege.

A high school diploma has been touted for decades as the goal all students should pursue, but evidence suggests that achieving the diploma may no longer be a sufficiently high expectation. The academic skill level many diploma recipients achieve may not be adequate to qualify them for many of the careers and occupations emerging in the new economy. In fact, being able to get an entry-level job is not enough; having the skill level to start work today will likely not be enough to retain a job for life, take advantage of new opportunities, or cope with changes in the economy.

Success in the future will be much more a function not simply of what people have learned but of what they are capable of learning. Schooling will truly need to be about enabling students to learn throughout their careers. Creating lifelong learners, a cliché that has been used often and carelessly by many, will become an increasingly critical and compelling goal of education. It's not at all clear what today's students will need to know throughout their lives, but it is likely that they will not be learning in school today much of what will be important to success over the course of their careers.

The Changing US Economy and the Changing Nature of Work

While schools have struggled to adapt to the changing needs of the workforce, the US economy has continued to evolve dynamically, having undergone a transformation over the past century that can only be described as remarkable and unprecedented by any measure. Farming, manufacturing, clerical, and middle management jobs have declined dramatically as service-related occupations and professional careers have increased in an equally dramatic fashion. Where manufacturing and farming in 1900 together were something on the order of 70 percent of US jobs, these activities occupied about 13 percent of the labor force by the end of the twentieth century. Between 1950 and 2000 alone, manufacturing jobs decreased from well over 30 percent to around 9 percent of all employment. This rapid shift in the structure and composition of the economy sent shock waves through the workforce as jobs that required highly specialized skills or repetitive manual labor disappeared overnight, to be replaced by occupations for which the displaced workers were entirely unprepared and generally ill suited. Entirely new categories of work have rapidly emerged with the shift from agricultural and industrial jobs to service jobs. Knowledge workers and the creative class have become increasingly prevalent in the workforce.

Take one small example from Lane County, Oregon, the home of the University of Oregon but also a county that, if it were a state, would fall between Delaware and Connecticut in area. The economy of Lane County had been largely dependent on timber extraction and lumber milling until the 1990s, when logging in federal forests was effectively shut down. Fortuitously, the luxury RV business grew rapidly in Lane County during the 1990s and early 2000s. Many timber workers made the transition from logging to assembling the RVs through retraining programs that helped them learn skills in the trades as well as the use of technical manuals, wiring schematics, and other complex informational texts that hadn't been a part of the timber industry.

Unfortunately for all of those workers who had survived one massive economic shift, the bottom fell out of the luxury RV industry less than ten years later in the mid-2000s, as first the cost of fuel skyrocketed and then the economy as a whole came unhinged. Almost overnight, nearly all of the five thousand jobs in this industry disappeared as manufacturers either went bankrupt or cut back to skeleton crews. Worse yet, the remaining companies consolidated and centralized their operations elsewhere in the country, which meant that the thriving after-market industry that had sprung up around providing attractive and expensive options to these customized RVs also evaporated. Another industry that did not require high levels of formal schooling disappeared in the space of just eighteen months.

Lane County did see a rapid increase in employment opportunities around this same time, though. Some of the jobs were in the client support, or call center, sector. Others were at high-tech fabrication plants. Companies such as Enterprise Car Rental and Royal Caribbean Cruise Lines established major centers and hired entry-level employees and managers. Sony Disc Manufacturing and Hynix opened high tech production plants in the county. The only catch was that the prerequisite skills required for entry-level employment at these companies included the ability to use technology and computers; read and interpret manuals and rapidly changing schedules; keep pace with new product and production lines; solve problems creatively and patiently with a strong customer orientation, often as a member of a team; speak clearly and concisely and listen carefully; and be prepared to adapt on short notice to new company priorities. Nothing from their previous work experience prepared former timber workers or RV assemblers for this type of knowledge-intensive, dynamically changing workplace. While the local community hastily instituted training programs for call center workers, these were beyond the reach of those who lacked prior experience with computers, who had difficulty with a range of written material, whose communication skills were not strong and well developed, and for whom teamwork meant not getting in the way of or in a fight with a fellow worker.

Variations on this story have played out around almost every part of the United States during the past two decades. The story illustrates the painful truth that the skills needed to be successful in this new economy are fundamentally different from those that the old economy required. Increasingly important are skills such as the following:

- Foundational academic knowledge and the ability to apply knowledge
- Communication capabilities in reading and writing and, increasingly, speaking and listening
- Technology proficiency
- Problem-solving strategies
- Flexibility, initiative, and adaptability

This dramatically shifting set of expectations has signaled the obsolescence of the previously well-established and fundamental distinction between what should be taught to students planning to attend college versus those who plan to enter the workforce immediately.

Economic Impact of Education

Most educators and many students are familiar with studies showing the increase in earnings over a lifetime based on a person's level of formal education. These studies find in general that workers without a high school diploma earn by far the least; those with a diploma and even with a little college earn marginally more; those with two-year certificates do substantially better; and those with bachelor's degrees or better fare the best of all. Of course, some of this has to do with the economic class in which a person starts out initially and the difficulty of moving up the economic class ladder generally, but the fact that success is tougher for those who start from a lower economic level only strengthens the argument for more education as a means to overcome initial socioeconomic status. The United States offers far more opportunity for social mobility than many other countries. Unfortunately, the country is also among the most polarized in wealth distribution, a trend that is increasing. Economic mobility for those who do not already have money is linked increasingly to education and the ability to acquire new skills and certifications over the course of a career. The economic gap between the skilled and the unskilled is growing. The era of succeeding with little formal education and lots of hard work is pretty much over.

> The era of succeeding with little formal education and lots of hard work is pretty much over.

The evidence of the effect on employment status is demonstrated most clearly and dramatically in data on job loss and creation during the Great Recession and the tepid recovery period that followed. The trends identified in a report prepared by the Center on Education and the Workforce at the Georgetown Public Policy Institute are striking. Between December 2007, when the downturn began in earnest, and January 2010, when it was declared to be over, people with bachelor's degrees or better actually gained 187,000 jobs. During the recovery period from January 2010 through February 2012, this same group saw their employment numbers grow by an additional 2 million jobs. Those with an associate degree or

FIGURE 1.1 EMPLOYMENT CHANGES DURING THE RECESSION

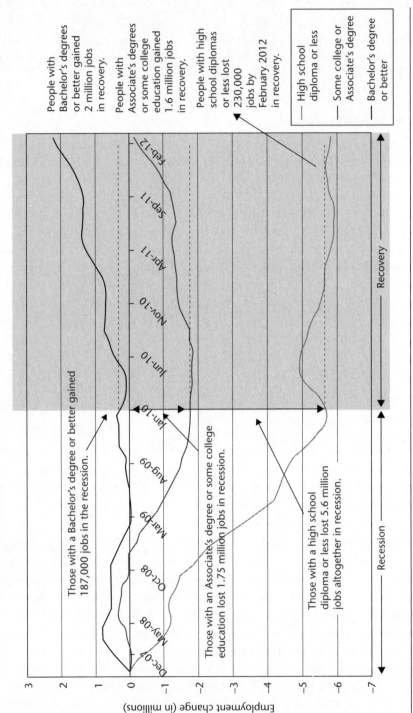

Source: Carnevale, A. The College Advantage (Washington, DC: Georgetown Center on Education and Workforce, 2012). Author's estimate of the Current Population Survey data (2007–2012).

Note: The monthly employment numbers are seasonally adjusted using the US Census Bureau X-12 procedure and smoothed using four-month moving averages. The graph represents the total employment losses by education since the beginning of the recession in December 2007 to January 2010 and employment gains in recovery from January 2010 to February 2012.

some college lost 1.75 million jobs during the recession and saw 1.6 million jobs added during the recovery, more or less a wash. The effects on the
final group, those with a high school diploma or less, are truly dramatic:
the recession cost these people 5.6 million jobs, and the recovery has not
reached them at all. Between January 2010 and February 2012 they have
lost an additional 230,000 jobs (figure 1.1).

Note that this final group includes those with a high school diploma,
the standard that most states set as the goal for all their students to reach
and to which many high schools then aspire. Also note how completely
inadequate the diploma is as a means to gain employment and secure a
livable wage over the past 40+ years (figure 1.2). The new measure of a
sufficiently prepared student is one who has knowledge and skills to keep
learning beyond secondary school, first in formal settings and then in the
workplace throughout their careers, so that they are capable of adapting to
unpredictable changes and new economic conditions and opportunities.

> The new measure of a sufficiently prepared student is one who has
> knowledge and skills to keep learning beyond secondary school.

FIGURE 1.2 ANNUAL EARNINGS AND EMPLOYMENT OF MEN WITH A HIGH SCHOOL DIPLOMA AND NO POSTSECONDARY CREDENTIAL

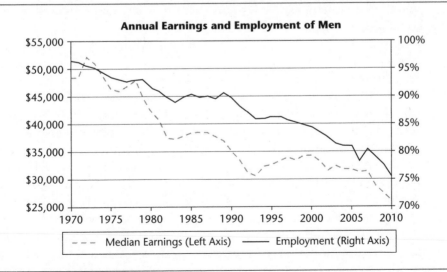

Source: US Census and Current Population Survey, 1970–2011. Data analysis by the Brookings Institute.

Note: Male-only data used due to substantial changes in women's participation in the labor force over this period of time.

From Vocational Education to Career Technical Education

Before continuing this discussion of the current state of college and career readiness, it is necessary and useful to look back on how the concept of career readiness has evolved over the past one hundred or so years. Throughout most of the twentieth century, what is now called *career readiness* was labeled *vocational education* or *job training* and took the form of specific programs designed to prepare students for an entry-level job in an area of work, a job they could then theoretically do without change for their entire working lives.

From the 1920s on, many large school districts physically separated vocationally oriented students from students going on to college. Denver's High School for the Manual Arts and Benson Polytechnic High School in Portland, Oregon, are but two examples of names that lived on well beyond the period when these were institutions that attracted students citywide for specific vocational training. These early magnets offered high-quality training, with state-of-the-art equipment and instructors who possessed real-world experience in the vocational area they taught. They also provided related academic preparation for their students, but the emphasis was on the practical and the applied, and a high school diploma for students graduating from these schools was generally seen to be terminal, the final formal education they needed. The good news was that the training these schools provided prepared students well for entry into the workforce, and their graduates had an advantage in securing employment over applicants without such formal training.

By the early 1960s, a model commonly referred to as the "comprehensive high school" had become dominant. Often referred to as the "shopping mall" model, these schools attempted to meet student needs by offering different programs based on student aspirations. The physical layout reflected the philosophy that students were headed toward different futures that would require different knowledge and skill sets and that they would not likely need to interact with students pursuing other futures. Academically oriented students took classes in parts of the building that were designed to emphasize contemplation and reflection, while vocational students were mostly separated from their college-bound peers at the opposite end of the campus, ostensibly because their programs were noisier. This model, with its assumptions about the separation of college and work preparation, remained strongly rooted through the end of the century in many high schools and has only recently begun to be seriously questioned.

This discussion of traditional vocational education is not intended to ignore or discount the rise of career technical education (CTE) programs that offer students high-quality and challenging courses built around applied academics. However, in many schools, much of the sorting that existed during the era of vocational programs continues under the guise of CTE. Students continue to be grouped and physically separated based on differences in their post–high school goals.

The point is not that it never makes sense to provide separate programs for students who wish to follow different paths. For example, many jurisdictions offer high-quality regional vocational-technical institutes or skill centers devoted to specific occupational training; these are of high quality, very successful, and valuable, and they generally address student academic skill development as well. The larger question, though, is what steps today's secondary schools, saddled with the remnants and physical space legacy of vocational programs, are taking to ensure that all students have open to them the option of pursuing college or a high-quality career pathway, not just a job, immediately after high school.

The vocational education model worked well in part because students could be taught skills that were generalizable across many work settings, even if they were specific to a particular occupation. Someone skilled in metalworking could be a pipefitter or machinist in any of a dozen industries. Woodshop courses opened the door to a host of occupations ranging from construction to cabinetry that required the ability to use the machinery and methods students learned. Employers were eager to hire workers with these skills, and this training was not narrow or dead-end. Vocational education worked well within the economic context within which it existed.

What these students also gained was an orientation to the world of work—what I call "work readiness." Values such as commitment to quality, attention to detail, and pride in craftsmanship were conveyed, along with behaviors such as safety, teamwork, punctuality, cleaning up after one's self, and following supervisor-given directions. These skills were as important in many ways as the specific skills associated with operating machinery or creating products. For many of the students who struggled in traditional academic courses, the structure and regimen of the vocational courses offered a haven where they knew what was expected of them and where they could be successful.

Although young women had access to some programs, such as home economics and office occupations, vocational education was largely a male-oriented and male-dominated activity. The programs never were designed to reach or appeal to all students, particularly the full range of young women. The notion of universal readiness was not central to this model. Vocational education in the shopping mall high school simply perpetuated aspects of the pre–World War II social sorting model without being as explicit, overt, or rigid about it. Students could theoretically change tracks, although this happened rarely in practice.

The Academic Core

Students not in a vocational-technical program had two choices. One path took them toward college. The other, the "general" track, took them nowhere in particular, preparing them for neither a job nor college. As high school participation increased during the 1920s and 1930s, a trend that accelerated after World War II, the core academic programs in high schools struggled with what to do with students whose futures were unclear. The strongly held belief was that most students were not suited for the rigors of the academic track. The students in the general preparation track inhabited an intellectual no-man's-land of sorts, without clear guidelines or reference points for what they should be learning and why they were learning it. This group became the largest one in many postwar high schools.

The long-time high school academic core consisting of English, mathematics, science, social studies, foreign languages, and art was more or less consistent throughout the twentieth century, and key elements of it look to be important for the foreseeable future. The content of this core may omit additional knowledge and skills that all students will need during their lives, a point taken up in chapter 7. At the moment, however, it is most relevant to this discussion to understand the ways in which this core has been taught to and learned by students.

Because college was not seen as a goal for all or even most students, educators had little reason to believe that academic core courses should be designed in ways that resulted in most or all students succeeding in them. After all, didn't many college freshmen fail the introductory courses they took? The teaching methods in core courses took on a decidedly abstract bent. The expectation was that students needed to work hard to understand and retain what they were being taught. That not all students would be able to do so was taken as something of a given.

In the absence of agreement on what constitutes an appropriate challenge level for core courses, high school instructors have been left to follow the tradition of the entry-level college class, where high standards meant a sizable number of students did not pass. The introduction of competency-based instructional models is leading to a movement away from this mind-set. However, it is still possible to encounter teachers and schools that display remnants of this old Darwinian model, where course rigor is viewed as a function of how many students fail and only the strongest survive.

Many schools are now valiantly attempting to enroll all students into core academic courses without necessarily changing much about how these courses are taught or what is in them. In essence, the general track is being merged with the academic track. The challenge level of such courses can now be calibrated against the Common Core State Standards. However, enrolling more students in academically challenging courses without paying attention to the instructional methods used or the strategies needed to engage students at the cognitive levels envisioned by the Common Core is unlikely to result in more students being college and career ready. Students will need more reasons and more support if they are all to learn at a high common level. Breaking down formal and informal tracking requires significant redesign of core courses. Integrating students from the general education track can be even more challenging than involving CTE students in the core.

These changes can be achieved without lowering standards. They will require focusing on the most important content in the Common Core State Standards, making expectations crystal clear to students, providing formative feedback that lets students know where they really stand in a course, and supporting students who are struggling academically.

Perhaps most important is an idea that appears in multiple places in this book: all students need to take more ownership of their learning. Schools can help this process along by creating stronger links between the content and student aspirations and goals, and by redesigning core courses consistent with findings from brain and cognitive sciences, best practices pedagogy, and commonsense observations about how students learn best. The traditional core will need to change dramatically if the Common Core is to be taught successfully to the full range of students—CTE, general education, academically oriented, and students with special needs.

Creating College Readiness and Career Readiness for All

Schools follow changes in the economy; they do not lead them. Schools find themselves struggling to play catch-up as the economy continues to morph with dizzying speed and unpredictability. With no longer a need to sort students into the academically capable and the manually proficient, how will schools adapt rapidly enough to enable all students to be ready for college and career? The process has been underway for some time now, although not all educators may have recognized the linkages between state actions and the larger economic context of schooling.

 Schools find themselves struggling to play catch-up as the economy continues to morph with dizzying speed and unpredictability.

The first acknowledgment by states that schools need to have all students succeed with a core set of content came during the 1990s when essentially every state adopted education standards that defined key knowledge and skills. The underlying rationale for the standards, in most cases, was to define what was required for success in a twenty-first-century economy and society. In some states, though, the standards were little more than codifications of basic skills and current content taught at each grade level, while in other states, the standards soared to rhetorical heights, waxing rhapsodic about students who would be global citizens who contributed throughout their lives to making the world a better place.

The challenge level of the standards varied dramatically from state to state, but they were almost always silent or intentionally vague on what the ultimate goal was that students were being prepared to reach. Rather than confront the issue head on, most states linked their standards at least indirectly to the goal of high school completion, with the implied assumption that graduates would be prepared for entry-level employment. Students who aspired to postsecondary education almost always needed to complete course work that exceeded the state standards. In other words, states were not anxious to embrace the expectation that all students would be ready to learn beyond high school and would be likely to do so.

Perhaps ninth-grade algebra courses are the example of the way standards played out in many schools. This course continues to have high failure rates even as it has become a universal expectation in many high schools. Failure in this one course can cut in half the proportion of students aspiring to college. The effect of failing algebra is even more pronounced on student aspiration to careers in science, technology, engineering, and mathematics (STEM). Biology courses, which often have similarly dismal pass rates, combine for a one-two punch that takes many students off the STEM pathway. The effect of failing one or both of these courses is to truncate the pool of students who will be eligible for post-secondary programs or majors that require solid foundational math and science knowledge. Many students choose vocation-oriented options at this point, not because they are not capable of learning algebra or biology but because the price for continuing in the academic track, in the form of passing courses in which little of what they learn is applied, seems too steep to them.

The rise of two de facto sets of educational programs in many schools, one for students focused on completing high school and another for those going on to college, has been a troubling trend in the standards era of the past twenty-five years. Theoretically all students have been learning what the state standards call for, but not all students have been held to the same academic standards. While many state education leaders opine that their standards prepare students for a range of futures, little evidence exists to confirm this is the case, and few state standards have been specifically aligned to the knowledge and skills required for success in college and career programs. Under the standards model of the past two and a half decades, all students theoretically graduate with at least basic skills. However, access for all to college and career pathways was never the goal or the criterion measure.

The evidence supports the conclusion that states did not specifically target college and career readiness for all students. Although college-going rates continued to climb from 1990 to 2010 (with the exception of a 5 percent decline from 1997 to 2001, a time of rapid economic growth that created more immediate employment opportunities), remediation rates have remained stubbornly high, and national measures such as the SAT and ACT have not registered a significant increase in student performance. First-year college success rates and overall graduation rates have also been relatively stagnant overall.

The Rise of College Readiness Standards

By the late 1990s, the issue of the purpose of state standards was beginning to come into sharper relief. Several states by that point had already revised their standards at least once, some twice, often with great fanfare. Postsecondary institutions began to take note that the "standards" thing was not going away and that secondary schools were shaping what they taught based on state standards and the exams used to test those standards. It occurred to some leaders in the postsecondary community that their ability to influence the high school curriculum, which had been well established from the time of the higher education–dominated Committee of Ten in the early 1890s, which had specified the college preparatory curriculum, might weaken if states were to write their own learning objectives and goals independent from what colleges wanted.

The less cynical view is that colleges wanted to be supportive of high schools preparing students properly to attend their institutions, and helping high school educators to understand what exactly students needed to be ready to succeed in college might be an important way to contribute. What better way to do so than to develop standards that defined what it meant to be college ready? Given the importance of evidence in the postsecondary world, the process chosen to develop these college readiness standards was to establish empirically what it took to be ready to succeed in entry-level postsecondary courses. The aim of the initial studies undertaken was to create a new standards-based specification of college readiness that paralleled and could be linked to the academic content standards that states had developed for their K–12 schools.

This work built on previous large-scale efforts to develop high-quality standards, most notably the New Standards Project. Founded in 1991, New Standards was a joint project of the National Center on Education and the Economy, the Learning Research and Development Center, and the University of Pittsburgh to develop internationally competitive performance standards in English, mathematics, science, and applied learning at the fourth, eighth, and tenth grades. The standards were accompanied by a "reference examination" that was calibrated to national content standards. This system was seen as a framework within which students could pursue certificates of initial mastery, which would serve as measures of readiness for college and careers. While not explicitly tied to college and career readiness, New Standards provided a model for high-quality standards and assessments that spanned multiple grade levels, had a content component, and pointed toward success after high school.

The first study specifically focused on college readiness was Standards for Success, which I designed and directed beginning in 2000 under the sponsorship of the Association of American Universities, an organization composed of sixty-two prestigious and well-known research universities. The study engaged more than four hundred faculty members at leading US universities in a structured process to identify what it takes for students to be ready to succeed in the entry-level courses at their institutions. Although the results of the three-year study were not surprising in some respects, they were quite remarkable in others.

Faculty did identify a great deal of content knowledge in core subjects that was consistent with what high school teachers generally taught. More surprising was that they stated emphatically that this prerequisite content knowledge was not the most important measure of potential success in their courses. With near unanimity, they stressed in no uncertain terms on campus after campus that students needed to know what to do with the content they were learning. They needed to be able to use their content knowledge in ways consistent with the subject area's rules and premises to generate intellectually interesting outputs. Repeating information alone was not sufficient. Faculty noted time and time again that otherwise well-prepared students could not grapple with a task or problem that asked them to go beyond what they had been taught literally. Students struggled to make inferences, interpret inconsistent or novel data, posit multiple explanations for a phenomenon, generate an original thesis and explore it, or extrapolate from a given set of information to a new and novel setting.

> Students needed to know what to do with the content they were learning.

In essence, faculty were calling on students to have mastered what I describe as *key cognitive strategies*—ways of thinking and processing content at more complex levels to allow for its use and transfer to new settings and situations as needed. Chapter 3 contains a more in-depth discussion of these strategies because they are so important to understanding the difference between how the academic core is taught in high schools today and how it will need to change to prepare students for college and careers and to be lifelong learners.

Shortly after Standards for Success released its final report, *Understanding University Success*, and distributed it to every high school in the nation in 2003, the Washington, DC–based education policy-advocacy group Achieve undertook the American Diploma Project (ADP). Its goals were similar to Standards for Success: to define college readiness by gathering input from postsecondary faculty. This study queried postsecondary faculty regarding their expectations, but took the additional step of including instructors from two-year institutions along with economists and members of the business community. Achieve characterized the ADP standards as representing an "unprecedented convergence" of educator and employer opinions on what it means to be ready for college and careers. The two studies reached significant agreement on the key knowledge and skills that underlie postsecondary readiness, but they also had differences.

National admissions test makers ACT and the College Board, which administers the SAT, shortly thereafter entered the arena of college readiness standards by creating their own systems. Developed through internal processes that included expert judgment panels and the use of each organization's extensive database of student performance on admissions tests, the standards each organization produced had much in common with Standards for Success and the ADP. The College Board's version, the Standards for College Success, drew from the Standards for Success and was the only set of college readiness standards to span sixth through twelfth grades. ACT followed suit with its College Readiness Standards, which described the knowledge and skills students would be expected to have mastered at various score levels on the ACT exam system, also known as the Educational Planning and Assessment System, or EPAS.

Several states developed versions of college readiness standards, but most set their exit standards somewhere before the end of twelfth grade. The state that has developed the most complete and aligned set of college readiness standards to date is Texas, also one of five states not adopting the Common Core State Standards as of the spring of 2013. In 2009, the Texas College and Career Readiness Standards were released to the public. These standards are interesting for a number of reasons. They were developed under the sponsorship of the Texas Higher Education Coordinating Board in collaboration the Texas Education Agency, which is responsible for K–12 education. These standards were created by vertical teams comprising faculty from middle and high schools and two- and four-year postsecondary institutions. They drew on the research on college readiness standards, previously produced college readiness standards systems, and high-quality high school standards from other states to help inform the professional judgments of the vertical teams.

Texas law required that these standards be used as the reference point for high school end-of-course examinations in multiple subjects. In addition to English and mathematics, standards were developed in science and social studies as well. Finally, and uniquely among all the college and career readiness standards that had been created to that time, the Texas system includes a set of cross-disciplinary standards that acknowledge the importance of learning skills that students need to be prepared to succeed in postsecondary studies. These skills include intellectual curiosity, reasoning, problem solving, academic behaviors, work habits, and academic integrity, skills that vertical team members in a range of subjects specified as important to success in their subject area. The standards are being used throughout the state by groups such as Generation Texas in San Antonio as a focal point for local improvement efforts.

☾

This chapter has reviewed the importance of having all students ready for college and careers, the challenge to high schools to develop programs that challenge all students at high levels, and the emergence and rapid evolution of college readiness standards. But what exactly does it mean to be college ready, and how is this different from being career ready? The next chapter goes into greater depth to answer this question and offers a comprehensive definition of college and career readiness.

☾ Awareness and Action Steps

- Share information on the changing nature of the US economy by reviewing and discussing *The College Advantage: Weathering the Economic Storm* by Anthony Carnevale, Tamara Jayasundera, and Ban Cheah.
- Read and discuss the report *Pathways to Prosperity: Meeting the Challenge of Preparing Young Americans for the Twenty-First Century*, and consider the balance between career preparation and college preparation that is most appropriate.
- Determine whether tracking, formal or informal, is present in academic courses and how such practices affect student aspirations.
- Look at a blueprint or map of your school campus. Do you see evidence, either historical or recent, of the separation of vocational and college-track students built into the physical design of your school?
- Explore the degree of consensus in the school on the need for all students to be college and career ready.
- Consider how high-quality CTE programs that develop skills for twenty-first-century careers can help students become more college and career ready. Does viewing these programs through the lens of college and career readiness, not job training, suggest any necessary changes?
- Schedule a conference call with professionals who have taken nonlinear routes to their current positions. Have them share their pathway story to model how people change careers multiple times over their life, may have to move for a job, and may have to return to school or a training program at multiple points during a career.

- Visit the National Assessment Governing Board website to read the results of studies on the knowledge, skills, and abilities needed for different occupational areas (http://bit.ly/10utTvH) and the National Center on Education and the Economy's report, *What Does It Really Mean to Be College and Work Ready?* (http://bit.ly/1apPck1).
- Share with your students the comparison chart of the 2012 Bureau of Labor Statistics average salaries and unemployment rates across different levels of education attained, including occupational programs (http://bit.ly/18X2tSJ).
- Trace the story of your community's evolving workforce needs. How have these changes affected your students' families? How do these personal experiences influence and shape local conversations about the importance of having all students ready for college and careers?
- Identify how the national and international economies have led to changes in your local economy and what the future prospects are for changes that will affect the knowledge and skills students will need if they wish to work and live in the community.
- Analyze your school's data on student outcomes in ninth-grade algebra, subsequent course-taking decisions, and college matriculation. How does failing ninth-grade algebra limit future student options, particularly their ability to pursue STEM careers?
- Gather a small group of educators and guidance counselors to discuss the following question: What does it looks like, in concrete, observable ways, when students take ownership of their learning? What are three steps the school can take to increase student ownership of learning?
- Evaluate your school and local high school diploma requirements. For what types of jobs or employment tasks would a student who met just the minimum graduation requirements qualify? If you could design a set of diploma requirements that prepared all graduates for college and careers, what would the requirements entail?

CHAPTER 2

COLLEGE READINESS, CAREER READINESS: SAME OR DIFFERENT?

Even as college readiness standards began to emerge, the question of the relationship between college readiness and career readiness remained largely unexamined. Then, in 2006, ACT published an influential study that reached the conclusion that college and work readiness were the same in terms of the academic skills needed for each. ACT researchers first studied job requirements, which they cross-referenced against an ACT job skills assessment system. They then mapped the findings onto ACT's college-readiness standards and concluded that the readiness requirements in English and mathematics for both college and work were substantively comparable.

This finding was welcomed in many quarters at the time for several reasons. The process of defining college readiness was still ongoing, and adding the need to define work or career readiness was seen as a significant challenge. Many career and technical educators expressed the sentiment that the entire discussion of college readiness did not acknowledge the fact that their courses challenged students at a high level as well. States that were attempting to move to adopt college readiness as a systemwide goal were perplexed about what to do with students not on the college track. The ACT report was swiftly endorsed by a range of policymakers and educators because it seemed to solve the problem of how to educate a wide range of students with varied aptitudes, interests, and goals.

However, as the research on college readiness has progressed and results from new studies examining the English and math skills needed for readiness for particular careers have begun to be reported, the view that college and career readiness are exactly the same is being reconsidered. The next section explores the substantial overlap that exists, along with areas that are unique to each. While the foundational set of English and mathematics knowledge and skills that applies universally to college and career readiness is largely the same, the specific content students need to master is influenced by their goals and aspirations and the postsecondary program they wish to enter.

> The view that college and career readiness are exactly the same is being reconsidered.

Each set of college readiness standards described in the previous chapter has elements in common, and each has unique elements. This should not be surprising. College readiness is both complex and contextual. Part of this complexity stems from the fact that students in the United States can choose from over two thousand baccalaureate-granting institutions and over a thousand two-year colleges, with a range of missions, selectivity, and program focus, among other factors. Readiness means one thing at one institution and something slightly or dramatically different at another.

The other critically important point is that readiness needs to be considered in the context of individual student goals and aspirations. As expectations of what constitutes an educated person continue to increase, and they most certainly have increased during the past two decades, it is important to remember that if standards are too rigid, many students will fall just short in a subject area even though they are still capable of succeeding in a given postsecondary program. Better to learn how to gauge the knowledge and skill level of students in relation to their goals and then constantly encourage and challenge them to raise their aspirations than to tell them they are not ready because they fail to meet a rigid or arbitrary standard that may have little relevance to their probability of success in their area of interest.

It is important to view college and career readiness through the lens of its complexity and its application to the individual. Readiness has a lot to do with what the student wants to do next educationally. Although high schools will never be expected to adapt their programs to each individual student's needs and goals, the programs of study available to students need to recognize and accommodate student interests. To some degree, readiness can be judged in relation to the student and the future that the student wishes to pursue. The focus should always be on what students can do and not just what they cannot do.

Exploring Readiness More Deeply

The college readiness standards developed to date have been critically important. They help identify a set of common expectations that the Common Core State Standards authors were able to draw on as one frame of reference. It may seem that the adoption of common standards settles the issue of what constitutes college readiness and what constitutes career readiness. However, further investigation suggests it's somewhat premature to declare victory and go home.

Additional examination of what it means to be college and career ready is ongoing and continues to yield new insights. At the Educational Policy Improvement Center (EPIC) in Eugene and Portland, Oregon, my colleagues and I have been conducting studies over the past decade designed to provide greater insight into college readiness, career readiness, and the similarities and differences between the two. Our approach has been to focus on the first courses students take in college toward a bachelor's degree or in career programs leading to a certificate or associate degree. We collect and analyze key material from these courses, including syllabi, assignments, readings, and tests, and gather insights from instructors of these courses in order to specify the knowledge and skill needed to succeed in entry-level courses. By understanding what goes on in entry-level courses, we can identify in some detail what students need to know and be able to do to be ready for college, whether at a four-year or two-year institution or other postsecondary settings in which occupational skill training occurs, such as proprietary programs or the military. Some of the results from this line of research are shared here.

Academic Content and Cross-Disciplinary Skills

One study that EPIC conducted analyzed courses in accounting, drafting, introduction to computers, marketing, and business English at Texas two- and four-year colleges and universities. Participating instructors completed a course profile, uploaded a course syllabus, and determined the importance of the cross-disciplinary skills in the Texas College and Career Readiness Standards that included cognitive strategies, learning skills, and foundational knowledge necessary across all subject areas.

We found significant variation in the English and mathematics knowledge required, which should not be surprising. What was somewhat surprising, but consistent with previous studies, including Standards for Success, was the consistency with which instructors identified a set of learning strategies and techniques, such as study skills, problem solving, critical thinking, and goal setting, as being important for student success in the career-oriented courses.

A companion study analyzed nursing and computer programming courses in Texas. Here too the key finding was that the prerequisite academic content in English and mathematics necessary for readiness varied much more than did the learning skills, which were found to be common to all courses. For example, although the computer programming courses required significantly more mathematical skills than did the nursing courses, and nursing courses required significantly more scientific knowledge than did courses in computer programming, both expected students to have mastered a range of strategies necessary to learn the material being taught.

These and other analyses of postsecondary courses support our basic conclusion that while the English and mathematics knowledge and skills students need to be ready for a wide range of college courses varies, it is possible to identify a core that is foundational and prepares students for most postsecondary programs. Considerable differences do exist, though, between general education courses in four-year institutions and entry-level courses in career-oriented programs, largely at two-year institutions.

The Common Core Connection to College and Career Readiness

In 2011, EPIC completed a national study of the Common Core State Standards to determine the degree to which they contained the knowledge and skills needed to be ready for a wide range of postsecondary courses. We developed a data set based on the responses from a national sample of nearly two thousand faculty members who taught entry-level courses in twenty-five subject areas at more than five hundred two- and four-year postsecondary institutions. The course areas included fourteen subject areas necessary for a bachelor's degree and eleven associated with career pathways. Bachelor's degree–related classes were drawn from general education subjects in English, mathematics, science, and social sciences. Career pathways courses came from the fields of business, computer science, and health care.

We asked the faculty members how applicable and important the Common Core State Standards were as prerequisites for success in their courses. We found the following subset of the English language arts standards to be important across all course areas:

- Speaking and listening
- Reading informational texts
- Writing in a variety of genres

In mathematics, the Standards for Mathematical Practices, which include reasoning and problem solving, were the most highly rated across all subject areas in both academic and career-oriented courses.

As in the case of the earlier Texas studies of career-oriented courses, the specific applicable English and math content standards varied considerably by course area in both the academic and career-oriented courses. For example, reading literature was not emphasized outside English courses. Statistics was more important to science readiness, and computer technology courses required higher math skills across all math standards than did any other area studied. These findings are presented in greater detail in chapter 7 in a discussion of the research base underlying the Common Core State Standards as measures of college and career readiness. They have been presented here in summary form to establish early on that the Common Core State Standards do have a strong relationship to postsecondary readiness, as well as to illustrate the similarities and differences between college readiness and career readiness.

The Key Skills All Students Need

These studies suggest that college readiness and career readiness share many important elements, but they're not exactly the same. Beyond the foundational content knowledge that is common across a range of programs, the elements shared most consistently are the learning skills all students need to be ready for a variety of postsecondary learning environments:

- Study skills
- Time management skills
- Goal orientation
- Persistence (also called tenacity, determination, and grit)
- Ownership of learning (or human agency)

Others are important as well:

- Self-awareness, which constitutes knowing how well one is actually doing in a course
- Help seeking, that is, the ability to obtain necessary resources when needed
- Technological proficiency, which includes knowing how to use a range of technological tools effectively and appropriately

Postsecondary instructors at a wide range of two- and four-year institutions stress the importance of these skills across subject areas and programs. A lack of proficiency in these skills probably affects career-oriented students more adversely than it does students entering bachelor's degree programs—in part because career-oriented programs tend to offer fewer supports to help students develop these skills if they lack them on entry, and in part because students in such programs are more likely to be discouraged if they do not experience success initially in their program, and a lack of these skills often causes students to struggle even if they are capable of mastering the content knowledge expectations.

We have encountered a number of postsecondary instructors who espouse the extreme position that students don't need to know anything about the subject prior to taking the instructor's course; they just need highly developed learning skills. These instructors would prefer to teach key prerequisite content themselves rather than reteach or correct student misunderstandings. While it may not be true that incoming college students are better off not knowing anything except how to learn, the point here is that college instructors believe students do benefit from knowing how to learn, a skill many lack.

In addition, we found that students need to have a range of cognitive strategies at their disposal, such as the ability to formulate problems, collect information, interpret and analyze findings, communicate in a variety of modes, and do all of this with precision and accuracy. These strategies are particularly important when students are confronted with tasks that require them to apply content knowledge in novel and nonroutine ways.

Connecting Student Interests and Goals to College and Career Readiness

As convenient as it would be to declare college readiness and career readiness one and the same, evidence suggests it's more complicated than that. The good news is that secondary school programs of study can be designed in ways that don't require distinctly different courses or programs for students with different interests or aspirations. All students can be challenged with rigorous academic content and then build skills and nurture interests necessary to achieve more personalized goals. The Common Core State Standards will help because they are designed to include a great deal of content that is universally important to learners throughout their careers and lives. Beyond the Common Core State Standards, students can be encouraged to develop their interests and focus on areas of strength.

> Secondary school programs of study can be designed in ways that don't require distinctly different courses or programs for students with different interests or aspirations.

Perhaps the greatest challenge that a broader definition and conception of college and career readiness creates is acknowledging that not all students are going to follow the same path to college and career readiness, and that's okay. The genius of the US postsecondary system is that it creates so many options for so many students. Why should all students be required to have exactly the same set of knowledge and skills in order to go to college when they plan to pursue such a wide range of majors and programs once they get there? While all students need the opportunity to learn a curriculum that enables them to develop a strong foundation of academic knowledge and skills, preparation for postsecondary education requires more than just meeting a set of standards in English and mathematics. The secondary school program of study needs more opportunities for students to match what they are learning with their aspirations, interests, and ambitions.

This process begins with students starting to identify their interests at a much earlier age and then learning what knowledge and skills they will need to pursue their interests at the postsecondary level. This is not the same as advocating the old European model where students take a test in eighth or tenth grade and are sent on one track or another, an approach that Europe is largely moving away from.

What I am proposing is quite the opposite. The idea here is that all students need to be exploring the career options open to them in a dynamic global economy at the same time that they are developing an appreciation of how what they are learning helps them prepare for their future. This is the only way they will gain deeper insight into the challenging content to which they are being exposed and retain it. The goal is not to have students pick occupations, but to have them begin to make stronger connections between what they are learning and what they are interested in doing with their lives.

> The goal is not to have students pick occupations, but to have them begin to make stronger connections between what they are learning and what they are interested in doing with their lives.

Clearly most students will change their minds multiple times about their career goals, and this is not a problem given that most of what they are learning will be applicable across a wide range of career options. Focusing a bit too much on statistics and then having to sharpen one's algebra skills is probably not a dramatic problem, assuming the student possesses the learning skills and techniques described earlier. By middle school and certainly on enrollment into high school, however, all students should be thinking about both college and careers, at least in the most general of terms.

I readily acknowledge the danger that students could be tracked into different futures based on their race, ethnicity, and income level. Unfortunately, this occurs all too often in the current system, but in a quiet, almost invisible way. Explicitly giving students options to explore potential futures need not lead to more tracking. This needs to be done in ways that encourage students to raise their aspirations, not lower them. Getting them to do so will require encouragement from the adults in their lives, both parents and educators. More and better counseling can also help. So can online resources. However, fear of tracking should not stand in the way of helping students understand the world of options available to them, encouraging them to explore those options, and then helping them make the connections between the value of what they are learning and the future they may wish to pursue.

> ### ◑ Examples of Questions to Ask Students to Begin Their Thinking about College and Careers
>
> Does the student like:
>
> - Working with people?
> - Being outdoors?
> - Engaging in problem solving?
> - Designing things?
> - Applying logic to reach a conclusion?
> - Organizing processes?
> - Overseeing and directing a group toward a goal?
> - Helping others?
> - Creating visually interesting products?
> - Interacting across cultural and linguistic barriers?
> - Addressing social problems to improve the world?

In some ways, it does not matter precisely which choices students make initially as long as they are also learning about themselves and their interests. Student do not need to craft a customized program of study while in middle school or high school, but they do need to be making connections and applications between what they are learning and what they wish to do next in life. Ideally, students gradually refine their focus over time, or at least cross off from the list areas of endeavor that are no longer of interest to them.

The key way to accomplish this is not by trying to offer discrete programs in secondary school that prepare students for specific postsecondary programs of study, but through assignments, projects, and application-oriented activities that are more open-ended and afford students more opportunities to connect content to interests. An example of a generic assignment of this type is a research study in which students investigate the requirements and opportunities associated with various career and professional pathways. Beyond gathering information online from the increasing number of high-quality databases devoted to career exploration, they can interview people from various occupational areas, which need not always be done in person, as in the "career days" of old. Programs such as RoadTrip Nation have extensive banks of video interviews available online that open a window into a wide range of occupations and careers and what led people to choose them. Several states are expecting students to develop more formal career plans and even select an occupational pathway in high school. This movement reflects the emerging importance of having students become oriented toward their futures at an earlier age.

I am suggesting this approach to help students better learn academic content, including the Common Core State Standards, and retain key information more effectively because the material has meaning for them. Having students state a career goal or aspiration beginning in ninth grade sharpens their lens on what is important in what they are learning at the same time that it causes them to reexamine that career goal or aspiration regularly. Schools need to continue to challenge all students to increase their aspirations, but having an initial goal is a good starting place for that growth process.

Many young people today have no real idea if their actions and decisions in school are wildly inconsistent with their vaguely formed goals for their futures. Not every high school graduate is going to be paid a six-figure salary to test video games and drive around in a BMW right out of high school. The NBA is not going to expand to six thousand teams anytime soon to accommodate all of the would-be professional basketball players in high schools today. It's great for kids to have dreams, and nobody needs to be a Grinch. Fantasizing about the future is no substitute for preparing for it, but it is what constitutes career preparation in many schools. No wonder students do not focus on academics or see any relevance in the English and mathematics skills they are being taught.

 Fantasizing about the future is no substitute for preparing for it, but it is what constitutes career preparation in many schools.

Allowing all students to go through secondary school with no help on setting goals or shaping career interests creates a tremendous advantage for students who receive constant help, encouragement, and even pressure outside school from parents, siblings, and their wider social networks to prepare for their future. The students who do not get counseling and support are more likely to drift, disengaged from academic learning for which they see no point or purpose. Closing the achievement gap on English and mathematics test scores is an important goal, but will be largely meaningless if all students do not convert any improved academic proficiency into additional learning beyond high school, something they are less likely to do without a clear reason to aspire to college and careers.

Many tools and strategies exist and are already in place in many schools. In addition to curriculum materials that apply content to real settings and career exploration programs and materials, brief internships or career exploration opportunities can help students develop more specific aspirations, as can job shadowing and mentor relationships. Learning plans that include both academic and career exploration activities linked to post–high school goals will help more students prepare for college and careers. Students should not necessarily be trained for a specific job by the time they leave high school, but they should be focused on a career pathway or an area of study. This principle holds true for all students, regardless of whether they plan to pursue a certification in a two-year program or a bachelor's degree.

By pursuing programs of this nature, secondary schools need not be as concerned about the distinction between college ready and career ready. All students can be taught the Common Core State Standards while simultaneously acknowledging that students will demonstrate interests and strengths in particular areas, and that those should be cultivated and expanded so students remain excited about the possibilities for their futures. Even if students still need to buckle down and address areas of weakness, this is more likely to happen when they do so in the context of an instructional program that allows them to explore interests and apply learning to real-world situations and settings consistent with their interests and aspirations.

Levels of Readiness

While college and career readiness is of primary concern to educators and policymakers and is therefore defined in the most detail and specificity here, it is only one level of readiness among several leading to and even surpassing college and career readiness. This readiness continuum needs to be defined, specified, and understood by educators and students to help them know where they stand at any point in their education. The continuum also helps everyone understand better what schools are expecting from students by observing the level of readiness toward which the schools' instructional programs are gauged (figure 2.1).

FIGURE 2.1 READINESS CONTINUUM

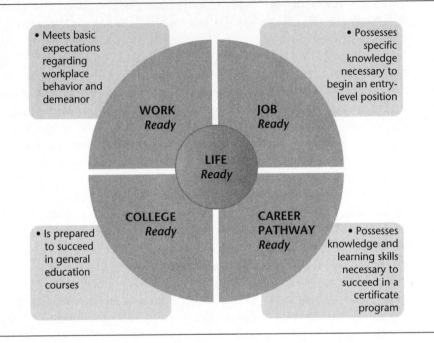

O   *Work ready.* At this most basic level, a student is prepared to enter the workforce in an entry-level position. Work readiness is defined by employers as the ability of an employee to show up on time for work, be free from drugs and alcohol while at work, and get along with supervisors and coworkers. As low as this bar is, employers note that many workers seeking employment in entry-level positions do not meet it. Unfortunately, far too many students with high school diplomas do not consistently reach the work-ready level. As a result, they are functionally ineligible for entry into the labor force, or they bounce around from one low-level job to the next, with no prospects of advancement. High schools that produce graduates who do not meet the work-readiness level have standards that are too low and are not addressing issues of student self-management and impulse control very well.

O   *Job ready.* At this level, an employee is capable of being trained by the employer for the job at hand. Workers who are job ready can participate successfully in the training program necessary for them to be accepted into the workforce in a very specific area. The range of skills required to complete employer training requirements or programs varies significantly, from simply observing someone else doing a job and then emulating what they do, to completing a formal training course that requires significant study and the use of basic literacy and numeracy skills. At the heart of most job training is the ability to follow directions and communicate with others. The job-ready level is higher than the work-ready level, but it consists largely of compliance behavior sufficient to follow directions and the foundational academic skills required by the training program. This is still a relatively low bar and not sufficient as the outcome level acceptable for large numbers of students. Being able to be trained for a job is not the same as being able to pursue a career pathway. This is a level that many high schools associate as sufficient for their graduates to have achieved. Students who reach this level need to be able to comply with supervisors and follow procedures, in addition to demonstrating the impulse control of the work-ready student.

O *Career pathway ready.* Students who reach this level have mastered the personal control, the compliance behaviors, and the foundational communication skills necessary to function in the workplace. The also have an academic foundation sufficiently strong to allow them to engage in focused study that will prepare them for a career pathway, not just a job. By *career pathway*, I mean the ability to progress beyond an entry-level position in an occupational area in which the potential for vertical advancement or horizontal branching exists. This is the first level that requires formal postsecondary education in some fashion, whether it is participation in a certificate program, training in the military, enrollment at a proprietary training school, or pursuit of an associate degree. Students who are career pathway–ready can have aspirations and goals that can be fulfilled only through postsecondary participation. Being career pathway–oriented in high school creates a stronger motivation and goal focus that encourages students to take on more academic challenges. These students may have some academic skill gaps, but they are sufficiently strong in areas necessary for a particular career pathway to succeed in their area of interest. They also possess the foundational academic content knowledge and skills and the learning strategies necessary to move along their career pathway as opportunities present themselves throughout their careers.

O *College ready.* This level is defined as being able to succeed in entry-level general education courses that lead toward a four-year degree at a broad range of colleges–both four-year and two-year institutions. Although we have found considerable variation in what colleges expect on entry, the content and challenge level is generally sufficiently consistent in general education courses to allow this standard to be clear enough for students to prepare to meet it. In addition to content knowledge, the postsecondary-ready and pathway-ready students have mastered knowledge and skills in three other areas, which will be discussed in detail in the next section.

○ *Life ready.* This level includes elements of all the previous levels to some degree, but life readiness becomes easier to attain as students move through each of these readiness level. Life-ready students are prepared to pursue successful careers and lead fulfilling lives as productive citizens. They have mastered impulse control. They communicate well and can follow directions when necessary. They possess foundational academic learning skills and have career aspirations. They are proficient with a range of additional skills needed to keep learning and adapting throughout their lives.

Much of what is taught in school does not necessarily relate directly to work, job, or career. It is about developing students as human beings who will enjoy their lives more fully if they have a broader appreciation of the human experience and if they can function in society without conflict or frustration. Education helps them develop this enhanced awareness, which can lead to a richer, fuller life. Life-ready students benefit from all schooling has to offer them and develop as complete human beings.

 Life-ready students benefit from all schooling has to offer them and develop as complete human beings.

My Definition of College and Career Ready

I conclude rather than begin the chapter with my own definition of college and career readiness because it was important to first establish the need for students to be college and career ready and then to understand the relationship between college readiness and career readiness and how high schools can enable students to achieve either or both. Now that you are armed with this deeper insight into the relationship between college readiness and career readiness, it is time to consider a definition of *college and career ready.*

Many groups are offering definitions of *college readiness, career readiness,* or both. My definition results from eighteen years of study and research on this topic. It draws from empirical studies as its primary reference point. Major research projects that my colleagues and I have conducted that led to this definition include the Proficiency-Based Admission Standards System, sponsored in the 1990s by the Oregon University System; Standards for Success; multiple analyses of entry-level college courses sponsored by the College Board; college and career readiness standards developed under the sponsorship of the Texas

Higher Education Coordinating Board and the Washington Higher Education Coordinating Board; the Reaching the Goal study of the alignment between entry-level college courses and the Common Core State Standards sponsored by the Bill & Melinda Gates Foundation; and two studies of job training programs and entry-level college courses sponsored by the National Assessment Governing Board.

The definition refers to readiness for postsecondary study, where *postsecondary* refers to any formal setting in which students pursue additional instruction beyond high school. This is broader than college readiness and includes two- or four-year degree institutions, certificate or licensure programs, formal apprenticeship training programs, and the military.

Here is the definition. Students who are ready for college and career can qualify for and succeed in entry-level, credit-bearing college courses leading to a baccalaureate degree, a certificate, or career pathway-oriented training programs without the need for remedial or developmental course work. They can complete such entry-level, credit-bearing courses at a level that enables them to continue in the major or program of study they have chosen.

However, not every student requires the same proficiency in all areas to be ready. Student interests and post–high school aspirations influence the precise readiness profile that each student needs to demonstrate to be deemed fully ready for postsecondary studies.

Therefore, a single score on a test given to high school students is not an adequate measure of college or career readiness because it does not take into account any possible individualization of the match between knowledge and skills, on the one hand, and aspirations, on the other. A program of instruction at the secondary school level should therefore be designed to equip all students with the full range of necessary foundational knowledge and skills and help them set high aspirations and identify future interests.

The measure of success should be students' ability to pursue their chosen field of postsecondary education or post–high school training. In other words, readiness is a function of the ability to continue to learn beyond high school, and particularly in postsecondary courses relevant to students' goals and interests, as represented by their choice of major or certificate program.

Readiness has a universal component in the form of the foundational skills needed for any of a wide range of programs of study students might choose to pursue, as well as for subsequent learning throughout a career and an individual component in the form of the knowledge and skills needed for success in the specific major or certificate program they choose to pursue. (Chapter 10 explores how this process can be implemented through the creation and use of student profiles.)

🌐 Awareness and Action Steps

- Do teachers in your school know about student interests and aspirations? If so, how do they know? What systematic data are collected on student aspirations, particularly as they move across grade levels in high school?
- What percentage of students in your school do not aspire to a postsecondary education? Are any data collected on why they don't?
- Consider informal or self-made surveys or more formal means, such as Campus Ready in the appendix, to gather more information on student aspirations.
- Develop assignments that require students to do research on their interests and on postsecondary programs. For example, students could be required to do a research paper each year on college options and the cost of pursuing an option of interest to them. Online sites such as Naviance (http://bit.ly/14IkC2I) and Big Future (http://bit.ly/11MCsgw) provide many free resources to help students complete such assignments.
- Construct a research project where students collect information on three different jobs to report on the necessary qualifications (e.g., training, education, skills), job market outlook and salary predictions, and the day-to-day experience using O*net data on http://bit.ly/15h0rFM.
- Create an activity for students using Venn diagrams to explore how student interests and skills overlap with different career types. Brainstorm in small groups the types of jobs that would be fitting for team members.
- Host a "career jumping" event, where students conduct two- to five-minute interviews with professionals from a variety of fields. Have the professionals talk about challenge and how they overcame obstacles.
- Informally rate the readiness of graduating seniors. Approximately what percentage are at each level of readiness? Develop three interventions to move more students from job and work ready to career pathway and postsecondary ready.
- Discuss my definition of *college and career ready*. What are the implications of thinking about readiness as sufficient knowledge and skills for students to pursue their aspirations? What are the drawbacks of this definition?
- Have students orally present on their interests in relation to different career or educational pathways (http://bit.ly/14Il0Oj).

CHAPTER 3

THE FOUR KEYS TO COLLEGE AND CAREER READINESS

The previous two chapters have considered the need to have all students college and career ready, examined the difference between the two concepts, and put forth a definition of college and career readiness. This chapter explores in greater detail and depth what it means to be college and career ready. What does it take for students to be truly ready for credit-bearing courses in English and mathematics and for a range of career preparation programs? Central to this chapter and the next is a comprehensive model for college and career readiness, one that captures a wider range of factors than content knowledge in English and mathematics, which is what the Common Core specifies and tests. This model helps educators and students think about the full set of knowledge and skills that need to be developed to make students college and career ready.

The Four Keys: An Overview

The definition presented in chapter 2 forms a foundation for determining college and career readiness. The readiness continuum, from work ready to life ready, that accompanied the definition helps us understand how students become increasingly capable of managing their own learning and their own lives. The definition and readiness levels do not, however, tell us much about how schools need to organize instruction to get all students to this level or what students must do to be fully prepared to succeed in postsecondary programs of study.

Schools and students alike will benefit from a comprehensive model that captures all of the factors and important variables for which students must develop knowledge or skills. The model described here was presented in its initial form in 2007 in a monograph I wrote entitled *Toward a More Comprehensive Conception of College Readiness.* The four-part model presented in the monograph went significantly beyond traditional criteria that have been used to determine students' eligibility for postsecondary studies. Since then, the model has been refined, and several of the components have been relabeled without dramatically changing the model's overall structure and content. Now known as the *four keys to college and career readiness,* the model incorporates recent research that led to the addition of new skill and knowledge areas and to more precise specification of the commonalities between college readiness and career readiness.

This chapter first provides an overview of the four keys. It then looks at the first two of the four keys that comprise college and career readiness in depth: key cognitive strategies and key content knowledge. The next chapter details the other two keys in depth: key learning skills and techniques and key transition knowledge and skills. Table 3.1 provides an overview of the four keys.

Students are ready for college and careers to the degree to which they have mastered all of the elements in all four keys. Students who have not mastered all are not necessarily incapable of going to college, but they are likely to struggle more than students who possess knowledge and skills in all of these areas.

TABLE 3.1   COMPONENTS OF THE FOUR KEYS MODEL

Key Cognitive Strategies	Key Content Knowledge	Key Learning Skills and Techniques	Key Transition Knowledge and Skills
Problem formulation • Hypothesize • Strategize Research • Identify • Collect Interpretation • Analyze • Evaluate Communication • Organize • Construct Precision and accuracy • Monitor • Confirm	Structure of knowledge • Key terms and terminology • Factual information • Linking ideas • Organizing concepts Technical knowledge and skills • Challenge level • Value • Attribution • Effort	Ownership of learning • Goal setting • Persistence • Self-awareness • Motivation • Help seeking • Progress monitoring • Self-efficacy Learning techniques • Time management • Study skills • Test-taking skills • Note-taking skills • Memorization/recall • Strategic reading • Collaborative learning • Technology	Contextual • Aspirations • Norms/culture Procedural • Institution choice • Admission process Financial • Tuition • Financial aid Cultural • Postsecondary norms Personal • Self-advocacy in an institutional context

Key Cognitive Strategies

Key cognitive strategies are the ways of thinking that are necessary for postsecondary-level work. They include formulating hypotheses and developing problem-solving strategies, identifying sources and collecting information, analyzing and evaluating findings or conflicting viewpoints, organizing and constructing work products in a variety of formats, and monitoring and confirming the precision and accuracy of all work produced.

Key Content Knowledge

Key content knowledge refers to the foundational content and big ideas from core subjects that all students must know well, and to the understanding of the big ideas in core subject areas that enable students to gain insight into and retain what they are learning. Also included in this key are the technical knowledge and skills associated with specific career aspirations, the ways in which students interact with content knowledge, its perceived value to them, the effort they are willing to expend to learn necessary content, and their explanations of why they succeed or fail in mastering this knowledge.

Key Learning Skills and Techniques

Key learning skills and techniques consist of two broad categories:

- *Student ownership of learning*, which includes goal setting, persistence, self-awareness, motivation, help seeking, progress monitoring, and self-efficacy
- *Specific learning techniques and strategies*, such as time management, study skills, test-taking skills, note-taking skills, memorization and recall techniques, strategic reading, collaborative learning, and technology skills

Students need to master these to succeed in most academic courses and also to continue to learn once they have concluded their formal education. These skills are useful and important to success in all content areas.

Key Transition Knowledge and Skills

Key transition knowledge and skills are necessary to navigate successfully the transition to life beyond high school. This is information that is not equally accessible to all students. Least likely to have this information are students from families and communities historically underrepresented in higher education or certain career pathways. This key includes, among other things, knowing which courses to take in high school in order to be admitted to an appropriate postsecondary program, understanding financial aid options and procedures, being focused on a career pathway or major, understanding college-level and workforce norms and expectations, and knowing how to be a self-advocate who can take advantage of resources and solve problems encountered within the institutional framework of a postsecondary program.

Key Cognitive Strategies in Depth

Research conducted over the past fifteen years on the content of college courses and instructor expectations has yielded remarkably consistent findings: to be successful in entry-level, credit-bearing general education college courses and, increasingly, in occupational training programs that lead to careers, students must have developed a set of cognitive strategies that they can apply to varied learning situations. They need to know how to think in particular ways about the content they are learning. They need to be able to do more than retain or apply information; they have to process and manipulate it, assemble and reassemble it, examine it, question it, look for patterns in it, organize it, and present it. These more demanding tasks require cognitive strategies that are not generally developed very consistently in a typical secondary school education.

> Students must have developed a set of cognitive strategies that they can apply to varied learning situations.

A strategy is a systematic approach that anticipates the key issues or problems that will be encountered to complete a process. An effective strategy is adaptive based on the specific challenges and nature of the task at hand, and it draws from prior knowledge and expertise on how to achieve the goal of the process. An effective strategy derives from a series of decisions, some conscious, some more intuitive, in which the learner selects from among various options the most effective and efficient way to address the challenges that the particular problem poses. Strategy is more than following directions; it is the consideration and evaluation of the trade-offs and feasibility of the different options available as means to address the issue at hand.

Adults generally have a range of strategies to deal with daily life challenges. Think about how you approach the task of assembling something you purchased that contains numerous parts and pieces. You probably have a preferred way of doing this, and you start with that approach to see if it works. Your default strategy may be to read the directions, or lay out all the parts and pieces in groups, or look at the picture on the box and visualize how it fits together, or perhaps go online to view a YouTube video or visit a user forum to see what problems others have encountered assembling this same item. As you come across problems or challenges that your initial strategy can't help you resolve, you may employ other strategies, such as calling a help line or going back to an online forum and posting a question. You may ask for help from someone more skilled than you. Or you may simply hire someone else to do it for you. In short, you have at your disposal a lot of options and a lot of experience that lead you to have a host of options from which you can choose. You know what will likely work best if, for example, the directions turn out to be poorly translated or in such small text that you cannot decipher them, or if you end up with extra parts after having completed the assembly. You may not look forward to the task of assembling what you bought, but you don't let the task discourage you from buying the item in the first place.

Now think about how young learners approach learning situations where they have to complete a task or achieve a goal that is new or unfamiliar to them. Effective learners may have more than one way to go about it, but learners without strategies simply do what they are told and nothing more; in other words, they follow directions—literally. If that works, they proceed, but with little insight into why it worked. If it doesn't work, they stop, with little insight into why it didn't work. Without strategies for how to proceed when they encounter a problem, ineffective learners repeat the same mistakes over and over, not because they are not cognitively capable of learning but because they do not know what to do next or how to approach the task from another direction. This is particularly true for special populations of learners such as those with disabilities and English language learners because they are not given the cognitively challenging opportunities necessary to develop strategies in the first place.

Developing strategic learning techniques takes time and practice. Most students don't get enough opportunities to practice an array of learning strategies as they go through school. The effect is borne out in studies that the Educational Policy Improvement Center has conducted of college faculty nationwide who teach entry-level courses. With near-universal agreement, they assert that most students, even those with good high school grades, arrive unprepared for the intellectual demands and expectations of college. The courses students encounter when they reach college differ from high school courses in several important ways. Students are expected to be proficient in a number of cognitive strategies that require them to think more deeply about what they are learning. Skill in employing these strategies can be as important as specific content knowledge. Faculty across the full spectrum of postsecondary institutions, from selective universities to open enrollment campuses, are consistent in this regard: students must be able to think about and apply what they learn in order to succeed.

The Five Key Cognitive Strategies

Our findings led us to look deeper to see what types of strategies students were expected to demonstrate in these college courses. As we analyzed college course syllabi and assignments and as we heard from ever more college instructors, we identified five key cognitive strategies, each with two components, that represent the intentional patterns of thinking that students must be able to draw on as they complete college-level work (figure 3.1):

- Problem formulation: Hypothesize and strategize
- Research: Identify and collect
- Interpretation: Analyze and evaluate
- Communication: Organize and construct
- Precision and accuracy: Monitor and confirm

These strategies are applied throughout the learning process and can be thought of as revolving around the notion of inquiry, of thinking more deeply about what one is learning, of formulating ideas, seeking information, reflecting on findings to generate conclusions, reporting these results in a variety of ways based on the nature of the subject area, and doing all of this with the precision and accuracy required of the subject area and the specific problem or issue being addressed.

FIGURE 3.1 THE KEY COGNITIVE STRATEGIES

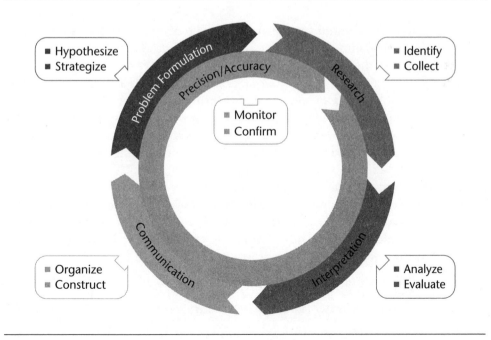

We examine the five key cognitive strategies and their components in the following sections. Note that each component is in the form of an action verb that identifies what students do to address each strategy.

Problem Formulation Students demonstrate clarity about the nature of the problem, identify potential outcomes, and develop strategies for exploring all components of the problem:

> *Hypothesize:* Students formulate a complete, comprehensive hypothesis that contains a cause-and-effect or thesis statement that is sufficient to formulate a potential solution to the task.
>
> *Strategize:* Students consider one or more plausible approaches that could lead to a solution and generate a feasible plan of action to implement the approach. In the process, students may revisit and revise the hypothesis as a result of thinking about potential methods to solve the problem.

Research Students explore a full range of available resources and collection techniques or generate original data. They also make judgments about the sources of information or quality of the data, and determine the usefulness of the information or data collected:

> *Identify:* Students consider a full range of appropriate resources and determine how and where to locate available informational material and source data.
>
> *Collect:* Students make judgments about available informational material and data sources, considering validity, credibility, and relevance. In addition, they collect information and data necessary to address the hypothesis. Students may revisit their resources and information collection process as their thinking evolves.

Interpretation Students identify and consider the most relevant information or findings. In order to make connections and draw conclusions, they need to use structures and strategies that contribute to the framework for communicating a solution. Reflecting on the quality of the conclusions drawn is an important part of this strategy.

> *Analyze:* Students deconstruct information and data, select evidence, and use analytical tools to structure findings or insights. They look

for patterns and relationships as the basis for developing ideas and insights relevant to the problem and its solution.

Evaluate: Students group information into usable pieces, connect ideas and supporting evidence, and draw conclusions. They also reflect on the quality of the conclusions they have drawn.

Communication Students organize information and insights into a structured line of reasoning and construct a coherent and complete final version through a process that includes drafting, incorporating feedback, reflecting, and revising:

Organize: Students incorporate ideas and supporting evidence purposefully using structures that demonstrate the line of reasoning.

Construct: Students create a draft, incorporate feedback to make appropriate revisions, and present a final product that is appropriate for the purpose and audience.

Precision and Accuracy Students apply this strategy throughout the entire process. They are appropriately precise and accurate at all stages of the process, determining and using language, terms, expressions, rules, terminology, and conventions appropriate to the subject area and problem:

Monitor: Students determine and apply standards for precision and accuracy appropriate to the subject area throughout the task.

Confirm: Student confirm that the final product meets all discipline-specific standards for precision and accuracy in language, terms, expressions, rules, terminology, and conventions.

Teaching to the Key Cognitive Strategies

Teaching in ways that emphasize and develop the key cognitive strategies can open up thinking about student learning and what constitutes sufficiently challenging assignments. For example, problem formulation is often difficult for students because they have little experience formulating problems. Teachers tend to give students the problem. In cases where students do have to formulate a problem, their instinct is to ask the teacher what the problem is. Even well-intentioned teachers often inadvertently formulate the problem for the students when they don't need to do so.

The instinct of many teachers is to structure and guide learning, to turn any task into a series of directions and procedures to follow. Allowing students to formulate problems requires tasks or situations that are sufficiently challenging or open-ended enough to accommodate multiple possible solutions or resolutions.

Similarly, what passes for research by students is often just a rudimentary trip to Wikipedia or a randomly selected set of online sources from a Google search without a great deal of thought about the credibility, value, or appropriateness of the sources. Instead of interpreting what they find after they gather information, students are more used to repeating verbatim their basic findings. When it comes to communicating, more often than not, students would prefer to go right from being given an assignment to writing their response without the intermediate steps of problem formulation, research, and interpretation. They either don't want to or don't know how to go through the process necessary to think about what they are trying to do, and it shows in the end. Similarly, when students get to the communication key cognitive strategy, their natural tendency is to write or otherwise complete their assignment without revising, editing, or reviewing what they produce in their first draft. One-and-done is all too often the way students approach assignments, even assignments that clearly require time and attention to detail, precision, and quality.

> One-and-done is all too often the way students approach assignments.

However, the whole point of the key cognitive strategies process is to cause students to have to think about what they are doing. This extra time, energy, and effort results in the brain's consolidating knowledge, building new neural pathways and connections, and learning from the experience. In this fashion, new strategies are identified, developed, and incorporated for future use. For example, teachers might give students an assignment like this one:

Natural disasters affect people and society. Identify a natural disaster and describe its effects on civilization, historically and in the present. Be sure to describe the ways this natural disaster disrupts the economy and people's lives. List three things that could be done to lessen the effects of this type of natural disaster in the future. Tell whether you agree or disagree with these types of ways to reduce the impact of the natural disaster you are describing.

This assignment has nothing wrong with it, but it doesn't give students much opportunity to think or formulate a hypothesis. Students can complete this assignment successfully merely by looking up information and incorporating it. But note how the hypothesis is essentially given to them. Note also how the assignment can be completed by following directions literally and not making very many independent decisions about the strategies to use.

This same assignment reformulated in a fashion that creates an opportunity for students to develop a hypothesis before proceeding might look something like this:

Natural disasters have been a part of the human experience throughout history. Consider the reasons humans are affected by natural disasters and how this interaction with natural disasters might have shaped human society in specific ways. You may pick one type of natural disaster that best illustrates your point of view on how society might be affected by this type of disaster, or you may compare and contrast the effects of different kinds of disasters. Identify means humans could adopt to deal with disasters and how, in doing so, this might change how disasters affect society. Conclude with a discussion of your observations about the relationship between human society and natural disasters in which you offer insights and observations you have not encountered in your research.

The assignment still has an overall structure to it, but it expects students to make a series of critical decisions throughout the process, beginning with the reasons they identify for natural disasters affecting humans, then choosing to present a case study of one disaster or a comparative analysis of multiple classes of disasters, then offering observations on effects and remedies, and concluding with an invitation to offer original ideas on the topic. Yes, it will be difficult for students to do this with no prior instruction in how to think strategically, but if they have been taught the key cognitive strategies model for multiple years, with opportunities to practice using it on increasingly complex tasks, this assignment will not be overwhelmingly difficult for them.

This assignment is aligned with the organizing concepts in the scoring guide presented in chapter 6: insight, efficiency, idea generation, concept formation, integration, and solution seeking. You will see that the assignment presents opportunities for students to demonstrate expertise on many of those concepts.

Teachers who look at an assignment like this may conclude that it is beyond the current capabilities of their students, and in many cases, they would be correct. However, this is not because the students are simply incapable of doing this sort of work; it is because they have not been taught how to or been given the opportunity to do so with sufficient frequency. Developing cognitive strategies requires considerable practice over time with increasingly more complex assignments. The ThinkReady system described in the appendix spans grades 6 to 12 and develops student thinking skills by means of progressively more challenging tasks that are closely aligned with the key cognitive strategies.

Key Content Knowledge in Depth

This key is somewhat different from the other three, which contain more specific elements. If this key were of similar organization, it would consist of a specification of the precise content knowledge a student needs to know. It does not because the college and career readiness level of the Common Core State Standards or other college readiness standards presented in this book, such as Standards for Success and the Texas College and Career Readiness Standards, are assumed to specify content knowledge necessary to be college and career ready. It would serve little useful purpose to repeat what is in those standards. Instead, this key explains what it takes for students to learn important content effectively and efficiently:

- The content is well organized.
- Key ideas are identified.
- Students believe that effort will make a difference in their learning it.
- The content is valuable to learn in the first place.

What's Important to Know?

Educators probably spend less time thinking about the content knowledge that students need to know than the myriad other issues associated with running a classroom. Content is often taken as a given, although the advent of standards has resulted in periodic reevaluations of what is important to include. However, most subject areas at the secondary level include much of the same content they always have. The Common Core State Standards provide all educators with a convenient framework to determine if the English language arts and mathematics they are teaching and emphasizing are most important for college and career readiness. These standards also offer guidance on how literacy and mathematical knowledge and concepts should be applied in other subject areas. They do not provide any guidance in other subject areas, however, a point considered in chapter 7.

The key content knowledge students need to know derives from research on college readiness content knowledge that is somewhat encouraging. Students need strong foundational knowledge in core academic subjects, and they also need to have an understanding of the structure of knowledge in the subject areas. By *structure of knowledge*, I mean they need to know the big ideas and how those ideas frame the study of the subject. They need to see how the big ideas provide an umbrella under which reside in each subject area a set of enduring understandings and organizing concepts. These in turn create the structure within which the topics and objectives that make up daily instruction in most classrooms are located. Students come to understand that high school classes represent separate academic disciplines—each with its own way of knowing, its own rules for organizing information, and its own ways of communicating its understandings of the natural world. When students gain this insight, they are vastly better prepared for college than students who have no idea how the pieces they are learning fit into a whole.

Armed with this understanding of the structure of knowledge and the underlying logic of the subject area, students can make more sense of the key terms and terminology they learn. Each subject has its own vocabulary, and much foundational learning is the act of comprehending these key terms and terminology. Teaching this requires awareness of how the brain organizes and retains bits of information into structures—what psychologists call a *schema*. The understanding of structure and big ideas creates the scaffold on which terms and terminology can reside and be connected. The two go hand in hand. Without a structure, it's difficult to retain key terms. Without the terms and terminology, it's tough to do much with the big ideas.

When the brain has the overarching structures in place and has mastered key terms and terminology, it can manage factual information much more efficiently and effectively. It's difficult for learners to retain facts in the absence of any connections to larger structures in the brain. For many

3

THE FOUR KEYS
TO COLLEGE AND
CAREER READINESS

learners, the jumble of information coming at them daily never gets organized, and as a result, it never gets retained. It's the reason that something like the concept of a noun can be taught at six or seven different grade levels and still not be retained. Without an understanding of the structure of language and the nature and purposes of grammar, students must rely on remembering the rules for the use of nouns. Forget the purpose of a noun, and you've forgotten what a noun is.

As students learn the big ideas, key terminology, and factual information, they need organizing concepts and linking ideas to serve as intermediate structures for grouping information. Without these, the learning chunks are too big. As an oversimplified example, if I were ask you to remember the names of the twenty-some streets in downtown Portland north of Burnside Street, you would likely have difficulty doing so. However, if I told you they were ordered alphabetically (Burnside, Couch, Davis, Everett, Glisan, and so on), you would likely have a much easier time of it. This is one way an organizing concept makes it easier to sort, categorize, and make the connections between specific bits of information and larger organizing concepts.

Understanding that biology is the study of systems of living organisms and that these systems can be very small or very large is another type of key organizing concept. Biology can entail the study of molecules, cells, groups of cells, organisms, populations, communities, ecosystems, and the biosphere. Each has its own set of organizing concepts as well.

An example of this type of organizational system can be found in the redesigned Advanced Placement Biology course and examination, which employs what it refers to as "four big ideas"—for example:

- *Big Idea 1:* The process of evolution drives the diversity and unity of life.
- *Big Idea 2:* Biological systems utilize free energy and molecular building blocks to grow, to reproduce, and to maintain dynamic homeostasis.
- *Big Idea 3:* Living systems store, retrieve, transmit, and respond to information essential to life processes.
- *Big Idea 4:* Biological systems interact, and these systems and their interactions possess complex properties.

Nested under each of these big ideas is a set of "enduring understandings." Each of these then contains "essential knowledge" statements that are accompanied by learning objectives (LOs)—for example:

AP Biology Organizing Concepts

- *Big Idea 1:* The process of evolution drives the diversity and unity of life.
  - *Enduring understanding 1.A:* Change in the genetic makeup of a population over time is evolution.
  - *Essential knowledge:* Evolutionary fitness is measured by reproductive success.
    - LO 1.2 The student is able to evaluate evidence provided by data to qualitatively and quantitatively investigate the role of natural selection in evolution.

In this way, the overall conceptual structure of the course is developed and expanded through multiple levels until reaching each specific learning objective. The reason for each one being taught can be ascertained by simply tracking back up the conceptual chain to see how it explicates the essential knowledge, enduring understanding, and big idea in which it is nested.

If students understand that axioms and organizing concepts specify the key ideas of their studies in biology, they have a framework within which to organize much of the very specific information and vocabulary they will be presented. They also know if they do not understand an organizing concept, they need to do what's necessary to make sure they do so that they retain the information related to the concept. Additional organizing concepts can be presented with increasing specificity to help students connect their conceptual understanding across each succeeding level of specificity until they reach the declarative knowledge level of factual information and terms.

In addition to equipping students with deeper understandings and stronger retention of ideas, concepts, terms, and facts, strong programs of college and career readiness attend to the ways in which students approach learning. Perhaps the most important single thing to know about learners is how they attribute success in learning the subject. The two basic ways to think about this are aptitude-based and effort-based attribution theories.

Teaching Key Content Knowledge

It is not enough simply to have students learn high-quality content knowledge, even when that knowledge is carefully organized, structured, and presented clearly. Understanding student explanations of how they learn content knowledge is as important as the content itself they are being asked to learn. Their beliefs are a key factor in their ultimate success. One of the first and most important things to establish is that success at learning content is a function of effort much more than aptitude.

 Success at learning content is a function of effort much more than aptitude.

Students who believe success is based primarily on aptitude subscribe to the notion that ability is innate—that you can either learn something or you can't. This mind-set leads to explanations of success based on someone being "good at" a subject and of failure based on "just not being good at" the subject. The problem with this belief system is that no amount of effort can make a difference. Learners who think this way basically have little control over their success or failure. They have little to learn from their failures (or successes) or from those who do well in the subject. If ability is predetermined, these students have little left to do except go through the motions, and avoid anything that doesn't come naturally—in other words, that requires effort.

Students who adopt an effort-based approach to learning know that their behavior and the decisions they make matter. They know that learning is not necessarily easy for anyone and that the difference in most cases is the time, energy, and learning strategies devoted to understanding a subject area. These students are more receptive to developing new learning skills and techniques. They realize that good study methods are crucial, that they must be able to manage their time and know exactly what's expected of them. They are not shy about seeking help because they do not view doing so as an indication of some sort of deficit on their part. They are not surprised or chagrined when they get an answer wrong or struggle to solve a problem, learn a concept, or complete a project. In fact, they expect to encounter a modicum of frustration and are prepared to confront obstacles.

Interestingly, research suggests that students with aptitude-based explanations of their success tend to be more concerned about failing than those who view effort as more important. These successful students take fewer chances because they expect everything to come easily and they expect to get good grades consistently. They strive to maintain the public perception that they are "smart" at the subject, and they avoid anything that might not conform to this viewpoint. They may dismiss a difficult problem or assignment as not being clear or "fair" and explain their lack of success by placing blame on the teacher for any of a range of shortcomings. Explanations for failure are generally externalized and attributed to factors outside their control. The net effect is that they learn little or nothing from their mistakes or failures.

Students who consistently do poorly often have an odd combination of the worst of the aptitude and effort mind-sets. They adopt an aptitude explanation of their difficulties by saying they are "just not good at" the subject. But they also don't usually take chances, extend themselves, or make a full effort. By holding back, they can continue to tell themselves that they could have done better if only they had tried. They guard themselves psychologically from the devastating effects of having to reach the conclusion that they might be unable to do the work.

The other major consideration regarding teaching content knowledge is the challenge level of the material itself, which must follow the Goldilocks rule: not so challenging that students cannot hope to succeed, not so easy that they do not have to struggle. The material must be in what psychologist Lev Vygotsky labeled the *zone of proximal development*, which refers to the need to stretch students in order to get them to engage but not to overreach and ask them to do things they are legitimately incapable of doing yet.

Learning progressions help teachers and students see the sequence of content and, more important, define the cognitive challenge level so that it is possible to gear material to students in a more individualized way that makes sure they are always stretched or pushed just enough to make learning meaningful. When this is occurring, student self-confidence as a learner is increased, even if the student isn't successful all of the time. This type of orientation to learning is important if students are to enter postsecondary education and career pathways confident, self-reliant, and comfortable engaging with content that is challenging to them.

❧

The key cognitive strategies and key content knowledge establish the thinking methods closely associated with content understanding, retention, and mastery and the structure of knowledge and the learning relationships needed to master important content. The next chapter examines the other two keys, key learning skills and techniques and key transition knowledge and skills, which address learning processes and the high school-to-college transition process. Students must seek to master all of these if they are to be fully ready for college, careers, and lifelong learning.

☺ Awareness and Action Steps

- Review and discuss the four keys model. Refer to table 3.1, which contains the forty-one aspects of the model.
- Examine one or more programs, such as AVID (Advancement Via Individual Determination), and identify which aspects of which key the program helps develop.
- Think of a situation in which you, as an adult, select from among a range of strategies to complete a task or deal with a problem or challenge. How did you develop that range of strategies? How do you choose among them?
- What percentage of students would be able to complete an assignment that required them to use the key cognitive strategies? Which key cognitive strategy would cause students the most difficulty? See the website for this book for programs and techniques to teach cognitive strategies to more students (www.collegecareerready.org).
- View the sample ThinkReady task in the appendix. Which elements would be challenging for students? What kind of support or scaffolding could be provided to help them complete it successfully?
- Using the Advanced Placement example as a model, design a simple poster, or work with students to do so, that shows the big ideas of your subject, the enduring understanding, and the organizing concepts. Often this information can be found on the websites of content organizations and other groups concerned with teaching in the subject area in question. Post the resulting product in the classroom. Refer to *Essential Questions* by Jay McTighe and Grant Wiggins for ideas and examples.
- Survey students to determine what percentage think success in each content area is a function of aptitude and what percentage think it's a result of effort. Consider programs such as Carol Dweck's Brainology (http://bit.ly/11JxZdw) or your own approach to get more students to believe effort is the key to success.
- Add a section to each course syllabus that identifies how the course builds on knowledge and skills from the previous course or grade level and how it prepares students for the next course or grade level.
- Require students to expand their research skills using *Research Methods Knowledge Base*, a free web-based textbook that familiarizes students with the diverse aspects of social research: formulating questions, choosing a sample, data analysis, ethics, and so on (http://bit.ly/1bSpZMV).
- Have students use the online site Pinterest to collect sources for research, visualize a new concept, or catalogue colleges or careers they are interested in.

CHAPTER 4

THE FOUR KEYS CONTINUED: LEARNING SKILLS AND TRANSITION SKILLS

While mastery of content knowledge and proficiency with cognitive strategies are unquestionably important, student ability to employ a range of skills and techniques essential to the learning process and to master the transition to postsecondary programs may over the long term end up being as important as their content knowledge and cognitive strategies. Unfortunately, important learning skills and techniques are not necessarily taught systematically in school, and students have little formal preparation for the sometimes-wrenching transition they are about to make from being high school students to college students. This chapter outlines the knowledge and skills students must have to be effective learners and to be able to handle major life transitions, specifically moving from high school to college.

Key Learning Skills and Techniques in Depth

The key learning skills and techniques comprise a series of elements that specify how students can take greater ownership of their learning and another set of teachable skills that enable students to learn more efficiently and effectively. Success in postsecondary education and job training programs is contingent on learners being able to learn with greater independence and efficiency. The key learning skills and techniques identify what learners need to do after high school to learn successfully in a wide range of settings. They prepare students to be lifelong learners.

When educators and policymakers speak of an achievement gap, they generally talk entirely in terms of student knowledge and skills in English and mathematics. The only way to close this gap, it is said, is to raise test scores in these subjects by reteaching content in areas where students perform poorly on the tests. And yet schools that follow this approach rarely close the gap, and even if they do, their students still experience difficulty when and if they do get to college. Why? Why do many students who manage to learn college-ready content end up struggling in college? What other skills beyond subject-matter knowledge might be necessary for those students to succeed?

The Achievement Gap

One key unexplored reason is that little to no attention is given to developing the learning skills and techniques students need to own and manage their learning. In the absence of these critically important skills, students remain dependent learners who struggle when expected to work independently. In essence, they lack the tool kits to manage their own learning process. Just as students who lack a repertoire of cognitive strategies stop short when they confront a task requiring them to employ a new strategy, so too do learners who need to adopt a new learning strategy when the one they are using proves ineffective.

Yet some students do develop the requisite skills to be effective self-directed learners. They may learn these in school because their teachers diligently develop these skills, they may acquire them from their home environment where they are given tips and support on how to handle challenging situations, or they may acquire them in other ways, such as when they learn a musical instrument, play a sport, develop a hobby, or participate in extracurricular activities that require adaptation and improvisation.

Ownership of Learning

No single factor may be more important to student success than the degree to which students take ownership of their learning and are allowed to do so. Not only does this key learning skill result in improved achievement, it is a more efficient and cost-effective way to manage the learning process. When students take ownership of learning, many more approaches to learning are possible, ranging from self-guided methods to online courses. Absent ownership, the traditional teacher-student didactic approach is the only real option, but this approach may not be sufficient when deeper learning is desired and the goal is for students to master the Common Core State Standards and become college and career ready.

At the heart of student ownership of learning is a complex of intersecting skills and dispositions. Among them are the topics explored in the next sections:

- Goal setting
- Persistence
- Self-awareness
- Motivation
- Help seeking
- Progress monitoring
- Self-efficacy

> No single factor may be more important to student success than the degree to which students take ownership of their learning and are allowed to do so.

Goal Setting Perhaps none of these skills and dispositions is more important than having a goal or reason to learn. That goal can be as broad as desiring to develop more fully as a human being or as targeted as wanting to become, say, a medical records technician. In some ways, it doesn't matter what the exact goal is as long students see the academic programs in which they are engaged as somehow contributing to achieving their goals. Having the goal to become a rock guitar player or professional snowboarder is not a bad thing in and of itself. It can lead students to develop skills of disciplined practice and stronger self-control and self-direction, but only rarely does the goal connect very directly to classroom academic success. For far too many students, goals of this nature aren't really goals at all; they are fantasies or diversions that can hinder them from coming to grips with the reality of what it takes to be ready to succeed in their lives.

Learning how to set goals should begin when students are young and then be incorporated into schooling at all subsequent grade levels. Students should learn how to set and achieve short-term, medium-term, and long-term goals. A short-term goal might revolve around doing better on the next assignment. A medium-term goal might require improving a skill area such as time management by learning how to manage time better over the course of an academic term. Longer-term goals should be specific enough to focus student behavior but broad enough to acknowledge the multiple pathways available to achieving the goal. Goals of this type generally are stated in terms of some sort of desired academic or career accomplishment, for example, attending college, pursuing a major or career area, or developing an interest. Long-term goals can take many forms and can be quite fluid. The key thing is for all students to have one or more throughout school.

Goals need to be recorded, and progress toward them needs to be measured regularly. One of the key things this accomplishes is a sense of causality—that students' actions matter and that students can influence or control their lives through their actions. It's worth noting that many young people come from communities in which cause and effect does not seem to hold sway, where bad things happen to good people for no apparent reason, where goals are rarely achieved and are often thwarted by the most arbitrary and unfair of circumstances or occurrences. Students from such backgrounds have a difficult time buying into the notion that hard work now pays off in the future. Giving these students tools to create some sense of control in their lives by setting and achieving goals, however modest those goals might be initially, can be incredibly empowering. Knowing how to set goals also puts them on the road to developing the self-reliance they will need in order to succeed in postsecondary education and the workplace.

Persistence Achieving goals requires the development of a constellation of skills. Most goals worth pursuing require persistence—the ability to continue in the face of frustration and failure. Many well-intentioned educators (and parents) attempt to minimize student frustration and failure by limiting challenge or by oversupporting. The effect can be to create young people who are not aware of their limitations and overestimate the significance of their accomplishments. The result is fragile learners who avoid situations that might shatter their carefully crafted illusion of competence.

Others have used terms such as *grit* and *tenacity* to describe the necessary behaviors to support goal achievement. I prefer the term *persistence* because the implication for me of terms such as *grit* and *tenacity* is that learners first must have obstacles to overcome in order to be gritty or tenacious. *Persistence*, on the other hand, connotes sustained effort over time and not necessarily triumphing over barriers, institutional, personal, or otherwise. Persistence does accommodate grit and tenacity but does not require adversity to demonstrate a commitment to maintaining effort sufficient to complete the task at hand or achieve meaningful goals. Students do not need obstacles placed in their paths for them that they must overcome tenaciously, such as poor teaching, poor facilities, unclear ends and aims, and irrelevant content, in order for them to demonstrate they are worthy of college and career opportunities. Learning challenges need to be carefully crafted to reward persistence, not create additional barriers.

> Learning challenges need to be carefully crafted to reward persistence, not create additional barriers.

Self-Awareness and Locus of Control Competent learners are cognizant of how good their work is. They know, independent of the teacher's judgment, whether what they are doing is of high quality. Students with experience in the performing arts and competitive sports perhaps understand this phenomenon best. They know it doesn't matter what a parent, teacher, or coach tells them. The true judgment is in the performance itself, and the final judgment often emanates from an external audience that has its own criteria by which it is judging the performance.

Self-aware learners are capable of saying a work product is not good enough even when they have received a high mark or praise for it. They can do this because they have sufficient confidence in their abilities to improve, largely through hard work, that they do not need to explain away a less-than-stellar performance by blaming others. They are comfortable discussing the strengths and weaknesses of their work, taking pride in what they did well and planning how to improve in areas where they did not. Self-aware learners have an internal mechanism of sorts that tells them how well they are doing. They do not need to be perfectionists who cannot take any satisfaction even from a very good performance or product. They are, however, realists who on occasion come to grips with the fact that they must settle for less than their best effort because they do not have the time or because the improvements they know they could make would not be noticed. They do not, however, kid themselves about what they have done and what they need to do.

This type of internal locus of control manifests itself in many ways. Effective learners who possess a range of key skills and techniques know how to become motivated to complete challenging tasks and assignments, even in areas where they may be less interested in the subject. They use a combination of internal and external motivation. Although many educators extol the virtues of intrinsic motivation, wherein students do things for the sheer joy of doing them, extrinsic motivation has its place as well. Knowing they need good grades in order to meet admission standards if they are to pursue their goal is just as important for successful students as completing an assignment for the sheer interest or excitement generated by the topic.

Students need help learning how to identify and harness both forms of motivation and to recognize that they are unlikely to do well in most classes without a combination of the two. While teachers and other adults can create systems that maximize student motivation, ultimately the students must manage their own motivation. They need to learn how to gear up even in situations where they are not naturally excited. They need to be given the tools that effective learners use to get through the tough times that all learners experience over the course of their schooling. Equipped with these tools and strategies, learners are ready for postsecondary environments, workplace training, the military, and other environments that expect them to be motivated and engaged.

These types of learning skills can be taught to all students. Currently the tendency is to view many of the key learning skills as personality traits that some students possess and others don't. Evidence, however, suggests that these skills are all highly teachable, but that they are going to be more challenging for students from some backgrounds to learn. When students don't necessarily believe they can be successful, it is harder to get them to internalize these skills. In this case, success can breed success, and students can be taught these skills incrementally and come to see that they are better and more successful learners as a result.

Help Seeking Skillful learners know when they need help. It's surprising how many learners do not know when they are in over their heads. And even when they do, they don't know how to get help they need or simply don't get it. Our research and that of others suggests that the students most in need of help are the least likely to pursue it on their own. Students from low-income families, members of certain ethnic minority groups, and those who are first in family to pursue postsecondary educations tend to struggle in college because they don't know how to get help or they believe that accepting help indicates they aren't really college material in the first place. They inadvertently set a high bar for themselves, in part because they believe that all the students who are succeeding are doing so without the need for help.

> The students most in need of help are the least likely to pursue it on their own.

In contrast, high achievers know how to seek help so well that sometimes they institute a near-monopoly on such resources. Perhaps online learning environments will level the playing field because all students can pursue help anonymously, but it is more likely that the anonymity will play against those who most need help. A more effective approach is to teach the students who most need it how to access available resources on their own. They need to develop a mind-set that seeking and accepting help is not tantamount to failure. They need to know that everyone needs help at one point or another; they may just not see how others are receiving the help they need.

When these students reach college and training programs, they will have potential access to a range of resources to assist them. Most colleges have academic support programs, tutors, advisors, and study groups available to aid students. However, accessing these resources almost always requires assertive action on students' part. They will no longer be able to depend on someone telling them to come to a study session or go to office hours. They will have to do so on their own. They will need to know:

- How to join a study group and participate effectively
- How to use campus-level and departmental academic advisors
- How best to use office hours or course study sessions, the library, peer tutors, and campus academic support centers

The only way this will occur is if they have developed the habit of using and seeking out available resources to help them succeed.

Another way to think about many of these self-monitoring behaviors is the notion of student self-efficacy, which is the idea that learners can produce the effect or outcome on the learning that they desire. Self-efficacy is the sense of control over the factors that make a difference for success in a chosen endeavor. This concept is closely related to empowerment because learners can legitimately advocate for and pursue their own success and have the power to do so.

Learning Techniques

In addition to assuming ownership of learning, students need a set of techniques to succeed in challenging and demanding learning situations generally and to reach the college- and career-ready level of the Common Core State Standards specifically. These techniques are numerous and varied. A few are discussed here to illustrate what they are and why they are important. Numerous commercial programs and products exist that teach these techniques. In addition, teachers can use their own methods. The website that accompanies this book, found at www.collegecareerready.org, offers examples of ready-to-use programs, as well as examples of teacher-developed approaches.

Time Management A key aspect of being an independent learner who can manage challenging assignments is the ability to manage time. The skills include:

- Scheduling
- Prioritizing
- Knowing what is a realistic amount of time to complete a task
- Pacing and distributing work over the course of a term
- Balancing competing demands
- Determining the highest return on time invested when confronting multiple competing deadlines
- Understanding how to break complex assignments into pieces that can be tackled sequentially

Time management begins with the simple act of writing down assignments, something many students fail to do in the first place. Once they have a reliable system for recording work in place and are using it reliably, they need good calendaring tools along with a to-do list system. With this basic infrastructure, students can then devise numerous plans and strategies for organizing their time. Teachers can help students develop the habits of recording assignments and keeping track of what they need to do. They can also reward students for demonstrating that they are managing their time well and hold them accountable for not recording assignments or being able to produce a to-do list of course-related tasks and activities.

While some young people are naturals at time management and others are not, this is a skill that every student can learn. Teachers need to be well organized themselves. They need to be able to let students know what will be going on in class. Detailed course syllabi with all requirements and due dates clearly spelled out are key to helping students organize their time. Even in competency-based settings where material may be retaught as necessary, students still need to know what they are expected to do, and by when. It is also important to have some assignments that require time management, for example, research papers that expect students to assemble resources first and then complete more than one draft. If all work or all assignments can be done the night before the work is due, students have little reason to learn time management skills.

Study Skills Study skills consist of a host of techniques and strategies necessary to learn material and complete assignments outside class. Some examples of study skills include knowing how long to study, where to study, how to break material down into manageable chunks to study, and who to study with. Many students devote time to studying but do not have well-developed study skills. The result is that they think they are doing what they need to do to succeed in class, but in fact they are not learning the necessary material or completing assignments at a sufficient level.

Many students unfortunately can never begin to study in the first place because they never get organized enough to plan for and then engage in a productive study session. Personal organization is a key prerequisite skill to studying successfully. Writing down assignments or having a copy of the syllabus available to refer to is the first step. Having all necessary materials available at hand enables students to get focused immediately and make the best use of study time.

It is also important to know how long to study in one sitting. The time-honored tradition of cramming, a technique that many students swear by, has been shown to be far less effective than study distributed over time. Students need to know how to pace their studying. This is different from time management in the sense that students need to make decisions about which material they need to study when and how to organize and sequence their studying to lead to completion of key assignments and culminate in readiness for important exams.

In his book *Brain Rules*, Jim Medina suggests that students benefit by varying the location and time of studying somewhat for different subjects, which runs counter to the time-honored tradition of always using the same place at the same time every day for all subjects. His argument, drawn from brain research, is that the brain can associate information with the place or

4

THE FOUR KEYS CONTINUED: LEARNING SKILLS AND TRANSITION SKILLS context in which it was learned. Some material might best be learned while walking down the street with headphones on, while other material should be studied in a quiet place conducive to deep concentration. Another subject might be studied in a place that has a view. Even changes in which room students study different material can help the brain form associations between the circumstances of studying and the material being studied, which helps retention and recall.

Finally, students need to know how to study with others. Study groups are a very important and ubiquitous study method in college, and being able to organize a study group when needed or participate in an existing group when possible can make a difference in the grade a student receives in a course. Study groups work best when they are composed of students with different skills and perspectives, not necessarily of people who all think alike or of best friends. A good study group can create a social obligation to study, which further increases the likelihood students will do so.

Test Taking Closely related to time management and study skills is test taking. While test taking is certainly common in entry-level general education courses, more and more career pathways have licensing or certification exams that students are going to have to pass before they are allowed to enter the field. Students who do not know how to perform well on exams generally may have their access to their career of choice blocked because they can't get past the certification exam. In addition, some majors or certificate programs rely on testing more than others. To succeed in these areas, students need a range of test-taking skills.

Being able to prepare for a test is not the same as being able to take a test. Being truly ready to take a test begins well before the actual event and is predicated on effective studying techniques that lead to students' feeling well prepared and confident entering the test. While different tests require specific strategies, the overall approach to test taking is relatively similar for all tests:

- Knowing what will be on the test
- Understanding how content or skills will be tested
- Learning how to organize to study for the test
- Identifying areas that are not yet well understood
- Discerning which material to memorize versus material to understand and apply

Students benefit by having the opportunity to take a number of tests of varying length and format before they reach college because formal testing is an important part of most postsecondary programs, and students in these programs seldom have the luxury of drawing on extra credit to compensate for a poor test score, as is sometimes the case in high school classes. Teachers should not be afraid of putting reasonable emphasis on tests, assuming the tests are of high quality. Students should not become so anxious that they are immobilized, but they should know how to handle the natural anxiety that surrounds a test and how to use that anxiety to their advantage, to focus, and also to take the necessary steps to be prepared and confident, a key way to reduce test anxiety.

Note Taking Note taking continues to be important, even in the digital age where lectures may be recorded and then reviewed out of class. Students still need to know how to identify what is important from among all they listen to and record. They need to know how to go beyond the basics contained in a PowerPoint presentation to delve deeper into areas they do not understand well and how to apply concepts from a lecture to other material. It is becoming increasingly common for college instructors to hear college students, particularly freshmen, complain when the instructor asks questions on the test that do not derive directly from material contained in one of the class slide presentations. Good note-taking skills enable students to understand better the material that has been presented to them in a variety of media and formats.

In addition to traditional methods of note taking that can be taught via well-developed systems, a host of new technology-based methods are available. These include ways to annotate live or recorded lectures so that notes are associated with particular times in the lecture, ways to highlight and organize important information, and methods for compiling all key information into databases for easy reference throughout the course and after. Students should become comfortable using both traditional, nontechnological methods and new technological tools and techniques to facilitate effective note taking.

Memorization Memorizing key material remains an important skill. Research on memorization has begun to yield more specifics on how best to practice and retain material, and much of the traditional wisdom regarding memorization is being called into question. The idea that repetition, generally in the form of flash cards or lists, is the best way to remember key facts is being displaced by the finding that the brain learns and retains information in context and that facts in particular need to be given hooks that enable the brain to grab onto and hold all the specific bits. Over one hundred years of research has shown that lists of spelling words, for example, do not work well to teach meaning or spelling, and yet they persist.

Memorization needs, first, to focus only on material that's truly important to raise to the level of automatic recall, and, second, on how to give that material sufficient meaning in context for the brain to capture it and move it from working memory to long-term memory storage. This generally requires practice distributed over time and in different contexts, not a one-time cramming of everything.

Furthermore, practicing remembering things seems to help with retention. In other words, the more that students practice strategies for recalling specific information, the better they become at it over time. Teachers can help this process by having reasonable amounts of material students are expected to learn to the level of automatic recall and then by helping students place this information into context in order to attach greater meaning to it. Novel and nonroutine uses of the information help consolidate recall, as do ways of personalizing the information. If the curriculum is organized around big ideas, organizing concepts, and linking ideas from the start, students will have a structure within which to memorize the key elements and building blocks of the subject that they must retain at the level of automaticity.

Strategic Reading Although students are taught how to read, they are not necessarily given much instruction in how to read strategically, a skill that increases in importance in secondary school and becomes critically important in college, where the amount and type of material to be read increases over what students have encountered previously. In addition, the time available to complete the reading is often insufficient, which requires them to develop more efficient reading strategies. The purposes for reading also shift, with a greater emphasis on extracting key meanings from informational texts and materials and a reduced emphasis on comprehending a story or narrative in its entirety.

Those who use strategic reading employ, as the name implies, any of a range of strategies or techniques appropriate to comprehending the material being read. For example, many readers simply begin on the first page of an assignment and read sequentially. Strategic reading techniques suggest a different approach:

1. Quickly preview the assignment to get the general idea of which parts of the reading will be most important to completing the assignment.
2. Continuing with a scan of the material, determine the structure and challenge level of the material. Then decide where to focus and where to skim.
3. Identify key unknown terms and terminology identified during the scan and define them before going into the material in depth.

In other cases, when everything can be close to equally important, as in many textbooks, students should recognize this before beginning to read and then annotate the material more thoroughly, identify and record unfamiliar words, and highlight key concepts. This requires the ability to identify which terms and concepts are truly important and then to limit highlighting to these. Of particular importance is knowing when to infer meaning from context, as in a novel, and when to define key words before proceeding, as in a science or social science text.

Many strategies and programs for effective reading have been developed. The problem is that formal reading instruction tends not to continue much beyond third grade, after which students are expected to use reading skills to learn new materials rather than be taught to read better or more strategically. Making the shift from children's books to academic content in particular requires new reading strategies that many students who can read narrative well will not possess. They need to be taught explicitly the strategies and techniques for reading the types of material they will encounter in college classes and career preparation programs.

Collaborative Learning One of the changes that has occurred over the past twenty years or so in many secondary and postsecondary classrooms is the commonplace use of collaborative or cooperative learning techniques as important instructional strategies. The term *teamwork* is often applied to this type of learning in order to make the connection with the work world in which adults more frequently function in teams to complete tasks and solve problems. While getting students to socialize may not be difficult, getting them to learn socially is nowhere as easy. It requires specific skills and techniques they must develop. Increasingly, students in college and occupational training programs are expected to work in groups to solve problems or complete tasks, just as they will later in the work world where almost all activities require a level of social interaction and teamwork.

Developing the skills of collaborative learning takes more than simply sticking students together in groups. Some tasks require group members who play specific roles, while other activities can succeed only with a leader who has a team willing to follow the leader's directions. Still others are leaderless and rely on collective understanding and equal contributions from all members of the group. Students need to be skilled and experienced in a range of collaborative learning techniques and models to be effective in postsecondary and career preparation settings. Students who are experienced with collaborative learning techniques will have an advantage in classes that have complex content and major assignments or exams that require intensive group work to complete successfully.

Technological Proficiency A final critical learning skill is the ability to employ a range of technologies that aid learning. Although almost all students may be able to send text messages or watch YouTube videos, this does not mean they are technologically proficient. Computers remain important tools, although portable devices such as tablets and smartphones are quickly closing the gap. Nevertheless, tools such as word processing and spreadsheet programs will continue to be important in college and the workplace for the foreseeable future. Most students possess only rudimentary skills with productivity software, and few have mastered the full feature set of a word processing or spreadsheet program. Students should be familiar with the full range of programs that they might encounter in college or occupational training programs. Similarly, it is not at all unusual for students to be required to prepare PowerPoint presentations in many courses, and few know how to organize material into the hierarchical format that a good PowerPoint presentation requires, how much text to put on a slide, or how to use graphics in a visually appealing fashion.

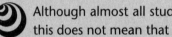

Although almost all students may be able to send text messages, this does not mean that they are technologically proficient.

Beyond these basic productivity programs, students benefit from experience with online research resources and strategies beyond Wikipedia and a basic Google search. Assignments that require specific source information that is contained in particular databases, for example, can help students learn to hone their search skills and their research skills at the same time. Digital bibliographic programs, on computers and online, allow students to store references where they can use them for the paper they are writing and find them again in the future. These programs also insert in-text citation markers and format the citations in the required style. Even exploring the advanced features of Google search (http://www.google.com/advanced_search) and learning how to use Boolean operators (*and, or, not*) will strengthen student research skills significantly.

Numerous other forms of technology are increasingly available and integrated into instruction. Colleges and universities in particular tend to upgrade on a regular basis the technologies that are essential to research in a subject area. Most training programs also tend to have access to the newest and most relevant technological tools for the particular job or career area for which students are training. These types of technologies range from projection microscopes to automotive diagnostic machines. While students cannot realistically be made familiar with the full gamut of technology, they should have enough experiences with a wide enough assortment of technologically based learning tools to be familiar with most forms of technology they will encounter after high school.

The goal is to have students think of technology not as separate from the learning process but as an extension of it. Armed with an array of gadgets, young people increasingly take for granted continuous and convenient access to technology and, with it, access to information. Today's K–12 schools do not always support this emerging mind-set well because they are obsessed with controlling student access to information. While educators have valid concerns about students viewing inappropriate content at school, schools can no longer respond by simply not allowing students access to the Internet or by restricting access so drastically that students cannot gather resources online.

Nor can schools rely primarily on outmoded approaches such as computer labs to meet student needs for access to technology. It will behoove secondary schools in particular to integrate technology as fully as possible into the learning environment and into learning tasks. This calls for hands-on, integrated uses of mobile computing devices in the classroom on a regular basis, formal instruction in and frequent use of foundational productivity software to solve complex problems and produce high-quality products, and less restricted access to the Internet, combined with more instruction on how to conduct sophisticated searches.

Valuing the Key Learning Skills and Techniques

This inventory of necessary learning skills and techniques can be daunting to consider. The good news is that all of the skills and dispositions I have described are actionable; in other words, students can learn them and become better at them through sustained application and practice. The challenge is that they cannot simply be taught one time and then checked off a list. These skills and techniques require years to incorporate fully to the point that they make a real difference for learners. This means they cannot be taught solely as separate classes, such as study skills or time management, but must be integrated into regular instruction on an ongoing and sustained basis. While the learning techniques in particular can certainly be introduced and refined through formal instruction, they must be practiced repeatedly over time to be retained to the point where they can be generalized to new situations and settings, the ultimate goal.

Schools should value proficiency in learning skills and techniques as highly as content knowledge and provide students with as much information about their capabilities as self-directed learners as they do about their content knowledge mastery. One possible way to do this is to give two grades in most courses: the traditional composite A to F mark, which is assumed to represent subject area mastery, and a measure of learning skill along the lines of "approaches, meets, exceeds." This is not too far off from a primary school report card that includes marks on academic skills in reading, writing, and math and a range of social skills associated with participation in the learning process. Grading these skills and dispositions at the intermediate and secondary levels in a low-stakes way can provide additional valuable information to students and parents, and potentially to postsecondary institutions that wish to provide proper supports to entering students. Teaching and emphasizing these skills and techniques is a key next step toward closing the achievement gap and toward enabling more students to learn the Common Core State Standards in ways that make them college and career ready.

Key Transition Knowledge and Skills in Depth

Educators and policymakers are used to seeing international comparisons on a regular basis that show the US public education system ranking well behind many of the countries with which the United States competes and with which its educational system is regularly compared. However, the US educational system is number one in an often overlooked area: the complexity of preparing for, choosing, applying to, and beginning studies at any of the country's more than four thousand postsecondary institutions and proprietary training programs. For a variety of reasons, the US secondary and postsecondary systems were developed and are governed completely separately from one another. The relationship between the two is so disconnected that K–12 and higher education governing boards in most states are just beginning to communicate with one another for the first time.

Getting ready for postsecondary studies is about preparing for a transition. It is a transition that entails multiple aspects. Some of these receive a lot of attention; most receive little or no attention. The net result is that students preparing to go beyond high school must navigate numerous potential pitfalls if they wish to make a successful transition. Most students are not even aware of some of the most important potential challenges they will encounter.

> Students preparing to go beyond high school must navigate numerous potential pitfalls if they wish to make a successful transition.

High schools and even some middle schools do pay a great deal of attention to the classes students need to take to be college eligible. In fact, in many cases, a school's entire transition program consists of encouraging students to take the courses they need to be eligible to apply to local state public colleges and universities. School personnel cannot be blamed too much for this because research on college success has focused on the relationship between high school courses taken and grades received in entry-level college courses. Because a relationship exists between the two, it's easy to draw the conclusion that taking a particular set of courses in high school is all students need to do to be ready to succeed in college. Were it only that simple.

In reality, students must do much more than enroll in a set of college-prep courses. They must attend to the development of key cognitive strategies, the acquisition of key content knowledge, and the cultivation and mastery of key learning skills and techniques. Beyond that, they need to have goals that a postsecondary program will move them closer to achieving. They need to understand more about college and career readiness than knowing they need to take courses with particular titles. They need to grasp the significance of the fact that they are about to embark on a life transition, one of the most significant and wrenching transitions they will ever face. Most students are not aware of the scope, scale, or severity of this transition.

The Five Aspects of Key Transition Skills

The complexity and multidimensional nature of this key is such that it requires an intermediate layer of organization. Five aspects capture the range of issues with which students must cope and changes they must make as they undertake the secondary-to-postsecondary transition:

○ *Contextual* issues, related to students' understanding their motivations to attend college and their options for postsecondary programs. Students need to know which types of institution they want to attend and why it is a good match for them. They need to research what it takes to qualify for the type of institution in which they are most interested. They also need backup options if their first choice does not work out for any of a variety of reasons. And, finally, something that few students really consider carefully, they need to have a sense of the probability that they are prepared to succeed in their institution of choice.

○ *Procedural* issues, which address the "how-to" of the admissions process. Knowing something about where one wants to attend college is the first step; knowing how to apply is the immediate corollary. Applying is not easy, often requiring multiple steps. Completing them all, and on time, is crucial to submitting a viable application.

○ *Financial* issues, which relate to how students afford their desired choice of postsecondary programs. Students and their parents must be aware of the actual costs and the options available to cover identified costs. This requires more than attending a single financial aid night where the Free Application for Federal Student Aid (FAFSA) is explained, and it requires more precise estimates of costs than most students or parents have.

○ *Cultural* issues, which address the behavioral norms students will encounter in postsecondary education. Those norms are generally quite different from those to which they have become accustomed in high school. Knowing what it means to be a college student and how best to take full advantage of the college experience requires an understanding of the postsecondary culture.

○ *Personal* issues, which involve students being able to advocate for themselves in an institutional context. Postsecondary institutions are complex environments, and students can easily lose their way if they are not effective self-advocates. Students need to be prepared to deal with a range of adults, including professors and instructors, financial aid officers, academic advisors, and staff in the business office, among others, all of whom are in positions of authority and can be intimidating to students who have to be ready to pursue their interests assertively.

Contextual The term *context* refers here to the need for students to understand the requirements for entry into postsecondary institutions and how those institutions align with their own interests and aspirations. This cannot happen without access to information about the options open to them. This is information secondary schools need to provide to all students. States and schools increasingly expect students to develop formal plans that go beyond listing the courses they will take in high school to thinking about what they want to do with their lives. Engaging in planning for the future requires students to have access to a lot of highly specialized information on how to make realistic and appropriate choices about which postsecondary options to pursue.

Students who know what they want to do with their future are better able to make the decisions necessary to arrive at the point of being fully prepared for college courses by the time they leave high school. Aspirations help establish the options they should be prepared to pursue. Absent some clear goal or target, students may be tempted to simply focus on prestigious schools or, at the other extreme, not to identify a target institution at all. Helping students develop an ever clearer and more appropriate sense of their options in relation to their aspirations is the first step in readying them to make a successful transition.

Doing this requires more attention to and information about student interests than most schools gather currently. Knowing how well a student can read, write, and do math is useful, but this information is only a first step. Students need not select a life career or occupation, but they need to be honing in on what interests and engages them and where they want to expend time and energy to become skilled. The school needs to be generating and collecting this type of information longitudinally so that all students can ascertain how ready they are at various points during high school to make a decision about where to attend college.

Procedural Knowing what one wants to do beyond high school is a good first step, but it is not enough. The application process in the United States is excessively complex and idiosyncratic, and therefore all the more challenging for students who are first in family to apply. Parents often figure out the drill only after the first child has gone through the process. Assuming they have other children, they can use this knowledge to help them apply. But pity the families with only one or two children who figure out the whole college application process the hard way and then have no way to use their hard-earned knowledge.

Rather than rely on this inefficient and ineffective trial-and-error approach, schools need to be organized to provide students and parents with the knowledge that is necessary to apply successfully. Much of this information is available online now, with multiple websites devoted to helping students accumulate the necessary information and organize it for entry into college or technical program applications. Students should begin this process in late middle school, be highly familiar with it by the end of sophomore year, and be ready to apply by the middle of eleventh grade, even though most applications are not due until twelfth grade. Ideally, students will be ready to apply six months before they need to submit an application, allowing them some time for remedying any errors or omissions.

Beyond the procedural aspects of applying are the actual accomplishments and life experiences students can include in their application to postsecondary program. While few postsecondary institutions have admissions processes that are so demanding or competitive that they require much beyond high school grade point average and an admissions test, students benefit nevertheless by participating in extracurricular activities, volunteering for service projects, working in meaningful jobs for no more than about ten hours per week, traveling, and developing expertise and demonstrating excellence in areas outside the academic subjects they study in school.

All students should be encouraged to develop this wider range of experiences and to document them. Although most colleges do not require specific extracurricular activities, such activities can be useful in gaining admission to special programs within less selective institutions, being more competitive for certain scholarships, and compensating in situations where their grades or test scores may be marginal. The most important reason to encourage all students to do these things is that these activities are all associated with greater success after high school. They will help students be ready no matter which postsecondary path they choose to pursue.

Financial Students and their parents need to be giving thought to how they will pay for college or a technical training program well before they begin the application process. As college tuition soars, more families are writing off the possibility of their children receiving a college education in part because they do not know about financial aid options or are unaware of the cost difference between various postsecondary programs. For a family that cannot afford to contribute to their child's college education, it matters little whether the program costs three thousand dollars or thirty thousand. Both seem equally out of their reach without specific information about how to make either program affordable.

Schools need to be providing more information much earlier to parents and students alike—information that helps them understand the options available for financial aid and the cost differential of community colleges, state universities, and private schools. Ironically, many private colleges have better scholarship options for high-performing students from low-income backgrounds than do state schools because these institutions are seeking to expand the diversity of their incoming freshman class and their overall student body, and they have fewer legal restrictions on how they do so. Although federal and state aid seldom covers the full cost of a college education, it can put college within reach when combined with work-study, summer employment, and judicious use of loans. Students and parents need to be doing the math on the financial aid equation early and often. Here, again, websites are useful resources, but most families need help accessing them and learning how to use them. Schools need to take a much more active role in this arena—one that goes well beyond a one-shot financial aid night for high school juniors.

In the area of the cost of college, middle-class families can be equally in the dark. Many believe they can negotiate a deal for their child with the admissions office, only to find out that this rarely happens, and certainly not to the degree parents think possible. Colleges make what is generally their final offer to accepted students when they send out financial aid information. It is surprising how few parents have realistic expectations for what they will need to pay and how much of a deal the college will give them. This can lead to disappointment, confusion, anger, and a last-minute scramble to find a college they can afford.

> In the area of the cost of college, middle-class families can be equally in the dark.

4

Secondary schools can be more creative about how they help students and parents prepare for the sticker shock of postsecondary education. Having students do research projects on college costs is one way to integrate this information into academic courses. Similarly, students in math classes can access databases that contain information on tuition trends, and they can create budgets from a range of sources. In social studies or economics courses, students can explore the value of a college education in comparison to its cost. Advisory periods can be times for accessing online sites with detailed information on two- and four-year college and proprietary program costs along with strategies to pay for them. Parents' knowledge of costs can be developed beginning in elementary school in concert with information on how they can help cover those costs for their children. In short, it takes a sustained, schoolwide effort to educate families on the financial aspects of postsecondary readiness and to help them prepare a plan to address the challenge.

Cultural While students are developing plans to choose, get into, and afford a postsecondary program, they also need to begin preparing for the culture of college. One of the primary differences between secondary and postsecondary educational settings is that colleges assume students are independent, self-reliant learners who take ownership of the learning process and their lives. Another way of saying this is that colleges expect students to be grown-ups in many (although not all) ways. This may or may not be entirely true when it comes to the individual student, but all students should at least understand that their role is changing and that expectations for their behavior will be more adult-like.

In college, students will no longer have teachers who remind them constantly to do their homework or prepare for a big test. To the contrary, they will receive a syllabus during the first class meeting that contains all key dates for assignments and exams. They will be expected to self-monitor from that point forward. If the initial assignment is not due for six weeks, it does not mean that they have the first five weeks off. They need to be studying and preparing for the assignment throughout the entire time. If they turn the paper in late, they may be penalized, or the paper may not be accepted at all. Excuses are less likely to result in students' being given an accommodation or modification of course requirements and more likely to result in a loss of points. Using extra-credit assignments to replace poor grades on key assignments or tests is rarely, if ever, an option.

At the same time, students need to understand why they are taking the course or are enrolled in the program. And while colleges increasingly sell their value based on the economic gain a certificate or degree will bring to students, instructors still are looking for students who are interested and engaged in the subject and not just going through the motions. Students may be shocked at the range of perspectives and points of view they encounter and may be unaccustomed to the give-and-take of an academic environment. They may be uncomfortable having their assertions challenged or opinions questioned. They may not be ready for the intellectual rough-and-tumble that is a central component in the college culture generally.

Personal At a personal level, young people need to demonstrate the ability to advocate for themselves more proactively and strategically when they are in college. Many things can go wrong, procedurally and otherwise, particularly during the first year of college. These issues often can be addressed only by students themselves. Failure to do so can lead to students dropping out before they really give college a chance.

Many issues can derail new college students, particularly those for whom college is a new experience for their families, who lack confidence initially, have trouble dealing with the bureaucratic complexity and depersonalized procedures and processes, and whose families cannot serve as a strong support system for them. For example, many students fail to remain in college due to some problem with their financial aid, which they do not address or do not know how to address. Similarly, some students run into housing or roommate problems that they cannot overcome. Others do not get signed up for classes in time or fail to get critical required classes when they need them. Some students encounter a family emergency but do not communicate with professors about the situation. All of these common situations require a personal self-advocacy capability.

College- and career-ready students aren't afraid to challenge a decision that affects them negatively. They know how to use appeals processes. They know how to communicate with and develop relationships with people in positions of authority who can help them. They get to know their academic advisor and their professors. They don't attempt to manipulate people, but when they need someone to be on their side, they have somewhere to turn.

> College- and career-ready students aren't afraid to challenge a decision that affects them negatively.

These skills become increasingly important as colleges become less personal and more dependent on online interactions. Students need to know how to manage online relationships with people in positions of authority, how to request and get personalized attention when they need it, and how to make sure they are exhausting every available option before giving up. Sending an e-mail to the financial aid office with a blank subject line and abbreviations more appropriate to text messaging is not an effective way to self-advocate. Knowing the right behaviors does not come naturally to all or perhaps most students, and students from certain cultural backgrounds have even more difficulty advocating for themselves with people in positions of authority. Helping these students be college ready requires opportunities for them to practice and develop self-advocacy skills while in high school:

- Reviewing their transcripts periodically and asking that corrections be made where mistakes or omissions exist

- Setting up meetings with counselors or anyone else who can help them with the college application process
- Taking the initiative to meet with teachers to resolve problems before the teacher calls the meeting
- Asking for adult help whenever they need it

Secondary schools should let students know these behaviors are not only permissible, they are strongly encouraged.

Preparing All Students for the Transition

One powerful way that high schools prepare students for the postsecondary transition that has been demonstrated to be effective is to have students participate in one or more college course or college-like experiences while still in high school. Options are expanding. Dual-enrollment and concurrent-enrollment programs are growing rapidly. These offer the opportunity for students to take a college-level course at their high school or at a local college and receive both high school and college credit and in many cases have this paid for by their local high school. And although these courses may not always transfer to all other colleges or universities, they generally carry credit at local postsecondary institutions. More important, they fulfill the goal of giving students an experience that helps them prepare not just academically but socially and personally for college.

Early-college high school programs are also on the increase. They will not work for all students, but for those for whom they do, they allow students to acquire significant amounts of college credit while in high school, and in some cases, they can complete an associate degree by the time of high school graduation. Advanced Placement® (AP) courses present another option for an expanding number of students. Some high schools have gone as far as to expect all students to take at least one AP course before graduation. An AP course may not provide the full cultural experience of a college campus, but it does help students develop the mind-set and work habits that they need for college success.

For students who may not be ready for a full-scale college experience or who live in rural areas without ready access to a local college, another option is a senior seminar in high school that emulates postsecondary education in important ways. Such a course can be set up in a variety of fashions. It can be a place to manage the college selection and application process along with financial aid form completion, including filling out the infamous FAFSA. In addition, the course can help students gauge their self-management skills by expecting them to record and complete assignments on their own. Students can be exposed to the somewhat higher standards of college grading by having a writing assignment graded at a college level of expectation. The intellectual culture of college can be simulated with discussions in which students must provide evidence for assertions and in which they learn how to question one another without attacking and how to accept critical feedback from peers and the instructor. The seminar can be as structured or open-ended as dictated by the needs of its students. The key is for it to address the broad range of issues associated with making the transition from high school to any of a range of postsecondary environments.

The Complexity of College and Career Readiness

The four keys model is complex, encompassing forty-one components. While it may seem overwhelming to try to get students to master them all, the more they know, the better. The process of introducing the four keys needs to begin at the latest in middle school, so that students can begin to master them a little at a time. Many of the components are simply good things for all students to learn regardless of their postsecondary aspirations. However, adopting the four keys model schoolwide and building instructional and support programs around them will help ensure that all students are being equipped to pursue postsecondary education if they choose to do so.

This chapter and the preceding one demonstrate the importance of the four keys to college and career readiness and illustrate the fact that college and career readiness cannot easily be captured in a single test score or by looking at academic performance in reading, writing, and mathematics alone. Many more factors come into play. This is something that most educators know intuitively because as they observe the differences between more successful and less successful students on a daily basis, they observe that aptitude is rarely the sole factor explaining student success. College- and career-ready students show skills and demonstrate effective behaviors that reflect competence in the majority of the aspects of the four keys model.

Aptitude is rarely the sole factor explaining student success.

This is important to know and act on in the era of the Common Core State Standards because these standards do not address all four keys, and in fact they were not designed to do so. This does not mean the college and career levels of the Common Core State Standards are not a valuable framework for designing a school's instructional program, simply that they do not comprise or address all the factors students must master in order to be truly ready for college and careers.

The potential danger is that so much has been invested in the assessments attendant to the Common Core State Standards that it is a short step to generalizing the results of the assessments far beyond what they are intended to measure. The two consortia, Partnership for the Assessment of Readiness for College and Careers and the Smarter Balanced Assessment Consortium, have taken steps to be clear that their assessments measure only the English and mathematics content knowledge associated with being college and career ready. This amounts to one aspect of one of the keys in two subject areas. The four keys help to illustrate how the Common Core State Standards fit into a larger framework of readiness, one that schools can address in all subject areas and across multiple grade levels. The four keys serve as the scaffold on which an overall program of college and career readiness Common Core implementation can be constructed.

◗ Awareness and Action Steps

- Which students are most successful and least successful in taking ownership of their learning? Are the expectations that students do so different for some groups of students? Think of three simple interventions that would improve ownership of learning without requiring major program redesign or staff training.
- Have students set goals in three time frames: short term, medium term, and long term. Short-term goals are those they can do immediately (e.g., improve study habits by devoting more time to studying). Medium-term goals may span a course or academic year (e.g., improve writing skills or get a 3 or better on an AP exam). Long-term goals relate to aspirations (e.g., prepare to become a commercial pilot, attend a four-year college locally). Collect and categorize their goals to see what they tell about the students and how their goals can be supported.
- Have students map their goals and the steps they need to take to achieve them. This site offers a series of ten steps to help students reflect on the intent and design of their goals. It also offers a mini-quiz to diagnose a student's ability to manage time and achieve goals (http://bit.ly/18X5z9p).

- Estimate student proficiency with the key learning techniques, such as time management and study skills. How many students do these things well? For those who don't, improvements in which areas would lead to the greatest improvement in their performance the most quickly? See the website for this book for a host of programs that address these techniques.
- Introduce students to time management by first having them track how they are using their time. This builds their awareness of the decisions they are making about which activities are important (http://bit.ly/11wb1HM).
- Look for evidence of how persistent students are when faced with a challenging task. Read *How Children Succeed* by Paul Tough.
- Access and share the resiliency quiz to help students reflect on how they learn and cope with stressful situations. As an assignment, ask students to describe how they will build off the ways they have handled unexpected difficulties in the past to persist in the future. Have students present and share these strategies with the class (http://bit.ly/191hJOG).
- Have students complete the 12-Item Grit Scale by Angela Duckworth and colleagues (http://bit.ly/1bSrniL).
- Provide high school students with examples of college-level writing assignments and examples of acceptable college-level work on these assignments. Have them then determine the gap between where their writing is now and what it would have to be for their work to be at the college level. Examples can be located on a number of websites—for example, Colby College, the National Council of Teachers of English, Standards for Success, the Purdue Online Writing Lab, and Appendix C of the English Language Arts Common Core State Standards.
- Many resources exist to help students improve their skills on a number of different learning techniques, such as time management and study skills. See the book's website for examples. Then identify students who could benefit by improving their skills in these two areas.
- Require all students to have a method for recording assignments regularly, and check regularly that they have done so. Do this schoolwide at all grade levels and in all courses that have assignments.
- Have all students sign up as ninth graders for a service that helps them identify potential colleges to attend (http://bit.ly/11MCsgw, http://bit.ly/14IkC2l).
- Access and share free resources on issues that students encounter as they make the transition to college and what they and their parents can do to alleviate difficulties (http://bit.ly/14llV1f).
- Encourage students to download financial aid videos to their playlists. Featured playlists include preparing for college, types of aid, who gets aid, and repaying loans (http://bit.ly/14gWiCC).

- Let students and parents know where they can get free help filling out the FAFSA (http://bit.ly/13Z0WEZ).
- Support students and parents with federal financial aid checklists. Different road maps, resources, and steps are displayed for each grade level, starting in elementary school (http://1.usa.gov/13QUUI0).
- Create assignments in which students can role-play how they might address a scenario through which an obstacle has arisen that threatens their ability to continue their enrollment in college (e.g., a problem with financial aid, roommate conflict, class registration delays, lack of availability for classes needed for major). How do they address the issue? How do they identify the resources they need to overcome the obstacle? What allies do they seek out? Who can they turn to for help? What are the appropriate methods for appealing decisions? What are the most appropriate methods for communication with authority figures regarding the obstacle?
- Create an assignment through which students research transition programs for new students on college campuses and offer meaningful critiques of the selected program. This gives students a glimpse of the kinds of programming available to first-year college students and prepares them for the gaps that may exist between transition programming and enrollment.
- Invite current college students to your classroom to talk with your students about their transition experiences. Invite speakers who had easy transitions and some who struggled.
- Have students create a free account at scholarships.com, a free scholarship engine that has customizable filters, including ethnicity, academic standing, and institute type, to help students target scholarships specifically for them.
- Teach students about college placement tests and their role in determining the level of college course they are eligible for. A majority of entering students don't know they need to take the placement test seriously. Understanding the role placement tests play in college credits, remedial education, and financial aid decisions will motivate students to study material prior to testing.
- Have students use digital tools for their presentations, reports, and projects. This website has tools in different categories for writing, research, organization, and creativity (http://bit.ly/13Z1evx).
- Have students register on EducationCents.org to build their financial literacy. It's an interactive site with a self-paced curriculum partnered with presentations and a printable guide. Students can even be rewarded with scholarships and free books just by participating.
- Develop a systematic program to encourage students' persistence. Assign projects that cannot be completed in one class period and require students to persist to solve multifaceted problems. In assigning projects, take care to provide appropriate scaffolding so that by the time students are seniors, they are capable of completing complex tasks independently.

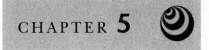
TOWARD DEEPER LEARNING

The primary issues considered to this point have been what it means to be college and career ready and the importance of having all students reach this goal. The main thesis, however, is that the Common Core State Standards goal of getting all students college and career ready cannot be achieved simply by teaching the standards and administering the consortia assessments. College and career readiness consists of much more than one set of standards and one battery of tests. A major concern of many is that the Common Core State Standards and consortia assessments will be taught and measured in small bits and bites—the "what" of a subject area and the "how" of applying that information in a formulaic fashion. If this occurs, students will not develop the deeper learning skills necessary for success in postsecondary education or an ever-changing workplace and society.

This chapter explores the importance of deeper learning—the notion that students need to go beyond the surface of facts and terminology to levels of thinking that require them to apply what they have learned in more complex ways. Deeper learning is achieved when knowledge learned in one setting can be applied in another. This is a challenging feat to accomplish and occurs only when students understand well what they have learned and know how to transfer that learning to other subjects and problems. Deeper learning also entails knowing how to learn in a variety of ways. Many of the principles of deeper learning reflect elements of the four keys and illustrate them in greater detail.

Some Framing Characteristics of the Learning Process

Basic content knowledge is critically important. About this point there is no dispute. As learners begin to study a new field or area of interest, they needs to know and master the basic vocabulary and terminology of the subject or topic. They have to understand how to apply this knowledge systematically in order to accomplish basic routines or tasks in the area in question. This is how a novice in a subject area begins to organize and structure these discrete bits of information along with the skills, experience, and understanding accumulated as information is used for a variety of purposes. In combination, this interaction between the acquisition of information and its application in increasingly sophisticated ways leads toward deeper insight into and connections among all the elements of the topic or subject.

The problem is that in many cases, learning never goes beyond the "what" and "how" levels. Learners continue to pile up more and more disconnected bits of information, algorithms, techniques, and methods without connecting them by using them to accomplish the broader aims for which they were intended in the first place. Students end up possessing knowledge without purpose, engaging in activity without meaning. No wonder so many learners have such difficulty retaining information that to anyone who is expert in the subject or on the topic seems like child's play.

 Students end up possessing knowledge without purpose, engaging in activity without meaning.

The expert has made the connections that result in the information becoming "sticky." For example, it takes only a few times of riding a bike to learn that putting one's foot down on coming to a stop is a key behavior, but once this behavior is learned, it is integrated into bicycle riding in a way that it is unlikely ever to be forgotten, even if some skills of bike riding, like riding with one's hands off the handlebars, may become fuzzy and have to be revived and practiced after some time. Once something that is learned becomes sticky, it is retained for much longer.

The mind has many ways to make things sticky, some feasible for use in the classroom and others not. Pain works, as in the example of the bike. A few crashes, and we get it through our heads to put our feet down. However, students can't be expected to learn math or any other subject this way. Experiences with strong emotional attachment tend to get remembered too, but every school experience can't be a strong emotional one because students are in school far too long for such a regimen to be sustainable. If every learning experience required a powerful emotional incident, school would soon become psychologically overwhelming.

What's more effective and sustainable are activities that cause students to engage actively in learning and provide them a chance to process and integrate what they have learned. The teacher's most effective strategy is to create opportunities for students to give material significance, personalize it, incorporate it into their experience, and imbue it with their own interpretations and value. When students do this, they are moving beyond the superficial and toward deeper learning and long-term retention of the material.

These general principles of learning help frame the remainder of the chapter and its explanation of how students can get to deeper levels of learning and why it is advantageous for them to do so. The next section presents and explores a knowledge complexity progression that illustrates how the principles of deeper learning can be understood more systematically.

Knowledge Complexity Progression

One way to think about creating this stickiness and building learner expertise is to identify the cognitive level at which students are processing what they are learning. This processing can be thought of as occurring along a continuum consisting of four levels (figure 5.1):

- Declarative knowledge—the what
- Procedural knowledge—the how

- Conditional knowledge—the when
- Conceptual understanding—the why

This model was introduced in the mid-1980s by educational researchers Ann L. Brown and Annemarie Panlincsar and has been used and adapted in many forms since then by educators, cognitive psychologists, and others. My interpretation of the model, which differs from the original in some minor ways, is explained in greater detail here:

○ *Declarative knowledge* is the "what" of content (figure 5.2). As its name implies, it is the type of information that students can declare, that they can repeat back when asked to do so. Declarative knowledge is important when students are learning the basics of a new subject area, such as vocabulary and nomenclature. It is also necessary for the elements of a subject that need to be committed to memory and raised to the level of automaticity—in other words, information that must be recalled instantly and accurately at a moment's notice in order for learning to progress. While most subjects have a significant body of declarative knowledge, it is difficult for students to retain all of this without the opportunity to process at the following three levels.

○ *Procedural knowledge* is the "how" of content knowledge (figure 5.3). In general, it involves the application of declarative knowledge in predictable, routine, and conventional ways. Most content knowledge has rules or methods associated with its use. English grammar defines how to use the declarative knowledge about parts of speech, for example. The commutative property in mathematics tells students about how certain mathematical

FIGURE 5.1 KNOWLEDGE COMPLEXITY PROGRESSION

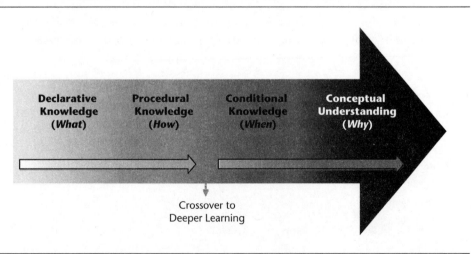

| Declarative Knowledge (*What*) | Procedural Knowledge (*How*) | Conditional Knowledge (*When*) | Conceptual Understanding (*Why*) |

Crossover to
Deeper Learning

FIGURE 5.2 DECLARATIVE KNOWLEDGE

Knowing That Something Is the Case

- Know the parts of speech.
- Know the dates of Civil War battles.
- Define what a whole number is.

FIGURE 5.3 PROCEDURAL KNOWLEDGE

Applying What Is Known

- Diagram a sentence, identifying incorrect use of parts of speech.
- Explain how the progression of Civil War battles affected the war overall.
- Use whole numbers to solve a range of problems.

relationships work. Students need to know these procedures and be able to follow them accurately. In many classes, instruction consists almost exclusively of introducing content in a declarative fashion and practicing procedures. Students who know and can use knowledge procedurally have reached a solid novice level in a subject area.

O *Conditional knowledge* is the "when" of the use of content knowledge (figure 5.4). As students progress from knowing the content to knowing how to apply that content, the next step is knowing when to use which sort of technique to apply or otherwise use the content. For example, understanding metaphor and simile and knowing when to use these literary devices to best effect requires conditional knowledge. Knowing under which conditions to use which statistical methods, based on the nature of the problem being studied, is another example. Conditional knowledge helps students know how to select from among a range of possible or potential methods the most appropriate, efficient, and effective approach. In other words, a procedure that may be perfectly fine in one context may not be as useful or the best choice in another. As students acquire and practice a wider range of procedural techniques, they reach the level at which they can begin to make choices among them. Students at this point have surpassed the novice level and are emerging as competent users of the content knowledge. They are becoming strategic learners.

 O *Conceptual knowledge* is the "why" of the use of content knowledge (figure 5.5). Whereas declarative knowledge gives learners raw material, and procedural and conditional knowledge enable learners to do something with that material, conceptual knowledge enables learners to know and understand why they are doing what they are doing. This ability then equips learners to make better and more strategic decisions about the ways in which they want to process information and apply it to a range of complex problems or

FIGURE 5.4 CONDITIONAL KNOWLEDGE

Using What Is Known in Context

- Write in a grammatically correct fashion, understanding when to use particular parts of speech.
- Decide which military strategies worked best under which circumstances.
- Know when whole numbers do not offer the best or even a possible solution to a problem.

FIGURE 5.5 CONCEPTUAL KNOWLEDGE

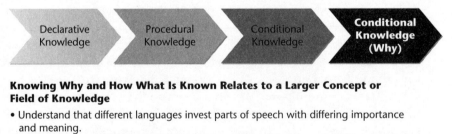

Knowing Why and How What Is Known Relates to a Larger Concept or Field of Knowledge

- Understand that different languages invest parts of speech with differing importance and meaning.
- Understand that combat in the Civil War rewrote or redefined many of the principles of warfare prevalent at the time.
- Understand the concept of whole numbers, of numbers generally, and of number systems, and how whole numbers and fractions are similar and different.

situations. Understanding that history includes multiple perspectives, some of which are contested, enables a learner to produce a far more sophisticated analysis of a time or place in the past, one that takes into account more than one possible explanation. Conceptual knowledge lets learners function at a metacognitive level to ask themselves if what they are doing makes sense and if they are accomplishing what they want to accomplish. Learners at this level are demonstrating emerging expertise in the subject area.

All four levels are critically important because as students move through each one, their retention of everything they learned at previous levels solidifies. Procedural knowledge reinforces declarative knowledge. Conditional knowledge reinforces procedural and declarative knowledge. Conceptual knowledge strengthens all three. Deeper learning occurs when students have the opportunities to experience each level as they progress through their instruction in a subject area. Not all students will reach the same ultimate level, but all need the opportunity to process information at each of the levels, in part to gauge their own understanding of the content but, more important, to begin to think more like an expert in the subject area.

These levels support the use of learning progressions that are more than just a series of concepts or topics taught in order. A true learning progression will consist of more than a sequencing of the content to be learned. It will also describe learning activities along all four levels of the knowledge complexity progression that build on content knowledge being learned. One of the true advantages of the Common Core State Standards and their culmination at a college and career readiness level is that content can be introduced, developed, and extended across grade levels until students are able to process the content at more complex cognitive levels, as specified in this four-level knowledge complexity progression.

The balance and proportion of teaching that is geared to each level says a lot about whether students are really being challenged and the degree to which they are encouraged and permitted to develop the types of cognitive skills associated with deeper learning. While different subjects and courses call for different proportions of each, students in general should have opportunities to process content at all four of these levels on a regular basis in all subject areas.

What Is Deeper Learning?

Deeper learning is defined as occurring when students acquire both declarative and procedural knowledge and then use that knowledge in ways that demonstrate deeper understanding at the conditional and conceptual levels. Deeper learning is the result of an interaction and interplay between the content being learned and the skills learners use in the learning process. To demonstrate deeper learning, students must develop their skills as learners. Students who can engage in deeper learning have moved beyond being novices and are emerging as strategic learners in command of a range of techniques and methods that enable them to attempt complex problems or sophisticated applications of knowledge and skills with confidence.

 To demonstrate deeper learning, students must develop their skills as learners.

Historical Summary

The idea of learning being the process of deep examination and understanding has been around in one form or another since the time of the ancient Greek philosophers, with the Socratic method and Plato's dialogues being two examples. Rousseau and others during the period of British and American romanticism espoused a philosophy that put the learner at the center of learning and in control of it. By the turn of the twentieth century, John Dewey and others were promoting a philosophy of education that came to be known as progressivism, which also emphasized the active role of learners in the learning process. They saw experience as the foundation of learning. Constructivist notions of learning—the idea that learners have to take an active role in constructing the meaning of what they are learning—extended progressivism and strengthened the notion of the learner as the arbiter of learning. Meaning is constructed from experience and mediated by the learner. Paying attention to the learner's role in the learning process, providing the learner with relevant stimuli, and helping the learner navigate the learning process are the important roles of teachers.

Another contrasting set of learning philosophies has assumed that the teacher is the font of all wisdom and that the child is an empty vessel to be filled with this wisdom. The role of learners is thus to follow the directions of the teacher and, in doing so, master the content knowledge that the teacher has organized and structured. This is largely a compliance-oriented approach to learning, where learners are assumed to be motivated to do what they are told or where motivation is simply not taken into account.

This approach does have several distinct advantages: content to be learned can be specified in more detail and precision, student learning can be measured more directly, and teachers can be trained how to teach in a more structured fashion. The mastery learning systems developed in the late 1970s were based on behaviorist notions of learning that employed these principles to the teaching and assessment of basic skills, and research evidence suggests that these approaches can lead to improvement in foundational skills in reading and mathematics. Direct instruction approaches that provide teachers with structured lessons to follow have shown positive results in getting students to learn specific academic content, particularly in the area of literacy skill development, and with students who benefit from this form of learning.

In all likelihood, no one form of teaching works equally well for all students. Ultimately learning requires a combination of techniques for most learners:

1. They need to understand the basic terminology and facts underlying the subject area they are studying, along with key methods and techniques for applying knowledge within the subject area.
2. They need to be introduced to linking ideas and organizing concepts that help them create an overall framework and set of connections for the detailed information or specific content that forms the foundation of the subject area.
3. As their understanding is strengthened, they become more aware of the structure and organization of knowledge in the subject area and are able to begin to apply what they are learning in new and novel ways, particularly to problems and situations outside the subject area in which the content was first learned.

Deeper learning, then, is not simply a combination of these two historical conceptions of learning, learner centered and content centered, although it certainly incorporates elements of both in important ways. Deeper learning also draws on findings from brain and cognitive sciences and experimental psychology that emphasize the importance of meaning and meaning making in the retention and use of information. The cognitive sciences increasingly are reaching conclusions about how the brain stores and organizes information that reinforce the value and validity of deeper learning.

Why We Need Deeper Learning Now

US presidents going back to Ronald Reagan have taken a certain perverse pleasure in highlighting the relatively poor performance of US schools on international comparisons and serving these up as a key indicator of the failings of the country's educational system and a harbinger of the imminent decline of the nation. While such comparisons potentially serve a useful purpose, the recipe for improving US schools may be more complex and nuanced than simply raising scores on the measures used to make the comparisons.

The entire notion of comparing nations' educational systems is new and fraught with issues—technical, cultural, and otherwise. Martin Carnoy from Stanford University and Richard Rothstein from the University of California, Berkeley point out some of the problems with comparing the United States to other countries, such as the fact that a larger proportion of students in the United States are disadvantaged and that, when compared on an apples-to-apples basis, US students at every socioeconomic level do better than it would appear based on a comparison of overall averages among nations. What is clear, though, is that students in some countries do a much better job than in the United States of performing well on the kinds of exams used in these comparisons. What is fascinating is that many of these high-performing countries are simultaneously turning their attention to the United States for guidance on how to improve their educational systems. Why is this happening?

When the US educational system works well, it is because it gets students to think. Students are engaging in deeper learning in the pockets of excellence that foreigners often observe. What visitors find is a type of learning they rarely see in their own countries. They see students who question assumptions, offer original hypotheses, use academic learning tools in new and novel ways, can generate multiple solutions to the same problem, can take charge of their own learning, are intensely motivated by their interests and aspirations, and use the basic skills they have been taught for a higher purpose than just answering tests questions correctly. This may not happen in every school with every student, which is the heart of the problem with US schools: the lack of consistent quality of engagement across all racial, ethnic, and income groups. But where it does occur, it is a model for the world.

> When the US educational system works well, it is because it gets students to think.

This is the genius of the US educational model. When and where it works, the results are stunning. These students:

- Excel in scientific inquiry
- Generate new solutions to old problems

- Create and manage self-directed teams that work with a high degree of independence to design original solutions to complex problems
- Are not afraid to make up their own rules and figure out how to take on ambiguous tasks

These are all key indicators of deeper learning, and the US educational system is looked to as a model internationally for getting a wide range of students engaged in this type of learning.

For all of their shortcomings, US schools have one potential advantage over those in most other countries: the US economy is probably the most dynamic in the world, and it values a range of skills and capabilities that can be developed only when students are deeply engaged in learning and are using what they know in creative, novel, and unique ways. The US economy values entrepreneurs, problem solvers, innovators—anyone with a new idea or a better way to do things. Technical skills are important, but they are not the only measure of one's value and worth. Creative insight, the ability to work with others as a team, strong research capabilities, and the ability to design and execute a complex project are all highly valued in an economy where manual labor continues to decline rapidly and knowledge work increases.

Another advantage the United States has is that its higher education system is still viewed as the model for the rest of the world. As country after country emerges economically, parents who are able to send their children to US colleges and universities do so. Many are also enrolling their children in US high schools. Why would parents whose students come from educational systems scoring the highest in the world want to send their children to a country whose system consistently ranks in the middle of the pack in mathematics scores in particular? Why do national education ministries send delegations annually to visit US schools? What is it about education in this country that is different and worthy of emulation? What are US schools doing right that educators in those schools may not fully recognize?

Even if the Common Core State Standards are successfully implemented, it is unlikely the United States will ever top the list of countries on international comparative exams. Schools in this country can and should strive to move up the list on international comparisons. However, US educators and policymakers should not miss the opportunity to legitimize and value the deeper learning skills that occur unevenly around the nation currently and to encourage their adoption and implementation broadly by every school and for every student. Many of the Common Core State Standards require deeper learning, and this characteristic of the standards

5

TOWARD DEEPER
LEARNING

should be constantly emphasized. The US culture and economy are more prone to value these types of skills—the skills for a twenty-first-century world. They should not be lost or pushed aside in a headlong rush to raise scores on content tests that paint only part of the picture of a well-educated US student.

If other countries are successful in adding deeper learning to systems that already teach content knowledge effectively, US schools will eventually find themselves in the middle of the pack on measures of deeper learning as well as basic skills. Such a result will be disastrous socially and economically. Deeper learning is key, not only as a vehicle by which students integrate the content knowledge they will be learning in the Common Core State Standards but also as the means by which US schools maintain their distinctive leadership role in the world.

Four Models of Deeper Learning

Several organizations have created the specifications for deeper learning. The four models that follow help to translate the general overview just presented into more practical and actionable elements against which educators can judge current practices.

Hewlett Deeper Learning Model

The Hewlett Foundation has spent several years and considerable resources supporting the development and implementation of deeper learning models in schools. The Hewlett deeper learning framework consists of six major areas, each with a number of subareas:

1. Master core academic content.
   a. Students understand key principles and relationships within a content area and organize information in a conceptual framework.
   b. Students learn, remember, and recall facts relevant to a content area.
   c. Students have procedural knowledge of a content area and know how knowledge is produced and how experts solve problems.
   d. Students know and are able to use the language specific to a content area.
   e. Students are motivated to put in the time and effort needed to build a solid knowledge base.

   f. Students extend core knowledge to novel tasks and situations in a variety of academic subjects.
   g. Students know that future learning will build on what they know and learn today.
   h. Students learn and can apply theories relevant to a content area.
   i. Students enjoy and are able to rise to challenges requiring them to apply knowledge in nonroutine ways.
   j. Students apply facts, processes, and theories to real-world situations.
2. Think critically and solve complex problems.
   a. Students are familiar with and able to use effectively the tools and techniques specific to a content area.
   b. Students formulate problems and generate hypotheses.
   c. Students identify the data and information needed to solve a problem.
   d. Students apply the tools and techniques specific to a content area to gather necessary data and information.
   e. Students evaluate, integrate, and critically analyze multiple sources of information.
   f. Students monitor and refine the problem-solving process based on available data as needed.
   g. Students reason and construct justifiable arguments in support of a hypothesis.
   h. Students persist to solve complex problems.
3. Communicate effectively.
   a. Students structure information and data in a meaningful and useful way.
   b. Students listen to and incorporate feedback and ideas from others.
   c. Students provide constructive and appropriate peer feedback to others.
   d. Students understand that creating a quality final communication requires review and revision of multiple drafts.
   e. Students communicate complex concepts to others in both written and oral presentations.
   f. Students tailor their message for the intended audience.
4. Work collaboratively.
   a. Students collaborate with others to complete tasks and solve problems successfully.
   b. Students work as part of a group to identify group goals.
   c. Students participate in a team to plan problem-solving steps and identify resources necessary to meet group goals.

5

TOWARD DEEPER
LEARNING

      d. Students communicate and incorporate multiple points of view to meet group goals.

5. Learn how to learn.

      a. Students set a goal for each learning task, monitor their progress toward the goal, and adapt their approach as needed to complete a task or solve a problem successfully.

      b. Students know and can apply a variety of study skills and strategies to meet the demands of a task.

      c. Students monitor their comprehension as they learn, recognize when they become confused or encounter obstacles, diagnose barriers to their success, and select appropriate strategies to work through them.

      d. Students work well independently but ask for help when they need it.

      e. Students routinely reflect on their learning experiences and apply insights to subsequent situations.

      f. Students are aware of their strengths and weaknesses, and anticipate needing to work harder in some areas.

      g. Students identify and work toward lifelong learning and academic goals.

      h. Students enjoy and seek out learning on their own and with others.

      i. Students anticipate and are prepared to meet changing expectations in a variety of academic, professional, and social environments.

6. Develop academic mind-sets.

      a. Students feel a strong sense of belonging in an academic community and value intellectual engagement with others.

      b. Students perceive the inherent value of content knowledge and of learning.

      c. Students see the relevance of schoolwork to their lives and interests.

      d. Students understand how work they do now will benefit them in the future.

      e. Students value their intellectual life and see themselves as academic achievers.

      f. Students trust in their own capacity and competence and feel a strong sense of efficacy at a variety of academic tasks.

      g. Students believe that hard work will pay off in increased knowledge and skills.

      h. Students delay gratification, refocus after distractions, and maintain momentum until they reach their goal.

     i. Students use failures and setbacks as opportunities for feedback and apply lessons learned to improve future efforts.

     j. Students care about the quality of their work and put in extra effort to do things thoroughly and well.

     k. Students continue looking for new ways to learn challenging material or solve difficult problems.

National Research Council Education for Life and Work model

A second model for deeper learning was presented in a report undertaken by the National Research Council (NRC). Entitled *Education for Life and Work* and published in 2012, the report describes deeper learning in terms of the ability of learners to transfer what they learn in one context to an unfamiliar context. Transfer of learning of this type is difficult for most learners to achieve, and when it does occur, it is an indication that learners know a subject well. Deeper learning emphasizes understanding of the fundamental concepts and principles of a subject area and their relationship to one another, not just the acquisition of isolated bits of factual information. The report presents a three-domain model of deeper learning derived from the research base:

- *The cognitive domain:* Includes cognitive processes and strategies, knowledge, and creativity. Examples of competencies in this domain are critical thinking, information literacy, reasoning and argumentation, and innovation.
- *The intrapersonal domain:* Consists of intellectual openness, work ethic and conscientiousness, and positive core self-evaluation. Competencies include flexibility, initiative, appreciation for diversity, and metacognition, which is the ability to reflect on one's own learning and make adjustments accordingly.
- *The interpersonal domain:* Consists of teamwork and collaboration, and leadership. Examples are communication, responsibility, and conflict resolution.

The Four Keys to College and Career Readiness Model

The Educational Policy Improvement Center's model, four keys to college and career readiness, discussed in depth in the previous two chapters, parallels in many ways the models just presented (figure 5.6).

5

TOWARD DEEPER
LEARNING

Three of the four keys align closely with the Hewlett model and overlap many NRC conceptions, although in a slightly different organizational structure:

- Key cognitive strategies (Think) are equivalent to the Hewlett category of "think critically and solve problems" and the NRC cognitive domain.
- Key content knowledge (Know) corresponds well with the Hewlett "master content knowledge category" and elements of the NRC cognitive domain.
- Key learning skills and techniques (Act) align well with the Hewlett "learn how to learn" and "develop academic mind-sets" categories and with elements of the NRC intrapersonal domain and, to a lesser degree, the interpersonal domain.
- Key transition knowledge and skills (Go) do not explicitly overlap the other models but are nevertheless important for students to learn and understand at a deeper level than declarative and procedural knowledge.

FIGURE 5.6 FOUR KEYS TO COLLEGE AND CAREER READINESS

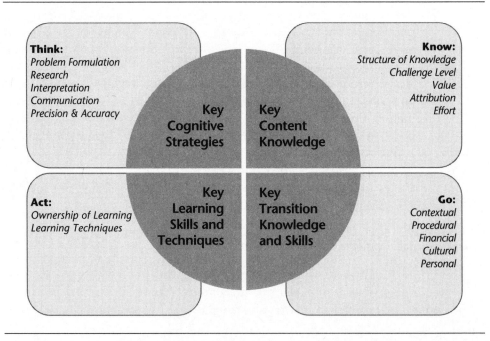

Partnership for 21st Century Skills Model

The Partnership for 21st Century Skills, an amalgam of national organizations and school districts, has developed its own framework that lays out the range of knowledge and skills students will need for success in the future. The framework consists of four elements:

- *Core subjects and twenty-first-century themes:* Global awareness; financial, economic, business, and entrepreneurial literacy; civic literacy; health literacy; environmental literacy
- *Learning and innovation skills:* Creativity and innovation, critical thinking and problem solving, communication and collaboration
- *Information, media, and technology skills:* Information literacy; media literacy; information, communications, and technology literacy
- *Life and career skills:* Flexibility and adaptability, initiative and self-direction, social and cross-cultural skills, productivity and accountability, leadership and responsibility

Although the Partnership for 21st Century Skills framework is organized differently and contains some elements not explicitly listed in the other three models, it addresses many of the elements of deeper learning that appear in the other models:

- Key content is specified and identified as a central focal point.
- The uses of knowledge beyond basic content acquisition are emphasized.
- Cognitive strategies and thinking skills are important and appear in several different places, along with an emphasis on communication in multiple formats and by a variety of means, including technology.
- Learning skills, both individual and those that occur in a social context, are emphasized.

Comparison of Models

It is worth noting the strong similarities among the conceptual organization of these models. Recognizing that all four of the models share a common vision of students engaging deeply with meaningful and challenging content, as well as specific components related to the learning process and students' social and intellectual development, helps reinforce the conclusion that the definition for deeper learning, while not exactly the same among all groups examining the phenomenon, has large and substantive elements of overlap and commonality. This is useful for educators who are attempting to build instructional programs based on the kind of cognitive engagement these models suggest. While deeper learning may not have one undisputed definition, the components are similar enough across multiple frameworks to provide a core of common elements for those who wish to move their schools toward a deeper learning approach.

The models all identify the interaction of learners with appropriate, challenging content that causes them to have to think and use a wider range of learning techniques to comprehend, process, apply, and retain material. In all four models, students reflect on what they know and make decisions about what they need to do next to learn necessary material. They understand that almost all learning is socially mediated and constructed; that is, learning occurs as a function of interaction with others as well as a result of sustained individual effort. Students who engage in deeper learning know they have to work hard and persist when presented with challenging academic tasks and that learning requires a certain discipline on their part. Most important, all models recognize the need to allow students opportunities to process what they are learning and give material meaning in order to retain information and be able to transfer what they have learned to new settings. In essence, all four models emphasize the role of the learner as a processor of information and creator of meaning. For learning to be deeper, it must be active, engaging, social, self-monitored, and self-aware.

 Learning occurs as a function of interaction with others as well as a result of sustained individual effort.

Overview of Research Foundation for Deeper Learning

The evidence base for this type of learning is growing rapidly, and a full presentation of the literature that supports deeper learning is well beyond the scope of this book, although numerous publications do make the case that learning needs to follow the principles set out here. The NRC report contains a thorough synthesis of the literature, and some of its key points are useful in describing the research base that underlies deeper learning, although the authors are quick to point out that much more research is needed.

More research has been done on cognitive competencies than on interpersonal and intrapersonal skills. This research finds consistent positive relationships between cognitive competencies and desirable educational and personal outcomes. From among the interpersonal and intrapersonal skills, one emerges as particularly important: conscientiousness. Conscientiousness in the form of being well organized and taking responsibility for one's learning shows positive associations with educational achievement and success in life. Human agency, the ability of people to persevere and succeed when confronted with challenges, is being recognized as an important, if largely unexplained, component in educational achievement. Finally, participating in more formal education in and of itself predicts earnings, social engagement, and health. Staying in school is a good thing in and of itself.

The NRC report makes clear that transferring what is learned in one setting to an unfamiliar one is not easy. Students must work diligently over extended periods of time to develop emerging expertise in a subject area. In the process, they acquire not just the skills associated with the subject area, but they also begin to understand how experts think differently than novices do. This type of metacognition helps them when they begin to learn something new. They not only apply content knowledge they have learned elsewhere; they also understand the process of moving from novice to expert learner, and they can accelerate their learning in new areas because they know what expertise looks like and can compare their current state of knowledge and skill to a higher, desired level.

Students who have developed expertise in something, almost anything, have a distinct advantage over students who have never reached a level of high competency in any area. Think of students who are highly skillful musicians or have achieved a degree of expertise in particular hobbies or interests. These students know how to work hard to achieve a goal and the amount of work it takes to be successful in an area. They know and appreciate better the gap between where they are and where they want to be and how to close that gap.

The context of the classroom also influences how students learn, as does their relationship to one another and to the learning tasks. In other words, the kinds of interpersonal and intrapersonal skills students are developing and using in the classroom affect their ability to understand, process, and retain the content information and concepts they are being taught. This is particularly true when the goal is for students to engage with complex content organized around key ideas and concepts of the subject area.

Students need to understand the underlying principles of what they are studying if they are to apply these to new and novel situations beyond the structured opportunities to practice that they are provided in class. They need to understand the nature and types of problems they will encounter in the subject area, the solution strategies and options available to them, and how the two interact with one another. In other words, they need to develop the metacognitive skills necessary to make decisions about how to process what they are learning and, eventually, how to draw on their understanding of the content they have learned and the problem-solving techniques available to them to address challenges or complete tasks that are entirely outside the boundaries of what they have practiced previously.

🌀 Awareness and Action Steps

- View the PBS Newshour eight-minute video on deeper learning entitled "Teachers Embrace 'Deep Learning,' Translating Lessons into Practical Skills" (http://to.pbs.org/18X7F9n).
- Review articles from *Education Week*'s Spotlight on Deeper Learning.
- Download the free PDF version and review selected passages from the National Research Council's report, *Education for Life and Work: Developing Transferable Knowledge and Skills in the 21st Century* (http://bit.ly/100Jgtl).
- Download the *Partnership for 21st Century Skills' MILE Guide*, a tool kit containing a comprehensive description of the P21 Deeper Learning model and a self-assessment tool for administrators (http://bit.ly/16er2p3).
- Learn about the connection between the Common Core State Standards and deeper learning at cresst.org: "On the Road to Assessing Deeper Learning: The Status of Smarter Balanced and PARCC Assessment Consortia."
- Do your own comparison of the four models for deeper learning presented in the chapter and identify commonalities you think are important. Then think about how these commonalities could be used to focus the program of study at your school.
- Read Bob Lenz and Ken Kay's commentary on Common Core Implementation, appearing in *Education Week* and Edutopia (http://bit.ly/15h4UIn). Discuss your school's or district's approach to the transition to new college and career readiness standards. In what ways are implementation efforts focusing on compliance rather than achieving the goals of the Common Core State Standards?
- Review course syllabi to determine the balance of declarative, procedural, conditional, and conceptual knowledge. Is one type of knowledge overemphasized? Is any type underemphasized?
- Assign and evaluate student work that explicitly focuses on conceptual knowledge and deeper learning.

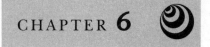
DEEPER LEARNING AT THE CLASSROOM LEVEL

A classroom in which students engage in deeper learning looks different from one that is focused on transmitting content knowledge without respect to its ultimate uses, long-term retention by students, or impact on student learning skills and strategies. The deeper learning classroom has crystal-clear learning goals, but those goals are not limited to a list of content topics alone. Also included are the big ideas and concepts being taught, along with the ways of knowing for the subject area. In a biology course, for example, in addition to all of the vocabulary and nomenclature that is important foundational information, a deeper learning classroom focuses on a half-dozen big ideas in biology and seeks to have learners gain greater insight into living organisms and how their systems interact. Knowing the nomenclature of biology and even knowing basic biological systems is not the same as understanding at a deeper level how living organisms function, a larger goal of a biology course.

Characteristics of the Deeper Learning Classroom

The deeper learning classroom has an explicit learning model that informs instruction. That model is composed of a number of assumptions about how students learn, many of which have been outlined in the previous chapter. The deeper learning classroom incorporates students as full partners in the learning process by being explicit about how learning is to occur. Teacher and students alike know how learning will be assessed, that assessments will be consistent with the goals of the course, and that assumptions about how students learn will include attention to deeper learning. This consistency helps students trust that if they truly engage and begin to go deeper into the content in order to develop conceptual understanding, they will not be punished by a test that values only low-level knowledge and does not acknowledge higher-order thinking about the subject.

Teaching to deeper learning begins with the use of effective and varied instructional techniques. It is certainly appropriate and necessary to present some information or explain some processes in a step-by-step fashion accompanied by examples and practice problems that allow the consolidation of understanding of a method. However, learning cannot stop at this point. The use of these types of directed instructional techniques (and they can occur at any step in the learning process, not just as the initial input) should be deliberate, purposeful, and not used to excess. Students need time to digest and integrate all the new declarative information they are being presented and to tag it with meaning through opportunities they have to use it in procedural, conditional, and conceptual ways.

This integration can be accomplished by presenting concepts in multiple and varied representations:

1. Introducing a concept first with a lecture accompanied by a visual aid, perhaps a graphic, table, or poster
2. Processing the material or concept through an exercise in which students manipulate information from the lecture individually or in teams
3. Integrating key learnings through an activity in which students apply the concept in a nonroutine fashion

Throughout the learning process, learners need to be challenged with thoughtful and provocative questioning that causes them to clarify what they understand and what they don't at the same time that they gain additional insight into the topic at hand by explaining what they have just learned. This is a process students can also learn to do with one another after it is modeled for them sufficiently.

Once material has been introduced within the learning framework and students have had a chance to comprehend and process it, they need a challenging task that enables them to gauge their competency with the content and concepts. This can be low stakes and provide formative feedback through a quick-and-dirty "brain dump" of everything they know about the topic, by means of an in-class assignment that requires solving a structured problem, or through a larger out-of-class project that is summative in nature and requires students to apply what they know to a more open-ended task in which they make decisions about the information that is needed, the most appropriate analytical techniques, and the best means to communicate the results.

Above all, learners must want to take ownership of their learning. Getting or helping them to do so is complex and highly contextualized, but creating a feeling of trust and support in the classroom is an important first step, particularly with students for whom getting deeply involved will require them to take a risk. Students need to know they can try and fall short of complete success and not be punished provided they are working diligently and conscientiously. They need to know they can get help without being made to feel inadequate if they do not understand the deeper meaning of the subject easily. They need help breaking the habit of doing only what the teacher asks them to do, which they are accustomed to doing at a low level of cognitive challenge. They need to make the transition to being learners who do more than the minimum and are proud that they are not afraid to attempt challenging learning tasks and even to fail occasionally.

> Students need to know they can try and fall short of complete success and not be punished provided they are working diligently and conscientiously.

Part of making this happen is the nature of the learning itself. It must be interesting and engaging, with a proper balance of intrinsic and extrinsic motivation underlying it. In a deeper learning classroom, students view grades largely as a by-product of conscientious work focused on understanding what they are being taught about the structure of knowledge and ways of solving problems in a particular content area, and not as the sole focus of their efforts.

Deeper learning classrooms help students make connections between what they are learning and their interests and aspirations. They also help students develop new interests and explore possibilities. Rather than relying on telling students that they will need to know something later, the deeper learning classroom explains why they will need to know the concept or material now *and* in the future. This leads to the applications of the material in concrete ways. As students grasp the importance of what they are learning, they come to understand that the content they are mastering opens up new possibilities for them in their lives. Learners need what they are doing to be meaningful and important, and the deeper learning classroom gives them the opportunity to make connections and create the meaning that they want to make.

Finally, the deeper learning classroom is a place where students learn to reflect on their own thinking:

- They analyze why they approach a problem the way they do.
- They consider alternatives they had not initially entertained.
- They conduct postmortems on significant assignments and projects to see how they could have gained deeper insight into the problem they studied, not necessarily how they could have gotten a better grade.
- They consider how they are organizing their time and how they are prioritizing the tasks necessary to complete a particular assignment.
- They assess their relations with others to determine who are good partners for studying and who thinks differently from them and may offer new ideas and insights as a result.
- They examine how they can be more efficient in how they work, not just generically, but in ways specific to the kinds of problems that they are encountering in the class.
- They think about the quality of their own thinking as objectively as possible and assess how innovative and original they are being in their thinking.

In short, they continue to improve continuously by examining all aspects of the learning process and how they engage in it.

Challenges of the Deeper Learning Classroom

Many educators would agree that this description of the deeper learning classroom is something to which they aspire, and many teachers do incorporate many or even most of these elements already. Teachers or schools that attempt to move toward deeper learning at the classroom level, however, will face a number of challenges.

Teacher Understanding of Subject Matter

The first and foremost challenge for the deeper learning classroom is having teachers who understand their subject areas well enough to engage students at deeper levels. While having state-of-the-art knowledge regarding the subjects they teach is certainly important, deeper learning requires them to have a strong understanding of the conceptual foundation of the content they are teaching and how what they are teaching fits within the large subject area and the academic discipline as a whole. They need to be comfortable with their subject's ways of knowing, the specific assumptions about what constitutes valid knowledge and the accepted methods of gathering and validating knowledge in a discipline, and conventions of problem solving employed in the subject area.

Armed with this deep understanding of what they are teaching, teachers can do more than present content. They can organize instruction around big ideas and discuss these ideas more fluently. Teachers who are unsure about their own understanding of big ideas tend to adhere closely to the textbook, teach facts and procedures, and close off opportunities for students to ask questions that might be uncomfortable or not answered easily. Teachers unfamiliar with the ways of knowing employed in a discipline, whether it is the scientific method, literary analysis, or mathematical proofs, are more likely to avoid giving assignments that allow students to use these methods. Instead, they rely on activities that limit students to coming up with right and wrong answers or following directions.

Challenge number one, then, is to have all teachers in a school be at a level of comfort with the subject or subjects they teach sufficient to let students explore content and concepts in greater depth and with wider latitude. Most school districts are reluctant to verify the depth of teachers' content knowledge directly and instead rely on indirect measures, such as a teaching license or certificate with an endorsement in a particular area. However, getting to deeper learning in a classroom or school starts with a candid examination of teacher depth of knowledge in the subject area. The purpose of any such determination is not to label or punish but to determine the proper set of supports teachers need to improve their subject matter comprehension so that they are more comfortable extending student thinking beyond basic content coverage.

Needless to say, assigning teachers to teach subjects in which they have scant expertise is a recipe for disaster when it comes to deeper learning. Central office administrators and principals need to work in concert to ensure the hiring pool and process are sufficient to yield highly qualified candidates who are willing and eager to go into depth on the material they teach. Principals need to follow up by observing in classrooms to ascertain the instructional strategies being used. If all that is observed are activities with low cognitive challenge levels, teachers aren't developing deeper learning. This signals the need for focused, sustained professional development.

Getting teachers to acquire this expertise need not be an exercise in drudgery. Resources abound to help teachers achieve greater conceptual understanding of and excitement about what they are teaching. Subject matter organizations offer videos, webinars, and courses, as do other leading organizations with interests in the subject matter. TED Talks, for example, can offer a new perspective on a topic, as can documentaries or television series that explore an area in depth. The Internet opens up a world of possibilities for accessing interesting materials. Finally, local post-secondary institutions can be called on to offer presentations or seminars to energize and excite teachers with a deeper understanding and love of their subject areas. Increasingly, online courses with lectures by faculty from some of the top higher education institutions in the country are available free of charge for viewing or through massive online open courses. Teachers may need help connecting with these resources, but such resources are abundantly available in every subject area.

Wide Range of Instructional Strategies

The second challenge centers on the instructional techniques used to facilitate deeper learning. Many of these have been alluded to previously, but several bear repeating. Teachers need to know how to:

- Organize lessons and focus them clearly on key ideas and concepts rather than just plow through content one topic after another
- Point out to students what is important and why
- Make connections between what has been learned previously and what is yet to come and how what is being studied currently fits in
- Make material meaningful and relevant to students by connecting it to their lives in some fashion and to their interests and aspirations
- Lead a discussion and question students in ways that cause students to reflect on their own thinking about the subject or topic

- Select or develop appropriately challenging assignments, tasks, or projects and then support students as they complete them
- Help students reflect on the learning strategies and methods they are using currently and then improve their use of those strategies in the future
- Organize, structure, and manage social learning situations and help students develop the ability to mediate their learning socially

In short, teachers need to become much more like conductors who know how to get the most out of a wide range of instruments and musicians. They need to know what it takes to cause deeper learning to occur and how to engage the full spectrum of students in deeper learning.

Many of the ways to develop these skills are not unfamiliar to educators:

- Professional learning communities in which teachers share ideas and strategies for dealing with particular challenges are places where they can explore and discuss new approaches in a safe, supportive environment.
- Professional development opportunities focused on teaching strategies give teachers opportunities to take ideas back to the classroom that they can test out immediately and then refine over time.
- Attendance at conferences and workshops in which specific techniques are taught helps inspire and motivate teachers and lets them develop broader professional networks.
- Mentorships and peer observations create opportunities for dissemination of effective teaching techniques quickly within a school and build schoolwide norms of collaboration.

The key element is the expectation that teachers continue to develop, refine, and expand their repertoire of instructional skills and that they receive regular feedback on the effectiveness with which they are implementing these techniques. This can and should be done from an instructional improvement perspective more than an evaluative one. Letting teachers know the instructional strategies and methods that enable students to engage in deeper learning, connecting them with necessary resources, and letting them practice their application in a safe, secure environment is a key function for all educational leaders intent on increasing deeper learning in their school.

Taking the Time for Deeper Learning

The third major challenge is the time it takes to teach to deeper learning. Some might argue this is the biggest challenge, but in fact much of the content taught in schools has already been introduced at a previous grade level, so the amount of entirely new material students encounter at any grade level or in any particular class is substantially less than what many teachers estimate. Up to two-thirds of the content of a typical curriculum at the upper-elementary or middle-school level can consist of material that students have already been taught at least once, with little adaptation of instruction to reflect this. If teachers are teaching all students the same material when half of the class already knows it, they are not making good use of classroom time. As a result, they do not have time to get any students to engage in deeper learning. The issue, then, is not necessarily always more time as much as it is how time is used.

A deeper learning classroom changes the tempo, pace, and length of time devoted to different types of activities. Instead of spending nearly every moment introducing material and practicing it in bits and pieces, the deeper learning classroom uses important concepts as the hub around which associated ideas, methods, techniques, and facts are introduced, practiced, applied, and then used strategically. Integrative activities, such as tasks and projects, let students make connections among all they have learned within the subject area and the application of their learnings to other subject areas.

> A deeper learning classroom changes the tempo, pace, and length of time devoted to different types of activities.

The trade-off here is that not as many topics can be covered, but it should be remembered that "cover" can mean "to hide from sight." It then becomes more apparent that simply covering material for the sake of covering it should not be the goal. As noted, much of the content that is introduced in elementary school is retaught in some form in secondary school, and the same phenomenon occurs again when students move from high school to college. So if the goal is to improve college and career readiness for all students, more time needs to be devoted to developing the deeper understanding of the subject area. Postsecondary instructors agree with near unanimity this is more important than having students learn factual information that they quickly forget. Keep in mind that much of the content students learn in high school will be reintroduced or retaught in college.

Time needs to be prioritized among content introduction, guided practice, explanation and discussion, deeper exploration and integration, and application for transfer, which can be facilitated by a wider range of more complex assignments and assessments. Also important to factor in is time for students to reflect on what they are learning and what this means to their lives, now and in the future. Time to explore interests and formulate aspirations that relate to the content being taught and the concepts and ideas being introduced creates powerful connections for young people and keeps them engaged in learning.

One of the first places to start to address this issue is the course syllabus. An often overlooked document, the syllabus is a window into the structure and content of the course. Even a poor syllabus says a lot, namely, that the instructor almost certainly has not organized the course around key concepts and ideas and likely has little idea how to pace instruction to allow opportunities for integration, reflection, and culminating assignments.

Building quality syllabi is not an easy thing for teachers unaccustomed to working closely from a syllabus to do, but tools exist to help them through the process, including one called CourseCreate, which is explained in greater detail in the appendix. Course content can be aligned to the Common Core initially to get the necessary focus. Then lessons can be balanced among declarative, procedural, conditional, and conceptual knowledge as focal points. No one rule can capture how best to allocate time among these. A good rule of thumb, though, is to see if more than a quarter of the class time is spent on any one area and, conversely, if one level of knowledge gets well less than a quarter of total course time (including out-of-class time for homework, assignments, and test preparation). Emphasizing quality syllabi as a means to allocate time more efficiently and effectively is itself an efficient way to help teachers see the potential for devoting more time to deeper learning activities, and to do so within the framework of college and career readiness and the Common Core.

Creating a Culture of Deeper Learning

The fourth challenge is the culture of the school itself:

- Does the school value the intellectual development of all its students, or is this important only for some students?
- Does the culture support student engagement in learning, or are students who care about learning viewed as social outcasts?
- Is the school ruled by youth culture or by an academic learning culture?
- Do the teachers publicly model the value of deeper learning through understanding and love of what they teach?
- Does the school value deeper learning in its award and recognition programs?

Deeper learning has little possibility of taking hold in schools where academic engagement is not seen as a centrally important activity. Teachers and administrators need to take serious stock of the culture of their school to determine the messages students are being sent about the need to engage in deeper learning. Seeking to improve test scores certainly is important, but it should not drive deeper learning out of the school. Students who dutifully strive to improve their test scores should also be given the message and opportunity to develop deeper understandings of what they are learning.

Schools do many things to encourage students to affiliate with the school, largely around a school identity. The challenge is to build affiliation around an identity tied to excellence in all its forms. Schools that do this successfully manage to recognize and value outstanding performance in all aspects of the school's program. They accept nothing less than the best of students, both inside and outside the classroom. They balance their nonacademic accomplishments with an equal emphasis on academic learning and achievements. They hire teachers who can demonstrate excellence in their classes as much as they hire coaches who can achieve victories in athletic competitions. They seek to instill the values taught so well in successful extracurricular programs—hard work and persistence, individual responsibility, understanding of one's role as a member of a team, the need to practice and to assess one's performance against high standards, the importance of respecting adult leaders—into every classroom and every student. They make academics as challenging, engaging, and rewarding as nonacademic activities.

One of the first steps in doing this is to assess the school's culture accurately. Many instruments exist to address this purpose. The appendix describes CampusReady, a survey instrument EPIC designed specifically to ascertain the degree to which the school and its instructional program is focused on college and career readiness. Part of what the instrument determines is the degree to which a variety of practices are followed that support deeper learning, and, more important, the values and beliefs of students and staff toward deeper learning. Armed with the results from a survey, a school can comprise a committee or work group to address areas of concern, recommend new activities and establish new traditions, and send a new message about what is important to the school.

Knowing How to Assess Deeper Learning

The fifth challenge arises from the assessments used to gauge learning in the school. Assessment in a deeper learning classroom should be multidimensional and well integrated with instruction and learning. In other words, the lines between teaching, learning, and assessing should be blurred to some degree. Students should be receiving formative feedback regularly and at more than just the level of the number of right answers on a test or quiz. Assignments and assessments should be carefully designed to address the full range of course goals, which will extend beyond low-level content knowledge acquisition. Students should be fully aware of the criteria by which they will be judged, including any scoring guides or rubrics that will be used on their papers or projects. All of this should be explained to students in plain language, with opportunity for discussion before any assessment is administered, to allow students to develop the same mental model the teacher has of what effective performance will look like on assignments, tasks, or projects.

Preparation for consortia assessments of the Common Core State Standards can and should certainly occur in a deeper learning classroom. Although the consortia assessments will be limited in their ability to assess deeper learning due to time constraints, among other factors, they will have more questions or item types that require extended thinking, analysis, and more complex application. Preparing in a deeper learning classroom goes beyond a procedural overview of the tests combined with a set of test-taking tricks. Ideally, instruction in deeper learning classrooms will be organized around the standards, and students will gradually but consistently gain mastery of the structure of knowledge and learning progressions that underlie the Common Core State Standards.

Test preparation in this context is largely a process of focused review with attention to the conceptual explanation of areas where weaknesses have been identified combined with guided practice of specific skills for which intensive practice is likely to make a difference in the short amount of time devoted to test preparation. A deeper learning classroom never uses test preparation as an occasion to reteach the entire curriculum or to drill students repeatedly on basic skills, a method that has been shown to produce rapidly diminishing returns and even to worsen scores when done to excess.

The appendix includes examples from ThinkReady, an assessment system that uses complex performance tasks administered and completed by students in and outside the classroom and scored by teachers using common scoring guides that gauge student thinking along a novice-expert continuum. This mode of assessment recognizes true deeper learning— not just clever thinking, but more complex understanding of the content knowledge and the ability to demonstrate conditional and conceptual uses of knowledge. ThinkReady works when it is fully integrated into instruction and teachers are explicitly teaching students how to think in ways that ThinkReady assesses.

The ThinkReady scoring guide looks for student performance in five broad cognitive areas. Within those areas, work is rated on a seven-level scale that spans emerging novice to emerging expert. To make more concise determinations about the level of expertise demonstrated in a piece of student work, the scoring guide breaks deeper learning down into a series of components. The next section explains a scoring guide designed to assess deeper learning in more detail.

A Closer Look at Scoring Student Work for Deeper Learning

The scoring guide explained here is built around six organizing concepts that each have seven levels of descriptions on a novice-expert continuum (figure 6.1). The organizing concepts are insight, efficiency, idea

FIGURE 6.1 CONTINUUM FROM NOVICE TO EXPERT

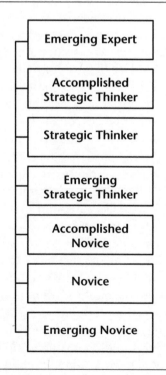

generation, concept formation, integration, and solution seeking (figure 6.2). As learners become more skillful, they progress in performance in each of these areas from emerging novice to novice and then to accomplished novice, emerging strategic thinker, strategic thinker, accomplished strategic thinker, and emerging expert. This creates forty-two cells, each of which would hold a description of student work. (See the appendix for a link to the complete scoring guide.) Teachers can use these six concepts and seven levels to analyze a range of sophisticated student work products along a continuum of cognitive development and learner competence.

Many educators find it challenging initially to cope with the complexity of a model with this much information and this many categories. However, capturing deeper learning does require some attention to complexity and performance along a number of cognitive dimensions. The good news is that as teachers use the scoring guide more, they quickly internalize the elements and become adept at rating the cognitive complexity of student work. In this case, teachers themselves must experience deeper learning before they can apply the scoring guide in an appropriate fashion. When teachers do understand the concepts embedded in the scoring guide, they

FIGURE 6.2 ORGANIZING CONCEPTS

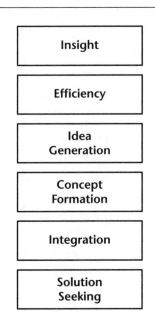

have a powerful lens through which to gauge the depth and complexity of student learning. Each of the organizing concepts is explained here in more detail:

O   *Insight* involves the ability to use the rules of the subject area in a procedurally correct fashion and then to become progressively more insightful about how to go beyond literal interpretation of subject area rules to combine or skip steps, ignore a rule if a more elegant solution is available, and, ultimately, use the rules intuitively rather than literally. Learners who become insightful in the use of disciplinary rules are able eventually to generate more original and interesting work.

O   One characteristic of novice learners is that they have difficulty completing tasks with *efficiency*. Experts spend much less energy than novices do on comparable tasks. This phenomenon can be observed in a wide range of fields, such as sports, where novices struggle to perform the same routine that the expert accomplishes effortlessly. Watch beginning skiers or snowboarders floundering on the slopes, expending vast amounts of energy just standing and maintaining their balance; then compare this with the accomplished skier or snowboarder who makes the sport look effortless. In deeper learning, efficiency is the ability to use the best methods possible to complete a task such that someone scoring the task would find few ways in which it could have been done more efficiently. Most learners complete some elements of tasks efficiently while struggling with others. A lack of efficiency can lead to a confusing final product. Students may even give up on parts of the task, project, or assignment. This then affects overall quality.

 One characteristic of novice learners is that they have difficulty completing tasks with efficiency.

O   *Idea generation* is another important variable that distinguishes levels of deeper learning along the continuum. Novices produce few original ideas, preferring to repeat well-worn observations and conclusions because this is what emerges from following a prescribed set of procedures. As learners develop strategic competence, they venture into the arena of idea generation, perhaps tentatively at first. Many of the initial ideas they put forth may be variations on conventional wisdom in the subject area. As they advance in expertise, they eventually come to the point where they are experimenting with ideas that are more novel and unconventional.

Although not all learners get to this point, most can reach the level where they are offering ideas that are their own and not simply restating what they have been told or have read.

○ *Concept formation* is the idea that as learners become more sophisticated, they begin to organize their work around concepts rather than simply presenting information in a series of statements. Concepts are a means to organize information, observations, or ideas. They are the next level up the cognitive structure chain from purely observational conclusions. More expert learners consciously design work products around a set of concepts, making sure the conceptual structure is firmly in place before beginning to generate the final work product. For example, students who are asked to complete an assignment in which they explore and explain the way truth and beauty are represented in three separate pieces of literature will need to be able to formulate concepts and organize a piece of work around them.

○ Work products that show high levels of *integration* avoid the novice problem of having each section of an assignment be essentially stand-alone in nature. Products that are integrated can have distinct sections, but they contain connections within and across sections. Novice literature reviews that describe study after study without making connections among the studies or summarizing the significance of them demonstrate novice-level performance. So too do papers that contain bulleted lists with scant explanation or elaboration accompanying each list and minimal connection among lists. Expert performance on such a task would include periodic summaries of the points being made in the studies, a section comparing and contrasting findings, and an overall summary that synthesized and integrated the observations and generalizations offered throughout the review. The paper would be a coherent whole that the reader would find easy to understand and would view as a value-added interpretation of all the specific information included in the review.

○ *Solution seeking* is the act of resolving the problem or issue that the task poses. This is not the same as getting the right answer, when there is one, although this is one component of solution seeking. Beyond the right answer, it is about proposing a result that is responsive to the question posed initially. Novices often do not answer well the question they are asked to address, in part because doing so requires either effort or insight that may be difficult for them to muster. It's easier to respond to the question they wish they were asked than the one they were asked. As learners become more strategic, their solutions improve and become better aligned with the challenge posed by the task. Expert solutions are cogent, coherent, and completely responsive to the task as posited.

The six constructs embodied in the scoring guide serve as examples of how deeper learning can be examined in ways other than conventional measures of right and wrong or of open-ended rubrics with terms such as *approaches, meets,* and *exceeds,* which provide little information to students about what they need to do to improve their performance. Assessing deeper learning does require thought by the assessor and attention to the quality of thinking demonstrated by the student, but employing a structured framework for feedback to learners tells them how to improve their technique as thinkers and the work products they create.

Note also that for students to move from novice to emerging expert as strategic thinkers requires many opportunities to practice and develop these skills, not one or two assignments in eleventh or twelfth grade. This type of complex cognitive development occurs over an extended period of time with multiple opportunities for practice and corrective feedback. For this reason, instruction needs to be organized around K–12 learning progressions that develop deeper learning in addition to content acquisition.

Deeper Learning, the Common Core State Standards, and College and Career Readiness

The Common Core State Standards do have the potential to take schools down the road to deeper learning:

- They establish a framework that accommodates complex instruction and assessment.
- They allow the incorporation of learning progressions that connect and link key ideas and concepts across grade levels and courses.
- They specifically address the foundation of important and relevant content that must form the basis for the investigations and applications that support deeper understanding and retention of key knowledge and skills.
- They include the Anchor Standards in English Language Arts and the Standards for Mathematical Practice that specify and emphasize incorporation of a range of cognitively complex skills into the instructional process.
- They align well with the research on the expectations students will encounter in postsecondary courses.
- They will be assessed in a way that will require more sophisticated forms of cognitive processing.

Given the complexity and challenge of deeper learning, how well will the Common Core State Standards and consortia assessments do in moving education in the direction of deeper learning? They are organized with the goal of fully representing the cognitive complexity of the mathematics and English language arts content they include. They include many specific standards that will require evidence that cannot be generated from online, on-demand computer-based or computer-adaptive assessments. (Examples of some of these standards are presented in chapter 10.) The Common Core State Standards include a range of verbs that suggest more complex forms of thinking and point toward academic tasks to achieve them that will demand students become more fully engaged cognitively. Many of the examples to date of performance tasks envisioned to be a part of the consortia assessments also suggest that students will need to demonstrate performances that reflect deeper learning to a greater degree than they do currently. A study by the Center for Research on Evaluation, Standards, and Student Testing at UCLA concluded that the consortia assessments will contain items of various types, including performance tasks, that will require more sophisticated forms of cognitive processing to answer correctly.

The Common Core State Standards and the consortia assessments represent a potential first step beyond the simple and simplistic notion that a well-educated student is someone who can recall the most specific factual information. They point the way toward more multidimensional systems of assessment and the notion of individual student profiles that contain much more information about knowledge, skills, and abilities in relation to student goals, not just in relation to the performance of other students. In this sense, they can contribute potentially to the strengthening of the unique ability of the US educational system to get students to think and engage deeply. They are, however, only the first step down the road to more universal deeper learning in US classrooms.

English language arts and mathematics, in addition to being disciplines in their own right, are important tools for learning in other subject areas. Deeper learning is best manifested not just in English language arts and mathematics, but in subject areas that require the use of sophisticated skills from these two disciplines. Although some states are moving toward end-of-course examinations that will include other subjects, they are not currently assessed in a high-stakes fashion nationally or in most states. Most schools still retain considerable latitude on how they assess areas outside English language arts and mathematics. These courses can become the natural setting and living laboratories for learning how to assess the more complex learning tasks that develop deeper learning skills.

One of the first steps on the road toward more fully integrating deeper learning into all US classrooms is to emphasize learning tasks, assignments, and projects in more science and social studies classrooms and in technical courses. (Some examples are presented in chapter 10.) To develop the strategic thinking skills necessary for them to engage successfully in deeper learning in college and careers, students need to practice and develop those skills across the curriculum and across multiple years. Integrating deeper learning thoroughly into classes beyond English and mathematics is an important first step.

When considering how to nurture deeper learning, it is important not to overlook the arts, visual and performing, as key environments in which student thinking and learning skills can be cultivated. The US economy is increasingly valuing creativity and a wide range of visual expression, including graphics and design. The skills students develop in arts-related courses contribute not only to their potential future employability; they open the door to the development of deeper learning skills and techniques that, with a modicum of practice, might apply in other areas as well. Students who are high achievers in core academic areas also benefit from strong involvement in the arts, which helps them to see possibilities for the creative applications of technical knowledge. Assessment in the arts, in particular, is well suited to the encouragement of student self-reflection and critiquing of work against explicit quality and creativity criteria.

 Students who are high achievers in core academic areas also benefit from strong involvement in the arts.

The US educational system is at a crossroads of sorts as it progresses toward implementation of the Common Core State Standards and consortia assessments. The effects on schools that these assessment systems will have are not yet entirely clear. One possible outcome is for US schools to become more test driven and for instruction to narrow around the lowest-common-denominator Common Core standards, that is, those that are the easiest to assess. Some of this may be happening already in a gradual, quiet process not subject to public scrutiny or debate as the assessments are developed and begin to target some standards more than others.

The road to deeper learning is far more difficult than the path to basic skills instruction. Developing skills for deeper learning involves the careful and thoughtful integration of a wider range of teaching and learning activities that are carefully focused on getting students to become involved in their learning, take ownership of it, and understand what they are learning. Students are then able to apply what they know in a wider range of contexts and situations and transfer their knowledge and skills to new and novel contexts in order to solve complex problems or complete interesting and challenging tasks. Going down this road requires schools to address the various challenges identified in this chapter and the rest of this book. If schools are able to implement the Common Core State Standards in ways that lead to deeper learning for more students, it's possible that the US educational system will regain some of its previous stature internationally as a model for excellence and as a system that produces students prepared for the US economy and the dynamic, turbulent future in which they are destined to live their lives.

Awareness and Action Steps

- Read the blog *Snapshot of a Deeper Learning Classroom: Aligning TED Talks to the Four Cs* (http://bit.ly/13Z2G0T) to learn how a teacher is integrating skills such as collaboration, communication, critical thinking, and creativity by using TED Talks.
- For a more policy-oriented perspective on deeper learning assessment, see Assessing Deeper Learning by the Alliance for Excellent Education (http://bit .ly/18X8i2s).
- Ten Macro Strategies to Promote Deeper Learning is a web posting that includes links to other sites with additional information on various aspects of deeper learning and ways to implement it (http://bit.ly/12TpZxS).
- Download sample ThinkReady tasks (http://bit.ly/17W85vj.) and have teachers do their own task development using these as a template. Set the goal of having all classrooms do at least one activity that requires deeper learning skills identified in chapter 5.
- Read *Brain Rules* by John Medina (http://bit.ly/16esLL3) for ideas on how to improve and deepen student learning based on principles from brain research.
- Partner with local colleges and universities for workshops that help faculty renew and deepen their content knowledge understanding. Such workshops need to go into depth on the big ideas of the discipline or subject area and how to teach them.
- Use the CourseCreate and CoursePathways tools described in the appendix and available at http://bit.ly/11MFZel to focus courses on big ideas, enduring

understandings, and key concepts, of the subject in order to create more time to go into greater depth in these areas.

- Institute awards and recognition for student work that reflects deeper learning, including projects and demonstrations that require research, analysis, and thought. Structure these awards and recognition programs with enough categories and opportunities for students who are not the highest achievers but who produce quality work to be recognized. Publicize the results schoolwide.
- Use CampusReady, which is described in the appendix, to gauge the aspiration levels of students and the general overall attitudes toward academic achievement.
- Watch the Education Commission of the States conference presentation on how to implement the Common Core State Standards in the classroom (http://bit.ly/19Oc1z0).

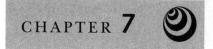
A CLOSER LOOK AT THE COMMON CORE STATE STANDARDS

Why does the US education system need a set of common core academic standards in English language arts and mathematics? How did the Common Core State Standards come into being? For most educators, the creation and existence of these standards came as something of a surprise, in part because they were developed so quickly and without the usual opportunity for multiple reviews and revisions, as has been the tradition in state standards development processes. Yet the general sentiment seems to be that the Common Core State Standards, however created, can be a useful tool to help improve teaching and learning nationwide and that they are likely to be influential in the states that adopt and implement them.

This chapter focuses on a deeper understanding of the Common Core State Standards for several reasons. Knowing something about the rationale for their existence helps ensure the implementation process will be consistent with the overall purpose and intent of the standards. These standards were designed to address a need and achieve a goal. Understanding the need and goal leads to implementation that goes beyond mechanical compliance and results in changes the standards were intended to achieve in the first place. To do so requires an understanding of the process by which they were developed, the organization and structure of each subject area, an examination of what they omit as well as what they include, and a consideration of issues that will arise in the implementation process. This chapter is not intended to be a substitute for the type of general overview of the standards available on the Common Core website and from many organizations. Instead, it is an opportunity to delve a little deeper into where they came from, what they are, how they tick, and what they don't do.

I am neither an unqualified cheerleader for nor a harsh critic of the Common Core State Standards. Given my experience developing college readiness standards, I understand the purpose and value of high, appropriate expectations for all students, particularly when those expectations progress toward the tangible goal of college and career readiness. I should note that I served as the cochair of the Validation Committee for the Common Core State Standards, an ad hoc group convened by the two organizations that sponsored the development of the standards. The committee's charge was to review the standards to determine if they were valid learning targets and if they were developed in ways consistent with best practices in standards development. (I should also note that I authored a supplement to the introduction to the English Language Arts and Mathematics Common Core State Standards that is designed to address some of the limitations in the original introduction that I discuss later in this chapter.) However, this chapter and the following one are not necessarily solely a review or critique of the standards. In these chapters, I adopt both descriptive and analytical perspectives to shine a light on the Common Core from a slightly different vantage point than offered by many reviewers: the usefulness of the standards as a means to improve college and career readiness for all students.

I hope the change in tone from descriptive to analytical, when it occurs, is not jarring and that it is clear when I am being descriptive and when I am being analytical. In places where I offer constructive criticism of the standards, I do so from the perspective that they can be made better and not from the point of view that they are fatally flawed. Pointing out limitations and ways to improve them is not the same as saying they can't or won't make a useful contribution to educational improvement in the United States.

Where Did the Common Core Come From?

The Common Core State Standards are in many respects the culmination of twenty years of standards-based education dating back to the early 1990s. States undertook the development of content standards voluntarily and optionally, at least until the 2001 passage of No Child Left Behind mandated states to adopt standards. By then, most had standards. The decentralized nature of educational governance in the United States, where states control education policy for the most part, creates the potential for tremendous creativity and experimentation across states when new policies take root, as was the case with academic content standards in the 1990s. This initial variation in practice led to new approaches, models, and strategies for standards development and standards content to be disseminated nationally without any federal presence or mandate.

This type of localized innovation and adaptation can be beneficial, but it can also lead to substantial inequity and inadequacy in the educational opportunities available to students in one state as compared to their counterparts in a neighboring state or in another part of the country. A great deal of variation has always been present in US schools in the content, sequencing, requirements, and challenge levels of the curriculum.

While most schools offer what appears on the surface to be broadly comparable content, studies of curriculum have yielded evidence of considerable variation across states in terms of the subject matter taught and the challenge level at which it is taught, in addition to how content is sequenced and the specific courses students are required to take. For example, recent research has highlighted the variation in the content in trigonometry, advanced math, and calculus nationally. Content varies among courses with the same title. Classes with larger numbers of minority students spend more time on basic math skills than those composed predominantly of white students. Students take the same course but end up having vastly different opportunities to learn comparably challenging material. Research by the Educational Policy Improvement Center has reached similar conclusions based on analyses of high school course syllabi in multiple content areas. Courses with the same title have vastly different content and challenge levels. Here, localism is a challenge to consistent quality and rigor and to the level of challenge.

Variation also exists at the elementary level, particularly in terms of sequencing of topics and instructional philosophy and methods, all of which can lead to dramatically different opportunities to learn for students in one classroom compared to the one next door and the one down the street. The elementary level does have the advantage, particularly in the primary grades, of significant agreement on its core and goals: language, literacy, and numeracy acquisition, and introduction to the core academic subjects, along with electives to develop the whole child. Often variations in sequencing of topics has been arbitrary and based on local preference, not research on learning progressions designed to link learning across grade levels.

In recognition of the fact that while variation is important, some degree of commonality is also needed, a group of the nation's governors in 1996 established Achieve, an organization devoted to improving educational quality across states. Achieve developed one of the first sets of college readiness standards, the American Diploma Project, with the goal of creating common and challenging high school graduation expectations for students in its member states. Initially, Achieve focused on getting states to adopt specified course requirements by subject area, with an emphasis on increasing the number of English, math, and science classes students were required to take in order to graduate.

The strategy of increasing graduation requirements seems like a relatively straightforward way to improve academic performance and still honor local governance principles. However, after a decade during which graduation requirements increased significantly in many states, vast differences in student performance still remain. When student scores on the National Assessment of Educational Progress (NAEP) are compared to those on state exams, a consistent pattern emerges: in almost all cases, students are being told by their states that they are doing much better on state exams than the results on NAEP would indicate. Furthermore, the state standards for proficient performance are so different across states that students who would be rated proficient in one state would be well below standard in another, sometimes adjoining, state.

This variation in state standards and assessments became more worrisome during the decade of No Child Left Behind (NCLB) because state tests came to be used as the basis for determining adequate yearly progress (AYP), an important NCLB benchmarking mechanism. Some states were having much less difficulty getting a large proportion of students to meet AYP targets, particularly at the elementary level, while others struggled almost from the start. The incentive clearly was for states to lower the score students needed to achieve on state tests so that more students would meet AYP goals.

While state graduation requirements and exit exams, NAEP, NCLB, and AYP are complex in their effects on schools, it would be an oversimplification to suggest that they led directly to the creation of the Common Core State Standards. What they revealed about the variation in the US education system, however, did provide a tremendous impetus to move toward some sort of common metric or frame of reference. While variation in educational practices across states is the hallmark of the US educational system, sometimes too much variation can be a bad thing.

> While variation in educational practices across states is the hallmark of the US educational system, sometimes too much variation can be a bad thing.

The two groups that represent state education policy leaders, the National Governors Association and the Council of Chief State School Officers, banded together to sponsor the development of the Common Core State Standards. They received help and support from Achieve and from philanthropic organizations, most notably the Bill & Melinda Gates Foundation. They resolved to act decisively to create one consistent set of high-quality standards that their constituents could then choose to adopt voluntarily as a means to ensure that their students were being challenged at a level comparable to other states and to the highest-performing countries in the world. This approach, the sponsors reasoned, would preserve the best of localism and state control while creating clear, high standards for all students that spanned multiple states. (See figure 7.1 for a timeline on these efforts.)

The method they chose for developing these standards was a departure from the way that states had historically gone about creating them. Instead of engaging multiple constituencies to generate an initial draft, the organizers commissioned a group of experts to develop the first version, which then became the point of departure for subsequent reviews and revisions. This approach made sense in part because so much evidence on and examples of high-quality standards had accumulated over the previous two decades. The development group was charged with taking into account all of this evidence and making sure that their draft was consistent with high-quality state standards, exisiting college readiness standards, and key standards and curriculum documents from other nations that were widely viewed as models.

FIGURE 7.1 TIME LINE OF STANDARDS-BASED EDUCATION LEADING TO THE DEVELOPMENT AND ADOPTION OF THE COMMON CORE STATE STANDARDS

1990s–2010 Twenty years of standards-based Education

Phase 1 Standards Development Workgroup Via membership in the CCSSO and the NGA Center

Phase 2 Feedback Work groups

Phase 3 Validation Committee: Independent experts review the standards to ensure they meet criteria

June 2010 Final Commons Core State Standards released

June 2011 Approximately 40 states adopt

2012 45 states adopt

- **Mid 1990s–2010:** Twenty yearsof standards-based education:

  - o States develop content standards voluntarily and operationally
  - o No Child Left Behind (2001) mandates steps to adopt standards
  - o Considerable variation across states in terms of subject matter taught and challenge level at which it is taught, sequenced, and required
  - o 1996 group of nation's governors established Achieve, devoted to improving educational quality across states and developing one of the first sets of college readiness standards, the American Diploma Project.
  - o Adequate yearly progress (AYP) data, required by NCLB, along with other national data sources such as those from the National Assessment of Educational Progress (NAEP), allow comparison of student performance across states

- **Phase 1:** 2009–2010 Standards Development, cosponsored by the Council of Chief State School Officers (CCSSO) and the National Governors Association Center for Best Practices (NGA Center

  - o Standards Development Workgroup : State-led effort made up of parents, teacher s, school administrators, experts, and state leaders through membership in the CCSSO and the NGA Center

- **Phase 2:** Feedback Group:Multiple rounds of feedback garnered from states, teachers, researchers, higher education, and the general public

- **Phase 3:** Validation Committee: Independent, national education experts nominated by states and national organizations review the CCSS to ensure they meet development criteria

- **June 2010:** Final CCSS released in June 2010
- **2010–2011:** Approximately forty states adopt CCSS
- **2012–2013:** Forty-five states have adopted the CCSS

The standards were to be "fewer, clearer, higher." They were to cut through the clutter of state standards that attempted to be all things to all people and incorporated the pet topics and content of every interest group that participated in their development. They were to be stripped down, stated in language that would enable the average person to understand their importance. And they would be pitched at a level of challenge that would stretch most US students to perform higher in existing skill areas and to develop new skills in areas key to success as twenty-first-century workers and citizens.

 The Common Core State Standards were to cut through the clutter of state standards that attempted to be all things to all people.

While numerous organizations, including those in the subject areas, were consulted and their input solicited, the process was not opened up widely until the initial draft documents were completed. This allowed for a certain consistency, logic, organization, and topical progression to be maintained, something rarely achieved in state standards development processes. This fast-track, rapid development approach to creating an intellectually coherent framework for K–12 English language arts and mathematics, while not universally embraced initially, particularly by some content organizations, did allow the work to continue on a fast pace and not become bogged down in repeated requests for more time to study and revise them, which would almost certainly have resulted in their demise before they ever reached the public comment stage.

Part of the logic of this development approach was almost heretical: that English teachers or professors did not own literacy development and that mathematics teachers or mathematicians were not necessarily the best or sole judges of how mathematical knowledge should be developed in students. As conceived of by the standards writers, the Common Core State Standards were to be foundational learning tools that would be used to facilitate learning in other subject areas, as well as within the disciplines of English and mathematics. This is not to say that experts in these subject areas weren't consulted, only that the process was not necessarily oriented toward creating better students for English and mathematics classes solely or primarily. All of this led to some controversy among teachers about who was responsible to teach what.

This unusual strategy was successful in part because the National Governors Association and Council of Chief State School Officers are not governmental entities that are responsible to the general public for the processes they employ. These standards are, after all, to be voluntary, and no government funds were used in their development, so the sponsors had some freedom to hold back the floodgates long enough to ensure that what emerged for public review initially was defensible; consistent with a vision of English language arts and mathematics as foundational, multi-disciplinary learning tools; and reflected the basic goals of having fewer standards that were clearer and were set at a higher level of challenge.

The ensuing public comment period did lead to significant revision and modification, and the input of relevant professional organizations, state education organizations, teacher organizations, leading researchers in both subject areas, and a host of individuals were influential in shaping the final products. As the review process progressed, however, a familiar pattern emerged: very little went out and quite a bit came in, not much was simplified, and quite a bit was amplified. Almost all recommendations led toward increasing the challenge level, although some state education departments did register alarm about how high the expectations were getting, particularly in mathematics. By the point of their adoption, the draft standards were not noticeably fewer than many state standard systems and were not necessarily any clearer (though they were very well written), at least if judged in terms of their structure and the ability of the general public to comprehend them, but they were definitely higher, a lot higher, than many of the state standards systems they would be replacing.

An Overview of the Common Core State Standards

Fast-forward to the present, and the Common Core State Standards are here: as of spring 2013, they were adopted by forty-five states and the District of Columbia and were being implemented by most states and a number of districts. What about them is different? What potentialities do they hold? What types of obvious changes will result from their implementation? What are the major challenges they pose? This chapter briefly considers the introductory material in the official standards document. It then presents the structure and organization of the English Language Arts and Mathematics standards and concludes with a discussion of some of the major issues associated with teaching the standards effectively.

One of the first observations that even a casual review of the standards yields is that the English language arts standards are very different in organization and structure from the mathematics standards. This occurred intentionally, if not deliberately, because the two subject area groups worked independently without making decisions based on what the other group was doing. It does make some sense to tailor the structure of standards to the nature of the subject area that the standards reflect. However, in the case of the Common Core State Standards, some differences are harder to explain. This is apparent in the introduction to each. Here, I switch to a somewhat more analytical critique of the introductions.

Most people who want to familiarize themselves with the Common Core State Standards begin by downloading each subject area separately, an approach that does not reinforce the notion of a common *core* very well. The next step would be to read the introductory section that accompanies each subject area. These sections summarize the views of the standards writers on a range of issues, but offer an uneven presentation of the overarching rationale for the Common Core State Standards that explains why they are necessary, what problem they solve, and what connects the two subject areas.

The English language arts introduction does devote several paragraphs to an overview of who sponsored the standards, the process used to develop them, and a brief concluding paragraph to explain why these standards are needed and which problems they address. This introduction explains key design considerations that shaped the standards and presents the overall structure of the standards. The ELA standards consist of college and career readiness anchor standards as well as specific standards for grades 9 to 12. The intent, the authors explain, is for the two sets to work in tandem to provide sufficient specificity for what constitutes college and career readiness while also guiding instruction and literacy development throughout each year of high school. In this way, the ELA standards are meant to specify what *college and career ready* means.

Next, the authors explain that the grade K–8 standards are grade specific and that the 9–12 standards are in two-year bands of grades 9 and 10 and grades 11 and 12. They emphasize that the standards are concerned about results, not means; in other words, teachers are free to teach them as they best see fit. Research and media skills, which the authors contend are or should already be embedded throughout a modern curriculum, are therefore integrated into the standards rather than being contained in separate sections. Finally, the authors emphasize, the development of student literacy is to be a shared responsibility within a school, and at the secondary level this will involve science, social studies, and technical-subject instructors as well.

The mathematics standards are silent on many of these issues. The mathematics standards document, for example, does reference college and career readiness, but not in the introduction. Readers must work their way through to the overview of the high school standards to find the reference to college and career readiness. The mathematics standards authors are clearly concerned about improving US competitiveness relative to other nations that do better on international comparison measures. They leave as an open question how mathematics instruction in US classrooms needs to change and which practices are causing poor performance by US students on international comparisons.

The mathematics introduction does contain a brief overview of the structure and nomenclature of the standards. It notes that the standards are not designed to dictate curriculum, and that learning progressions will be developed later from research on how students master the standards. The introduction concludes with a paragraph stating that the standards represent a new way of doing business that will help states learn from the results of two decades of standards-based reform. The document then turns to the presentation and explanation of the Standards for Mathematical Practice.

Why spend time dissecting the introductions to these documents? Because understanding what the standards are about, how they came into being, how they are organized, what they are trying to accomplish, and how they relate to college and career readiness is centrally important to being able to implement them successfully. The fact that the original introductions did not present as much information as they could about the context of the standards is probably more of an indication that the authors fortunately focused most of their attention on the content of the standards themselves, and not necessarily the introductions.

A supplement to the introduction is now available for download along with the standards. This supplement contains more information on the rationale for the standards, the process used to develop them, detailed descriptions of their organization by subject area, how they function as learning progressions, suggestions on how to use them, common misconceptions about them, and suggestions on how to implement them schoolwide. This supplement is a useful complement to what is contained in this chapter and aligns well with the contents of this book in part because, as noted earlier, I authored the supplement.

The next sections are purely descriptive in nature. They summarize the structure of the standards to help readers gain an understanding of them at a higher level before delving into them at a grade or subject level. Getting the big picture of the standards' overall organization helps illuminate the learning progressions that they seek to frame. This is particularly useful to teachers, curriculum developers, and administrators who need to connect and align the standards across grade levels and subjects.

Structure and Organization of the English Language Arts and Mathematics Standards

Several other differences are important to note between the two sets, even by educators who believe they are responsible only for ELA or mathematics. Each set of standards begins with what amounts to a unifying set of concepts designed to integrate the specific content that is spelled out subsequently. In mathematics, these are the Standards for Mathematical Practice. In ELA, they are the Anchor Standards. (The standards are explained in the sections that follow, and the chapter appendix groups them together.) Each is important to review and understand if the goal is to improve college and career readiness for all students. The temptation in many places will be to skip these sections in order to focus on the "what" of the specific content at each grade level and, for high school mathematics, each subject area. This would be a mistake for reasons that will be discussed later.

The Standards for Mathematical Practice

The Standards for Mathematical Practice are a set of general statements about mathematical processes and proficiencies, reasoning, and conceptual understanding. Because these are cognitive processes, they cannot be parsed into lists of discrete facts or algorithms. Instead, they are overarching organizers to be employed during the teaching and learning of all the mathematics standards. The following eight statements comprise the Standards for Mathematical Practice (these are also contained in the appendix at the end of this chapter):

1. Make sense of problems and persevere to solve them.
2. Reason abstractly and quantitatively.
3. Construct viable arguments and critique the reasoning of others.
4. Model with mathematics.
5. Use appropriate tools strategically.
6. Attend to precision.

7. Look for and make use of structure.
8. Look for and express regularity in repeated reasoning.

These framing standards are intended to create intersections between content knowledge mastery and conceptual understanding. They are to provide opportunities for students to develop and then demonstrate greater command of the mathematics content and procedures they will be taught when learning the material in the mathematics content standards. Their relationship to the content standards is not explicit, and it will be up to curriculum developers and teachers to make the precise connections. Clearly, they can and should be best addressed in a range of subject areas beyond mathematics classes. Students will need multiple opportunities to develop these skills through a range of projects and activities that go beyond traditional mathematics homework assignments, quizzes, and tests. Furthermore, as the description of assessments being designed to test the Common Core State Standards will illustrate, gauging student mastery of the Standards for Mathematical Practice poses particular challenges.

Organization of the Mathematics Standards

The mathematics standards have three levels of detail. The highest level is the domain, which encompasses a group of related standards under a topic that suggests the key skill being developed, such as number and operations in base ten. Standards are grouped into clusters within a domain.

For example, at the domain level of number and operations in base ten, one cluster of standards is grouped under "Use place value understanding and properties of operations to perform multidigit arithmetic." Clusters are further defined by more detailed standards. In the case of multidigit arithmetic, the cluster comprises three standards: use place value understanding to round whole numbers to the nearest 10 or 100; fluently add and subtract numbers that total less than 1,000; and multiply one-digit whole numbers by multiples of 10 in the range 0 to 90 (table 7.1). This type of organization is consistent with a subject that is taught largely as discrete skills and techniques that can be parsed into component parts and pieces.

The mathematics standards follow the same structure and mode of presentation across all levels. For grades K–8, a set of critical areas becomes the focal point, never more than a handful of high-level domain areas. All of fourth-grade mathematics, for example, should consist of multidigit multiplication; multidigit division; fractional equivalence and addition and multiplication of fractions by whole numbers; and analysis and classification of

TABLE 7.1 EXAMPLE OF ORGANIZATION OF STANDARDS, CLUSTERED WITHIN A DOMAIN OF 4TH GRADE MATHEMATICS

Domain	Numbers and Operations in Base Ten		
Cluster	Using place value understanding and properties of operations to perform multidigit arithmetic.		
Standards	Use place value understanding to round whole numbers to the nearest 10 or 100.	Fluently add and subtract within 100.	Multiply one-digit whole numbers by multiples of 10 in the range 0–90.

geometric forms on the basis of their properties. These are the domain-level statements.

The domains are fleshed out in narrative form for each grade level to provide an overall picture of what teachers should attempt to accomplish in terms of mathematical thinking and application, not just of content coverage. Next, the clusters of mathematical concepts and content for the grade level are presented. For example, fourth-grade mathematics has two clusters under the domain of number and operations in base ten: (1) generalize place value understanding for multidigit whole numbers and (2) use place value understanding and properties of operations to perform multidigit arithmetic. Finally, under the two clusters are specific standards—in this case, six standards under numbers and operations in base ten. An example of a standard under "use place value understanding and properties of operations to perform multidigit arithmetic" is, "fluently add and subtract multidigit whole numbers using the standard algorithm" (figure 7.2)

The high school mathematics standards are organized only slightly differently. They are listed by conceptual categories, but within the conceptual categories, they follow the same organizational conventions as the K–8 standards. The conceptual categories for high school mathematics are

- Number and quantity
- Algebra
- Functions
- Modeling
- Geometry
- Statistics
- Probability

None of these is new, all having been introduced and developed to varying degrees before high school. At the high school level, however, the

FIGURE 7.2 FOURTH-GRADE COMMON CORE STATE STANDARDS MATHEMATICS: NUMBERS AND OPERATIONS IN BASE TEN

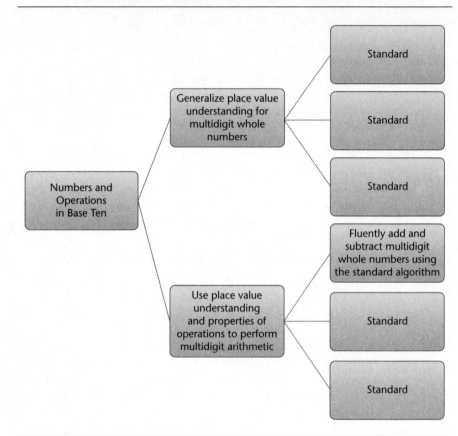

emphasis is specifically on getting to a level of performance consistent with readiness for college and careers, although the authors note that postsecondary success depends on thorough mastery of the mathematics taught in middle school as well, a conclusion consistent with research conducted by EPIC and others.

The authors have gone to great lengths to avoid dictating one sequence of mathematics courses for all high schools, thus the organization into conceptual categories that are not sequential in nature. This approach allows schools to continue with a traditional set of topics that begins with algebra 1 in eighth grade and continues with specific mathematics subjects each year, or to take an integrated approach in which all of the concept areas are taught and developed further each year.

The authors have gone to great lengths to avoid dictating one sequence of mathematics courses for all high schools.

It is also worth noting that the mathematics standards accommodate higher levels of mathematics for students going on to college majors or careers that are more mathematics intensive, such as engineering. The authors also attempt to integrate overarching standards such as modeling into a range of conceptual and topical areas in addition to identifying modeling as its own conceptual area. Finally, the Standards for Mathematical Practice appear in a separate box on each page where a new domain is introduced. The idea is to remind users that these standards are to be integrated into the more specific standards identified in each domain.

Reading College and Career Readiness Anchor Standards

The Reading Anchor Standards are derived from the College and Career Readiness Anchor Standards. These ten standards are restated in differing forms for reading, writing, language, and speaking and listening at grade bands K–5 and 6–12, and for history/social studies, science, and technical subjects, but they are the same within each broad topical area at K–5, 6–12, and for the other subjects.

There are four clusters for the Anchor Standards in reading:

1. Key Ideas and Details
   - Read closely to determine what the text says explicitly and to make logical inferences from it; cite specific textual evidence when writing or speaking to support conclusions drawn from the text.
   - Determine central ideas or themes of a text and analyze their development; summarize the key supporting details and ideas.
   - Analyze how and why individuals, events, or ideas develop and interact over the course of a text.
2. Craft and Structure
   - Interpret words and phrases as they are used in a text, including determining technical, connotative, and figurative meanings, and analyze how specific word choices shape meaning or tone.
   - Analyze the structure of texts, including how specific sentences, paragraphs, and larger portions of the text (e.g., a section, chapter, scene, or stanza) relate to each other and the whole.
   - Assess how point of view or purpose shapes the content and style of a text.

3. Integration of Knowledge and Ideas
   - Integrate and evaluate content presented in diverse media and formats, including visually and quantitatively, as well as in words.
   - Delineate and evaluate the argument and specific claims in a text, including the validity of the reasoning as well as the relevance and sufficiency of the evidence.
   - Analyze how two or more texts address similar themes or topics in order to build knowledge or to compare the approaches the authors take.
4. Range of Reading and Level of Text Complexity
   - Read and comprehend complex literary and informational texts independently and proficiently.

Writing College and Career Readiness Anchor Standards

Writing follows a similar structure, with College and Career Readiness Anchor Standards for writing serving to frame more specific content standards. The ten Anchor Standards here are organized into four clusters:

1. Text Types and Purposes
   - Write arguments to support claims.
   - Use valid reasoning and evidence.
   - Write informative/explanatory texts to examine and convey complex ideas and information clearly and accurately.
   - Write narratives to develop real or imagined experiences or events.
2. Production and Distribution of Writing
   - Produce clear and coherent writing in which the development, organization, and style are appropriate to task, purpose, and audience.
   - Develop and strengthen writing as needed by planning, revising, editing, rewriting, or trying a new approach.
   - Use technology to produce and publish writing and to interact and collaborate with others.
3. Research to Build and Present Knowledge
   - Conduct short as well as more sustained research projects based on focused questions.
   - Gather relevant information from multiple print and digital sources, assess the credibility and accuracy of each source, and integrate the information while avoiding plagiarism.
   - Draw evidence from literary or informational texts to support analysis, reflection, and research.
4. Range of Writing
   - Write routinely over extended and shorter time frames for a range of tasks, purposes, and audiences.

Language College and Career Readiness Anchor Standards

The Language Anchor Standards for College and Career Readiness address some of the more skill-specific components of language use. There three clusters are Conventions of Standard English, Knowledge of Language, and Vocabulary Acquisition and Use. The standards are cited or paraphrased as follows:

1. Conventions of Standard English
   - Demonstrate command of the conventions of standard English grammar and usage when writing or speaking.
   - Demonstrate command of the conventions of standard English capitalization, punctuation, and spelling when writing.
2. Knowledge of Language
   - Apply knowledge of language to understand how language functions in different contexts.
   - Make effective choices for meaning or style.
   - Comprehend more fully when reading or listening.
3. Vocabulary Acquisition and Use
   - Determine or clarify the meaning of unknown and multiple-meaning words and phrases by using context clues, analyzing word parts, and using references.
   - Demonstrate understanding of figurative language, word relationships, and nuances in word meanings.
   - Acquire and use accurately a range of words and phrases necessary for reading, writing, speaking, and listening at the college and career readiness level.

Speaking and Listening College and Career Readiness Anchor Standards

Finally, the Speaking and Listening Anchor Standards are organized into two clusters:

1. Comprehension and Collaboration
   - Prepare for and participate effectively in a range of conversations and collaborations with diverse partners.
   - Integrate and evaluate information presented in diverse media and formats.
   - Evaluate a speaker's point of view, reasoning, and use of evidence and rhetoric.

2. Presentation of Knowledge and Ideas
   ■ Present information, findings, and supporting evidence so that listeners can follow the line of reasoning and the organization, development of a presentation, and style are appropriate to task, purpose, and audience.
   ■ Make strategic use of digital media and visual displays of data to express information and enhance understanding of presentations.
   ■ Adapt speech to a variety of contexts and communicative tasks, and demonstrating command of formal English.

The Heart of the Challenge of Teaching the Common Core State Standards

The New York State Education Department contains a summary of the key shifts that need to occur in teaching practices for the Common Core State Standards to be implemented successfully. This list can be found on other sites as well, but on this site it is accompanied by a range of other useful resources (www.engageny.org). In the ELA/Literacy area, the following changes define the differences between much of current practice and the Common Core:

- *Teachers will need to balance their teaching of literary texts with informational texts.* This is a frequently misunderstood topic, one that is discussed in more detail in the following chapter. The major challenge of this shift is that no one has the responsibility and few have the training to teach how to read information texts currently.
- *Students will need to build knowledge of their subject areas through text more than through teacher presentation or activities.* Students will be expected to engage in texts more deeply and in ways that are more central to learning the subject matter. This increased emphasis on complex texts that are central to success in the course will increase the expectation that all students are competent readers and will value reading as a skill in place of workarounds that allowed students to complete courses without ever really reading a key text carefully and completely.
- *The progression of text complexity will become more explicit and systematic.* Teachers will spend more time for students to engage in close reading of key texts, and reading skills will continue to be developed across all grade levels, not only at the primary level.
- *Students will learn to use evidence from texts systematically to support and illustrate their arguments and responses to key questions.* In the process,

students will improve their logical thinking skills, but they will also need to master more techniques for analyzing texts, identifying key passages, and properly citing or paraphrasing them. This means that advocacy or unsupported opinion-based responses will not be as acceptable as they are now in many classrooms.

- *Students will develop, use, and retain a much broader academic vocabulary.* Teachers will need to introduce specific vocabulary associated with academic learning and then use those words in meaningful ways and not attempt to teach them through word lists. This topic as also taken up in more detail in the next chapter.

In mathematics as well, the focus of teaching and learning will need to change in important ways that will be challenging to teachers and students alike. Here are some key shifts:

- *Mathematics instruction will need to focus to a much greater degree on concepts and content prioritized in the standards.* This means students will need to think about and use mathematical concepts and techniques in a wider variety of ways so that they understand them more deeply and retain them better.

- *As in ELA/Literacy, mathematics instruction will be built on progressions of knowledge that extend and connect across grade levels.* In many cases, this will require teachers to incorporate content and skills learned at previous levels so that students recall and strengthen their mastery of that material as they learn new concepts that build on the prior material.

- *For some mathematical skills, students need to reach the level of fluency and automaticity in their ability to calculate or apply the technique.* Many fundamental skills have to be understood well enough and practiced long enough so that students do not need to think when they apply the technique. While this does not apply to all content learned, it is critical for a set of foundational mathematical knowledge and skills, much of which is introduced at the intermediary and middle school levels.

- *Students will need to understand deeply the foundational mathematical knowledge they are taught at each grade level.* This will involve new ways of explaining material and more interaction, use, and application of key knowledge. Teachers will be challenged to understand the mathematics they are teaching and be able to explain the whys along with the hows of lessons.

- *The mathematics in the Common Core is designed to be applied in a wide variety of settings and situations, most of them outside the mathematics classroom.* This is how deeper learning comes about: by transferring what is learned in one setting to a new and novel setting. Accomplishing this will require the application of mathematical knowledge in the sciences, career technical education, and social studies, at a minimum, as well as other subject areas where it is feasible to do so.

- *Students will be expected to practice and understand in equal measure.* Rather than emphasizing one at the expense of the other, mathematics lessons will be designed to seek a better balance between the two, enabling students to know why they are doing what they are doing but also to have sufficient opportunity to practice concepts and techniques in a range of settings that build the ability to transfer knowledge to new contexts.

The heart of the Common Core challenge and two of the key ways in which this set of standards is different from almost all previous state standards is that they represent progressions of knowledge, not just grade-level expectation, and that their implementation will require greater collaboration among teachers. Success in the twenty-first century requires much more than content knowledge alone. As today's young people enter postsecondary education and pursue career pathways, they will need to draw from and apply literacy and numeracy knowledge and skills across a much wider range of new situations and for more varied purposes than was required of those entering college and the workplace even a generation or two ago.

When educators understand the structure of the standards, the chances increase that they will implement them in ways that acknowledge their overall design and cognitive complexity. They are more likely not to teach them as isolated bits of content. The importance of this is more apparent from the students' point of view. They are experiencing the standards not just as content knowledge they are learning, but also as ways to develop their cognition and comprehend the structure of knowledge in these gateway skill subjects. Their brains are consciously and unconsciously trying to make connections among everything they are being asked to do. Given the design of the standards, which seeks to have learning and cognitive development progress across grade levels and subject areas in an integrated, connected fashion, deeper understanding of the structure is necessary for this to occur.

Relatively few students will go on to be English or mathematics majors, but all students will use the foundational knowledge and ways of thinking they develop in ELA and mathematics to comprehend content in other subject areas and to develop habits of mind and ways of thinking that they will employ throughout their lives in a wide range of learning situations. Students need to be able to transfer their knowledge of the ELA and mathematics Common Core State Standards to new learning settings and contexts, and to new content and different subject areas. Learning them as a coherent whole and developing an overall understanding of the sequence and progression of knowledge in each of these subject areas greatly strengthens learners' ability to retain and apply what they have learned.

This means that English and mathematics cannot be taught in isolation, with the hope that students make connections and retain understanding across classes and grade levels. The standards for English and mathematics are designed to be taught and applied in all subjects, connected to student interests and aspirations, and linked across grade levels through the use of learning progressions that go beyond content acquisition to address cognitive development.

> The standards for English and mathematics are designed to be taught and applied in all subjects.

English and math teachers need to be the leaders of a cross-disciplinary implementation process that pays close attention to how students are experiencing the standards and how they are developing integrated cognitive maps and models of literacy and numeracy that they can call upon when needed to tackle any of a wide range of learning or problem-solving situations. Implementation issues are discussed in more depth later in the chapter, but for now, it is important to emphasize the need for all teachers, and particularly ELA and math teachers, to have a complete understanding of the full set of Common Core State Standards, not just the content standards at their grade level or for their course. This is one of the reasons this chapter has presented the overall structure of the standards and not dwelled on the details or issues associated with a particular subject, topic, or grade level. Clearly this type of thoughtful, coordinated, comprehensive implementation approach will be challenging in schools that do not already have open communication channels and a culture of collaboration among all teachers.

What the Common Core State Standards Don't Do

The Common Core State Standards were designed specifically to do one thing well: create an overall structure for English and mathematics teaching, learning, and assessment in the United States. As a result and very intentionally, they do not do several things. Once again, calling out these points is not the same as finding fault with the standards themselves. The purpose of doing so is to help educators see additional areas that, if addressed, will strengthen the implementation of the standards and simultaneously make more students college and career ready.

Not All Subjects Are Included

While the Common Core State Standards do offer a tip of the hat to reading and writing in the sciences, social studies, and technical classes, they clearly are not a substitute for a comprehensive set of standards in these subject areas. National standards for science are in the process of being implemented in ways that will likely complement the Common Core State Standards in many states and school districts. Other areas, such as career and technical education, have developed standards that have the potential to align with the Common Core State Standards as well.

Social studies seems the least likely candidate to create common standards anytime soon due to controversies in the 1990s at the federal and state levels about the content of history standards. However, for those interested in social studies standards, the Texas College and Career Readiness Standards and Standards for Success address a variety of social studies subjects with a balanced mix of cognitive skills and a content framework. These two sets of standards fall short of a comprehensive list of all facts, topics, events, or important people to be studied at all grade levels. Educators therefore are free to make additions based on local preference, values, and traditions. They do outline well general expectations in the social sciences for a college-ready student.

The arts, both performing and visual, and second languages already have standards for those who wish to incorporate them. These subjects have the built-in advantage of lending themselves well to demonstration in the form of products, critiques, and performances. Second languages have proficiency standards developed by the American Council of Teachers of Foreign Languages. Standards for Success includes second languages and visual and performing arts standards as well.

Career and technical education courses, often referred to as CTE, can be important for a wider range of students to have the opportunity to learn the Common Core State Standards and apply them in meaningful ways. Various occupational areas are developing their own standards. For example, California has standards for fifteen career pathways. For each pathway, ten distinct areas are identified, such as Foundation Standards, Career Planning and Management, and Technical Knowledge and Skills.

These provide numerous opportunities for integration of Common Core standards, particularly through complex assignments in which the standards are applied in real-world settings.

Many high schools will encounter problems implementing the Common Core State Standards because faculty will assign ownership of the standards solely to English and mathematics faculty. But this is not how the Common Core State Standards are designed or how the authors intended them to be implemented. Schools that are seeking to achieve a full standards-based program will want to ensure that all teachers understand which elements of the Common Core State Standards apply to their subject area. Standards in other subjects provide numerous opportunities for integration and application of specific Common Core standards. If schools adopt standards in other subject areas, they will need to take care to cross-reference them against the Common Core or risk having the Common Core not be fully integrated outside of English and mathematics if teachers devote all of their energy to the standards specific to their subject area.

The Standards Are Not a Curriculum

The sponsors of the Common Core State Standards are careful to note in multiple places that the standards are not a curriculum, and it is not their intention that the standards be taught in a uniform fashion. This important acknowledgment of local control traditions in US schools makes sense, particularly because no one knows exactly how best to teach the standards yet. Experimentation and variation need to be the order of the day until and unless optimal ways of teaching many of the specific standards are identified and validated.

This decision, however, leaves a gap in the standards implementation process. Each district, school, and teacher is left to figure out the best curricular activities and instructional techniques to use. Although high-quality materials are available, including, for example, content frameworks developed by the Partnership for the Assessment of Readiness for College and Careers, these still require translation and additional development efforts before they can inform classroom teaching on a daily basis. Some states and districts have the capacity to create curriculum guides, but most will rely on commercially available products, which will be of varying quality, especially initially.

As the overview of the standards suggests, they are complex, multilevel, and detailed. Furthermore, they imply close coordination across grade levels because they are built around the notion of a learning progression. In short, they argue for a coherent, structured, highly intentional curriculum. These are characteristics on which most current school-level courses of study would rate poorly. While it may still prove true that the ubiquitous use of technology and social networking will allow teachers to develop and share materials much more directly, effectively, and quickly than in the past, the shift to teacher as curriculum developer, reviewer, and judge will require significant skill development for many teachers, as well as time to create new curriculum.

 The standards argue for a coherent, structured, highly intentional curriculum.

The significance of this lack of guidance on curriculum and instruction becomes more acute at the college and career readiness level. Here is where alignment with postsecondary practices and expectations becomes particularly important. While not all college teaching is good by any means, the expectations that postsecondary instructors have for student ownership of learning in particular are significantly different from those held by most secondary school teachers. Similar differences exist regarding the quantity of work that students are expected to produce, the pace at which they are expected to do so, and the cognitive challenge level the work must meet. Secondary school teachers cannot simply develop any curriculum they please and any activities they prefer and then label their courses as aligned with college and career readiness. Bridging the secondary–postsecondary expectations gap through carefully designed and sequenced curriculum and instructional techniques is a major challenge that exists today and that the Common Core State Standards are not designed to solve fully. Careful attention will need to be paid to alignment issues as curriculum is created in order to ensure that secondary school programs of study are built around learning progressions that lead to postsecondary readiness.

Proficient Performance Is Not Yet Fully Defined

The Common Core State Standards remain relatively silent on how well students must do on each standard or topic to be considered proficient. While to some degree this is the job of the assessments developed by the Smarter Balanced Assessment Consortium and the Partnership for the Assessment of Readiness for College and Careers, the reality is that teachers need far more guidance than can be provided by a test, even one with the capacity for interim and formative administrations. Performance on many of the standards can be defined only through student work, and collections of this nature have not yet been produced, although some are under development.

The reading standards are accompanied by example texts at different grade levels, which can help to suggest the performance expected. Little such guidance is available in the area of writing, although writing lends itself exceedingly well to the creation of exemplars, so it is likely this issue will be addressed soon. Particularly important are exemplary research papers because they can be judged more readily against common, widely accepted criteria. The language standards can likewise be made clearer using exemplars. Speaking and listening may prove somewhat more challenging to reach agreement on what constitutes acceptable performance, although digital audio files will likely be available from the testing consortia. It may take teachers some time to produce a wider range of speaking and listening exemplars.

Performance in mathematics could end up being more difficult to judge properly. Although mathematics knowledge and skill is often considered to be fully captured by a test score, the Common Core State Standards envision deeper conceptual understanding and the application of mathematics to a range of problems and settings, many outside of mathematics classes. The natural tendency will be to assess mathematics in math classes by means of tests or exercises that expect students to demonstrate declarative and procedural knowledge, where they show they know how to use particular algorithms or procedures in a specified fashion. This type of assessment is unlikely to result in students' demonstrating fully the conceptual understanding necessary to be ready for college and careers, a point that chapter 10 revisits.

Mathematics is also an area where complex performance tasks and example assignments are going to be very important to incorporate, particularly those that allow demonstration of the mathematics knowledge needed to succeed in other subject areas. These more integrated representations of proficient performance on a standard or set of standards can serve to highlight the distinctions and differences between what is occurring currently in most US mathematics classrooms and what is desired by the Common Core State Standards. The consortia assessments will provide some tasks, but additional examples will be needed, particularly those that take more time to complete than the tasks developed by the consortia.

Teacher Professional Development Must Be Addressed

The issue of teacher training and development to implement the standards is a book in its own right. I touch on this only to emphasize that this is another area that is locally determined. Many states and districts have already made great strides in orienting teachers and administrators to the

Common Core State Standards in order to raise initial awareness. Some have begun to convene educators to design units and identify instructional strategies to respond to the Common Core challenge. Kentucky and New York have gone so far as to develop and administer their own Common Core assessment ahead of the consortia, which gives their teachers much more insight into the areas they need to address.

Teachers must be able to identify their priority areas for knowledge or skill improvement and have resources available that address identified needs. However, the responsibility is two-way: teachers will have to take the difficult step of acknowledging that they need help in certain areas, and schools will have to be prepared to offer necessary help quickly and efficiently, without stigmatizing or punishing teachers who are professional enough to ask for the help they need. The first step in getting this information for secondary and elementary school teachers alike is an analysis of the relationship of the Common Core State Standards to the existing taught curriculum, not for content mapping purposes but to determine knowledge and skill needs for teachers.

When teachers go beyond awareness of the standards, a whole new world of needs arise. I addressed some of these in more specificity in chapter 6, when I explained what it takes to implement deeper learning and what a deeper learning classroom looks like. Those descriptions can serve to outline in more depth many of the likely professional development needs teachers will have as they implement the Common Core State Standards.

Awareness and Action Steps

- For anyone who has not already done so, review the overall structure of the Common Core State Standards by looking at the primary documents. Focus on the big ideas of the standards. Refer to Educore, a website sponsored by the Association for Supervision and Curriculum Development and devoted to Common Core implementation (http://bit.ly/13QXTjv).
- Watch and share the series of videos from the Hunt Institute and the Council of Chief State School Officers on the Common Core. The videos feature members of the Common Core State Standards writing team and are designed to help teachers, administrators, and parents better understand the standards' origins and implications for teaching and learning (http://bit.ly/129vaSO).
- If you're not sure what's going on in your state in regard to the Common Core State Standards, review material on the Education Commission of the

States website, which tracks all state actions related to the Common Core State Standards (http://bit.ly/14h13fx).

- Discuss the origin of the Common Core State Standards in small groups. Determine the degree to which you have agreement on the need for and value of common standards across states in English language arts and mathematics. Listen to concerns.
- Skim the introduction to the Common Core Standards in each of the subject areas. What questions are left unanswered? For a fuller discussion of the rationale and need for the Common Core State Standards, refer to John Kendall's book, *Understanding Common Core State Standards* (the first chapter of is available online: http://bit.ly/11JECMS).
- Connect your faculty with the Common Core resources developed by the National Council of Teachers of English. These resources specifically address the key shifts for the English language arts standards, including text complexity, nonfiction and informational texts, and literacy across the disciplines (http://bit.ly/15havOM).
- Introduce math teachers to the notion of learning progressions through material on the website of the Institute for Mathematics and Education (http://bit.ly/11Xpn7j).
- For an in-depth look into the history of standards-based reform, read Laura S. Hamilton, Brian M. Stecher, and Kun Yuan's *Standards-Based Reform in the United States: History, Research, and Future Directions* (http://bit.ly/16FN7ha).

7

A CLOSER LOOK AT
THE COMMON CORE
STATE STANDARDS

Appendix: Key Elements of the Common Core

Standards for Mathematical Practice

1. Make sense of problems and persevere in solving them.
2. Reason abstractly and quantitatively.
3. Construct viable arguments and critique the reasoning of others.
4. Model with mathematics.
5. Use appropriate tools strategically.
6. Attend to precision.
7. Look for and make use of structure.
8. Look for and express regularity in repeated reasoning.

Reading College and Career Readiness Anchor Standards

Key Ideas and Details

- Read closely to determine what the text says explicitly.
- Read closely to make logical inferences from it.
- Cite specific textual evidence when writing or speaking to support conclusions drawn from the text.
- Determine central ideas or themes of a text and analyze their development.
- Summarize the key supporting details and ideas.
- Analyze how and why individuals, events, or ideas develop and interact over the course of a text.

Craft and Structure

- Interpret words and phrases as they are used in a text, including determining technical, connotative, and figurative meanings.
- Analyze how specific word choices shape meaning or tone.
- Analyze the structure of texts, including how specific sentences, paragraphs, and larger portions of the text (e.g., a section, chapter, scene, or stanza) relate to each other and the whole.
- Assess how point of view or purpose shapes the content and style of a text.

Integration of Knowledge and Ideas

- Integrate and evaluate content presented in diverse media and formats, including visually and quantitatively, as well as in words.
- Delineate and evaluate the argument and specific claims in a text, including the validity of the reasoning as well as the relevance and sufficiency of the evidence.
- Analyze how two or more texts address similar themes or topics in order to build knowledge or to compare the approaches the authors take.

Range of Reading and Level of Text Complexity

- Read and comprehend complex literary and informational texts independently and proficiently.

Writing College and Career Readiness Anchor Standards

Text Types and Purpose

- Write arguments to support claims in an analysis of substantive topics or texts.
- Use valid reasoning and relevant and sufficient evidence.
- Write informative/explanatory texts to examine and convey complex ideas and information clearly and accurately through the effective selection, organization, and analysis of content.
- Write narratives to develop real or imagined experiences or events.
- Use effective technique, well-chosen details, and well-structured event sequences.

Production and Distribution of Writing

- Produce clear and coherent writing in which the development, organization, and style are appropriate to task, purpose, and audience.
- Develop and strengthen writing as needed by planning, revising, editing, rewriting, or trying a new approach.
- Use technology, including the Internet, to produce and publish writing and to interact and collaborate with others.

Research to Build and Present Knowledge

- Conduct short as well as more sustained research projects based on focused questions.
- Demonstrate understanding of the subject under investigation.
- Gather relevant information from multiple print and digital sources.
- Assess the credibility and accuracy of each source.
- Integrate the information while avoiding plagiarism.
- Draw evidence from literary or informational texts to support analysis, reflection, and research.

Range of Writing

- Write routinely over extended time frames (time for research, reflection, and revision) and shorter time frames (a single sitting or a day or two) for a range of tasks, purposes, and audiences.

Language College and Career Readiness Anchor Standards

Conventions of Standard English

- Demonstrate command of the conventions of standard English grammar and usage when writing or speaking.
- Demonstrate command of the conventions of standard English capitalization, punctuation, and spelling when writing.

Knowledge of Language

- Apply knowledge of language to understand how language functions in different contexts.
- Make effective choices for meaning or style.
- Comprehend more fully when reading or listening.

Vocabulary Acquisition and Use

- Determine or clarify the meaning of unknown and multiple-meaning words and phrases by using context clues, analyzing word parts, and using references.
- Demonstrate understanding of figurative language, word relationships, and nuances in word meanings.
- Acquire and use accurately a range of general academic and domain-specific words and phrases sufficient for reading, writing, speaking, and listening at the college and career readiness level.
- Demonstrate independence in gathering vocabulary knowledge when encountering an unknown term important to comprehension or expression.

Speaking and Listening College and Career Readiness Anchor Standards

Comprehension and Collaboration

- Prepare for and participate effectively in a range of conversations and collaborations with diverse partners, building on others' ideas and expressing their own clearly and persuasively.
- Integrate and evaluate information presented in diverse media and formats, including visually, quantitatively, and orally.
- Evaluate a speaker's point of view, reasoning, and use of evidence and rhetoric.

Presentation of Knowledge and Ideas

- Present information, findings, and supporting evidence such that listeners can follow the line of reasoning and the organization, development, and style are appropriate to task, purpose, and audience.
- Make strategic use of digital media and visual displays of data to express information and enhance understanding of presentations.
- Adapt speech to a variety of contexts and communicative tasks, demonstrating command of formal English when indicated or appropriate.

CHAPTER 8

THE COMMON CORE STATE STANDARDS AND COLLEGE AND CAREER READINESS

The previous chapter provided some greater familiarization with and deeper understanding of the Common Core State Standards. The discussion now turns to a consideration of the relationship between the Common Core and college and career readiness. To do so, EPIC's Reaching the Goal study, which describes college instructor ratings of the applicability and the importance of the Common Core State Standards, is presented here, along with the larger body of research on the expectations of postsecondary instructors who teach entry-level courses. Also considered are the role and importance of elementary school teachers and decisions they make to help students develop the language and vocabulary skills they will need for subsequent academic learning. The chapter concludes with an examination of a series of issues associated with implementing the Common Core State Standards in ways that are consistent with improving college and career readiness for all students.

The Common Core State Standards are designed to represent what students need to know to be college and career ready. The English language arts (ELA) standards state this more forcefully and explicitly than do the mathematics standards and are organized around the College and Career Anchor Standards to make the connection to postsecondary readiness all the more explicit. The mathematics claims are more muted and difficult to locate in the document, but the link to college and career readiness does appear explicitly in the introduction of the Mathematical Standards for High School. The Standards for Mathematical Practices do contain many attributes that are important to success in a variety of postsecondary courses, but they are not presented as college and career readiness criteria as in the ELA Anchor Standards.

So the question is, Do these standards truly represent what it takes for students to be ready for a wide range of credit-bearing entry-level postsecondary courses? Over time, the question will be answered by tracking students who are proficient on the standards into college and then seeing if these students perform better when compared to those who are not as proficient. However, some answers, even tentative ones, are needed before long-term studies can be fully completed, a process that can take five years or more. In the meantime, one way to gain some insight into the fundamental assertion that the standards will make students ready for college and careers is to ask postsecondary instructors whether their courses require students to know what's in the Common Core State Standards.

The Reaching the Goal Study

The Educational Policy Improvement Center set about to answer this question by conducting a study entitled Reaching the Goal: The Applicability and Importance of the Common Core State Standards to College and Career Readiness. We began by having a nationally representative sample of postsecondary instructors from a wide range of courses and institutions rate each Common Core standard on its applicability and importance to their course. We recruited instructors from over five hundred two- and four-year institutions in twenty-five course categories. Instructors from just under two thousand courses reviewed the Common Core State Standards. First, we asked them to rate the applicability of each standard to their course. If the standard was applicable, we asked them to rate the standard's importance to success in the course. Each instructor was given the opportunity to rate both ELA and mathematics. The two ratings, applicability and importance, and several supplemental questions provided the data for our findings.

The twenty-five course categories included fourteen from courses commonly associated with general education requirements for a bachelor's degree and eleven that might be better considered career oriented, often required for two-year certificates or, in some cases, a bachelor's degree in a career area. We selected courses to be representative examples of common offerings in seven major subject areas: English language arts, mathematics, science, social science, business management, computer technology, and health care.

The instructors rated the applicability of the standards for success in their course in five categories: prerequisite, reviewed, introduced, subsequent, and not applicable. If they rated applicability in the first three categories, they also rated the importance of the standards: least, less, more, and most. The percentages of all respondents who rated at least one standard as prerequisite, reviewed, introduced, or subsequent for both ELA and literacy and for mathematics are shown in figure 8.1.

In general, we found that all instructors rated the ELA and literacy standards for nonliterary reading and writing as being applicable, particularly when results from the English language arts strands of reading for informational texts and writing were combined with results from the literacy, subject-specific versions of these same strands. With few exceptions, a large percentage of instructors across all content areas rated the speaking and listening strand and language strand as applicable.

For the mathematics standards, instructor applicability ratings varied by standard type and domain. For example, the Standards for Mathematical Practice were rated as applicable by almost all mathematics instructors and a large majority of other instructors as well, whereas both functions and geometry were rated applicable to a relatively small percentage of the sample. Not every mathematics standard was applicable to every one of the twenty-five course categories. This should hardly be surprising given the wide range of courses we intentionally included in the study and the fact that we made all standards available for review by all respondents. Also not surprising were the variations in the applicability ratings for the eight ELA and literacy strands and the six mathematics conceptual categories and

FIGURE 8.1 APPLICABILITY RATINGS FOR THE COMMON CORE STATE STANDARDS

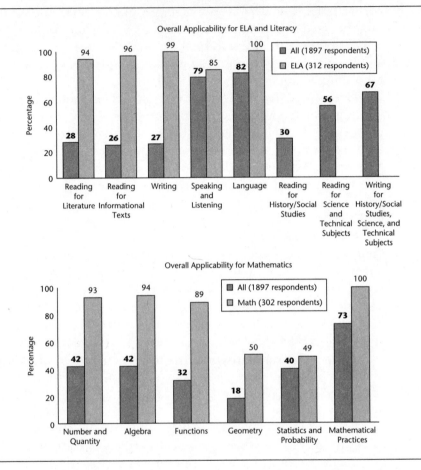

mathematical practices across different content areas. This variation does raise interesting questions—not so much about the standards as a whole, but about the knowledge and skill an individual student needs in order to be considered college and career ready for a particular postsecondary program of study. This point is taken up in the discussion of student profiles in chapter 10.

If essentially all of the Common Core standards are applicable to a range of postsecondary courses, how important to success in those courses are they? Almost every standard received an average importance rating well above 2.5, the midpoint between "less important" and "more important" on the four-point scale. Most exceeded 3, meaning they are "more important." Therefore, interpretation of the importance ratings is relatively straightforward: respondents who considered a particular standard applicable also considered it to be important.

The ELA and literacy standards on the whole received higher importance ratings than did the mathematics standards. Mathematics had more standards below 2.5—twenty-five of two hundred. Some of these were standards identified as being more specialized in nature. Only two of 113 ELA and literacy standards had means below 2.5. The language strand, while receiving high applicability ratings, also received the lowest importance ratings. These standards relate to use of the English language and include spelling, punctuation, and usage conventions and are specific in nature—more specific than other ELA and literacy standards. The lower importance ratings were taken to mean that the instructors felt that mastery of the basics of English grammar and conventions was necessary but not sufficient for success in their courses.

Standards that relate to students' mastering comprehension of nonfiction text with grade-appropriate complexity received high importance ratings, both generally and as they applied to specific content areas. Instructors placed relatively greater emphasis on standards that require students to extract key ideas and details from text, possess general writing skills—especially the writing process—use research to support written analysis, and write routinely over both extended and shorter periods of time.

Mathematics standards with the highest ratings included standards related to reasoning quantitatively and interpreting functions. Three algebraic concepts also received high importance ratings: create equations that describe numbers or relationships, interpret the structure of expressions, and solve problems with different equations. Figure 8.2 contains examples of some highly rated standards. All respondents rated the geometry category relatively lower. The Standards for Mathematical Practice, which authors of the Common Core standards stated should be applied across all applicable standards, are particularly noteworthy because they received the highest importance ratings and because the ratings came from a very broad cross-section of respondents.

The conclusion, then, is that postsecondary instructors across a wide range of subjects and institution types indicate that the standards as a whole are applicable to and important for success in their courses. Results from several additional supplemental questions reinforce this conclusion. When asked whether the standards were a coherent representation of the subject area they represented, nearly 84 percent of respondents indicated the ELA standards were, and about 62 percent of respondents said that

FIGURE 8.2 EXAMPLE OF A HIGHLY RATED COMMON CORE STATE STANDARDS

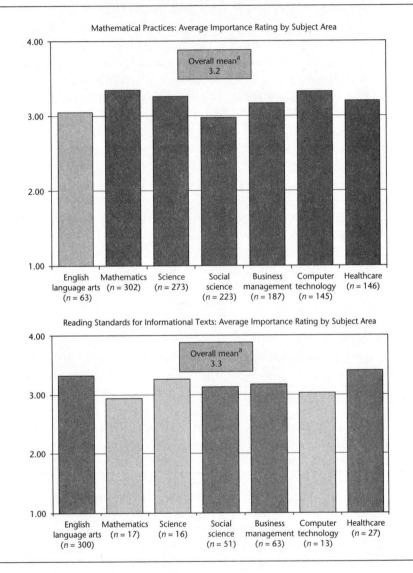

Mathematical Practices: Average Importance Rating by Subject Area

Reading Standards for Informational Texts: Average Importance Rating by Subject Area

the math standards met this criterion. Particularly telling and somewhat surprising, when asked whether the standards reflect a level of cognitive demand sufficient for students who meet the standards to be prepared to succeed in their course, over 95 percent of the nearly 1,800 respondents agreed that they did. This level of agreement across such a wide range of postsecondary faculty is rare indeed. The statement can be made with some confidence that the Common Core State Standards are applicable to and important for success in entry-level college courses and are at a level of cognitive challenge necessary to prepare students for those classes.

Implementing the Common Core State Standards to Improve College and Career Readiness

Implementing the Common Core State Standards begins with a deep understanding of them, something that is made all the more challenging by their complex structure, dense textual content, and significant number. Further complicating understanding of almost any set of standards is the difficulty of making the link between content standards and the expected level of performance associated with those standards. Many of the Common Core State Standards, particularly in English language arts, are virtually the same across grade levels, with only a change of a verb or addition of an adverb distinguishing one grade level from the next. Knowing what the language of each standard means in terms of expected student performance will be a significant implementation challenge.

> Implementing the Common Core State Standards begins with a deep understanding of them.

As noted previously, the standards are intended to function as a much more coherent system or progression than have many previous state standards, which consisted of lists of content to be taught and tested at each grade level. This suggests that school district central offices will have a new responsibility to bring about greater integration and coordination of the district's instructional program across grade levels without necessarily standardizing it entirely. The complex thinking and learning skills delineated in the Common Core will take time for students to develop. The ELA Anchor Standards in particular will require students to be writing earlier and more often in a wider range of genres, learning to rewrite and edit, and collecting and interpreting information through independent and guided research. Many of the standards, such as modeling in mathematics, are best developed through the use of projects that take more time and coordination than traditional assignments, and students will need to learn how to complete these projects successfully. This happens only if they are exposed to projects over multiple grades and become familiar with them. Speaking is another skill that requires coordinated action to practice and hone in a sustained fashion with carefully sequenced exercises that build skill and confidence. School districts will play a much larger role designing and overseeing the alignment, coordination, and integration of curriculum and instruction across grade levels rather than solely focusing on test scores at individual grade levels.

Who Owns the Responsibility to Teach the Common Core State Standards?

At the elementary level, it would seem that the responsibility to teach the Common Core standards would fall on the teacher with whom students spend most of their time during the day, and at the secondary level, the assumption will be that English and mathematics teachers will be primarily responsible. However, this assumes that elementary teachers are proficient in teaching all of the standards, which may not be true in all cases, and that the subject-area teachers at the secondary level are prepared to teach all the standards applicable to their subject area. Some high school English teachers may be uncomfortable teaching informational texts, for example, and some mathematics teachers may not wish to spend time on applications of mathematical topics to other subject areas.

While effective professional development can help address some of these issues, it may also be necessary or useful to consider some regrouping of elementary students during the school day to be with teachers who have particular training or strength teaching a subset of the standards. Because the standards are assumed to be a progression, any standard that is neglected, omitted altogether, or taught inadequately probably will lead to significant problems at the next grade level and beyond. Ensuring that all students have the opportunity to learn all applicable standards at a grade level is probably the first and foremost challenge of Common Core implementation.

The challenge at the secondary level is somewhat different. Here, the content of the standards has historically been clearly owned by English and mathematics teachers. And herein lies a dilemma. As noted previously, the Common Core State Standards are envisioned as being tools for use across all subject areas. The ELA standards make this case more clearly than the mathematics standards by having a slightly edited version of the standards written specifically for non-English teachers—those in science, social studies, and technical subjects. Ostensibly the standards also apply to other subject areas that use language as well, but only these three additional subject areas are called out by name.

How should secondary school educators respond to this apparent shared responsibility? As with their elementary colleagues, the first step is to ensure that secondary-level standards are being taught by instructors who understand them and apply them appropriately in the context of their subject area. In some cases, standards must be taught multiple times in multiple contexts in order for students to fully master them, and this must be taken into account as well. Getting agreement on who will be teaching what and when is an important first step toward establishing ownership of the standards. However, the goal is a coherent instructional program in which skills are reinforced in multiple subject areas. This requires a level of collaboration that will be unfamiliar in some schools.

It also requires explicit curriculum planning and agreement on who is teaching what. Most schools do not have a culture of collaboration and communication that supports this level of integration and coordination. Getting there will require some work, much of it focused on reviewing course content and redesigning courses. This type of work is not easy for teachers, who have strong attachments to what they teach. Central office administrators will need to be facilitators and coordinators of course development processes in individual school buildings to ensure consistency across schools and alignment across grade levels.

The appendix presents an overview of CoursePathway, a tool designed for analyzing the standards each course addresses and then creating a map that shows which standards are taught across a sequence of courses. CoursePathway can help answer these questions: Do students who take a sequence of courses have the opportunity to learn all of the relevant Common Core State Standards? Do some courses address the same standard? If so, do they do so in unique or different ways or in appropriately complementary fashion, or are they redundant? The CoursePathway analysis can then be used to add standards or remove them from courses, create curriculum that progressively develops skills in key standard areas across grade levels, and ensure that all students in the school are receiving a challenging program of study regardless of the courses they select.

Most schools do not have an explicit understanding of how courses coordinate and reinforce each other, particularly on standards that require progressive development over multiple courses, such as writing, research, and many of the text analysis skills. Engaging in the process of reviewing and updating syllabi and then analyzing course pathways helps address any deficiencies in this area and leads to a coherent, comprehensively integrated schoolwide program of instruction.

Understanding Key Areas Related to College and Career Readiness

Many educators are familiar with alignment or mapping exercises in which two sets of standards, one old and one new, are compared or mapped onto one another by identifying the language that is common between an old standard and a new one. Numerous states and districts are diligently assisting teachers with the transition to Common Core State Standards by having them participate in activities to help them see how state standards align with Common Core standards. These can be important starting points in understanding the standards. However, mapping old standards onto new ones alone is generally insufficient and potentially counterproductive if not done with other activities, some examples of which are described in the following sections, because such studies can reach erroneous conclusions if the matches are based primarily on word searches and matches.

Analyzing Verbs, Not Just Nouns

Most alignment activities focus on the nouns of the standards, not the verbs. For example, at which grade level are fractions introduced and taught? How many pieces of textual evidence are required of sixth-grade versus seventh-grade students to meet the key ideas and details standard? How many of which texts are to be read at which grade level, down to the percentage of each? These are all examples of aligning to nouns, a worthwhile starting place for determining the sequencing of content introduction and development.

The important and necessary next step is to analyze the alignment to Common Core verbs (figure 8.3). This type of analysis can take two forms: at grade level and across grade level. At-level alignment looks at the types of cognitive engagement required by a standard. For example, students from sixth through twelfth grades studying informational texts need to cite, determine, provide, analyze, explain, evaluate, integrate, and delineate. Some of these are more straightforward than others, but all require a degree of cognitive engagement that will be unfamiliar to many students. Even a verb that appears less challenging, *cite*, for example, requires multiple steps. To cite, students need to identify, locate, collect, evaluate, and summarize or reproduce the source material with which they are working.

FIGURE 8.3 VERBS FROM THE COMMON CORE ELA STANDARDS MAPPED TO THE KEY COGNITIVE STRATEGIES

Problem Formulation	Develop			
Research	Examine Conduct	Gather Interact		
Interpretation	Analyze Comprehend Determine	Develop Draw Evaluate	Infer Integrate Interpret	Reason Summarize
Communication	Argue Assess Cite	Collaborate Convey Demonstrate	Organize Produce Publish	Support Write
Precision / Accuracy	Edit Rewrite	Style		

So it is with almost all the other verbs. Analyzing content is a multistep process. In the case of the grades 11–12 key ideas and details standard, for example, students analyze a complex set of ideas or sequence of events in order to explain how specific individuals, ideas, or events interact and develop over the course of the text. This is a two-part process with subcomponents for each part. "Analyze" here requires assembling and organizing not just ideas but complex ones, or a sequence of events, and then applying some sort of explicit analytical framework to them. Examples of analytical frameworks that students could use include compare and contrast summaries, criterion-based analyses, pro-and-con lists, outlining, prioritizing, and matrix arrays. Most students lack training in specific analytical frameworks or methods and the application of such techniques to complex, sequential processes of assembly and organization. Teachers will likely need to master new tools and techniques to teach analytical methods to students. This need shows up more clearly when verbs are analyzed for their cognitive challenge and instructional implications.

In mathematics, analyzing verbs is a more complex undertaking because fewer verbs are used in the first place and their meaning is subject to greater interpretation in light of the content being studied and

FIGURE 8.4 VERBS FROM THE COMMON CORE MATH STANDARDS MAPPED TO THE KEY COGNITIVE STRATEGIES

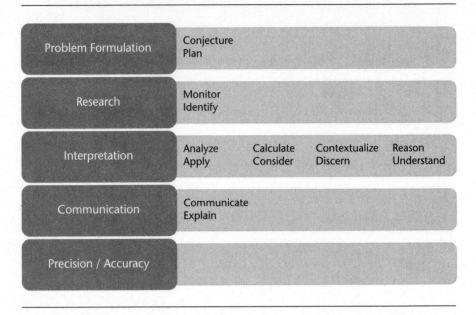

Problem Formulation	Conjecture Plan			
Research	Monitor Identify			
Interpretation	Analyze Apply	Calculate Consider	Contextualize Discern	Reason Understand
Communication	Communicate Explain			
Precision / Accuracy				

the potential actions students can undertake to demonstrate the level of understanding specified by the verbs (figure 8.4). Within the high school mathematics standards, the most common verbs are *understand, use, perform*, and *solve*, and these will be relatively familiar to mathematics teachers and students alike. Some verbs, however, are not necessarily encountered often in high school mathematics courses—for example, *include, create, construct, compare, model, visualize, summarize*, and *interpret*. The emphasis in the standards themselves is still primarily on the understanding, use, and application of a series of mathematical concepts, principles, and techniques but with some extensions beyond use and application. These extensions can be easily overlooked in favor of the four more common verbs that can be demonstrated more simply.

The Standards for Mathematical Practice echo some of the more complex verbs but also add a few new wrinkles. Recall that these standards are significant because they are meant to be applied across all of the other mathematics standards. Making sense of problems and persevering, reasoning abstractly and quantitatively, constructing arguments and critiquing reasoning, modeling, using tools strategically, attending to precision, looking for and making use of structure, and looking for regularity in repeated reasoning are the key concepts of the Standards for Mathematical Practice. They require skill development and practice by teachers and students alike. Achieving the goals of the mathematics Common Core State Standards will require attending not just to the verbs in the mathematics standards, but to their interaction with the Standards for Mathematical Practice as well. Any comparison of the Common Core State Standards to existing state standards should take their higher cognitive complexity into account and explore the instructional implications for math courses of verbs that imply deeper thinking and more interdisciplinary applications of math content and concepts.

Informational Texts versus Fiction and Literature: False Dichotomy?

One of the most frequently commented-on and perhaps least understood aspects of the Common Core State Standards is the specification of the proportion of time to be spent reading informational texts versus literature. The recommendation is for about half of the time in elementary school to be devoted to literature and half to informational texts, with the emphasis shifting by high school to 70 percent informational and 30 percent literature.

Some high school English teachers and others have interpreted this to mean that the amount of literature to be taught in high school English classes should be reduced by over two-thirds. Elementary teachers have decried the loss of time for imaginative and creative forms of fiction that fire the imagination of their students and make them want to read. What the authors of the standards intended, however, is that the *total amount of reading* done by students *across all subjects* conform to the suggested percentages, not just the time devoted to English language arts instruction.

This means that elementary school students would read literary nonfiction along with informational texts, such as news and magazine articles, in addition to text-based sources for other subjects they normally encounter, such as science and social studies. The increasing emphasis on nonfiction text at the secondary school level is a reflection of the prevalence and importance of these types of materials in other high school classes and at the postsecondary level. As high school students prepare for college, they need to become more proficient and efficient readers of textbooks, primary and secondary source material, technical documents and manuals, research reports, op-ed and political commentary, popular media, and a wide range of written material that they will encounter in college and career training courses. For this reason, the emphasis on nonfiction increases in high school when considered as a percentage of all materials read.

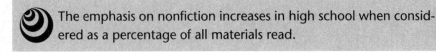

The emphasis on nonfiction increases in high school when considered as a percentage of all materials read.

Should English teachers be teaching students how to read these non-fiction materials? The answer is a resounding yes, although many would disagree with or qualify this statement to note that other teachers should take on this task as well. However, literacy now increasingly includes a wide range of nonfiction. It is in the best interests of English language arts teachers to possess the skills to help students access these materials. And while it is certainly desirable to have reading taught across the curriculum, it makes little sense not to have students acquiring specialized reading skills in their English classes at the same time. Ideally, all teachers become better at helping all students master a wide range of nonfiction content, while English teachers become the new experts and consultants to their colleagues.

Increasing the Quantity of Writing

The standards clearly demand a great deal of writing. This is potentially problematic at a time when many teachers are reducing the amount of writing they assign, a trend that has been borne out in several studies over the past ten years. The writing anchor standards, which were introduced earlier, lay out a blueprint for significant amounts and varying types of writing that go well beyond the six-paragraph essay, which has become commonplace in many schools located in states in which writing is assessed based on such a model. The Range of Writing anchor standard expects writing to take place both within a class period or two and over extended time frames. When, where, and how will this range of writing occur, and who will read, review, and score it?

Most teachers are reluctant to assign significant amounts of writing in part because their mode of evaluating the final product is very time consuming and, unfortunately, as research studies have demonstrated, not necessarily very effective in improving student writing. Reading and commenting on each student's paper takes many hours and yields little improvement in subsequent papers. Many teachers have learned how to use rubrics quickly and efficiently, and these represent a step forward. Some have tried student peer evaluation, though with decidedly mixed results. Is there a way to provide essential feedback to students on the quality of their work without being overwhelmed by the time required to do so?

Increasing the quantity of writing will require vastly more efficient means of scoring—for example:

1. The teacher scans all the papers from an assignment quickly, orders them from best to worst, and puts them into three piles: above standard, at standard, and below standard.
2. The teacher identifies a few papers from each pile to review more carefully. From this close analysis, general themes and categories of strength and weakness arise.
3. The teacher reviews just enough papers to identify the major problems students are having.
4. The papers are handed back, with no grade or teacher comments, but with a self-analysis sheet that contains the common errors and problems the teacher identified earlier through a close review of the limited subset of papers along with any other general criteria the teacher wishes to emphasize.
5. Students use the self-analysis sheet to review their own papers first and then participate in a focused peer review applying the criteria from the self-analysis sheet to the work of fellow students. The aim is not for them to score their paper perfectly but to learn about the mistakes they are making. This type of formative feedback can be repeated on the same assignment several times.
6. Students revise their papers based on their self-analysis and peer feedback.
7. Students hand in a final paper that is of very high quality.
8. The teacher reviews these final papers quickly to verify the quality and commends the students with comments of general validation and encouragement, not detailed in-text markups.

Although this process does not match a college course perfectly, it does contain several important elements that will help students be prepared for college courses in which written assignments are required. They learn about the importance of multiple drafts, self-review, peer review, understanding the expectations of their instructor, and then striving to produce a paper consistent with those expectations. Oddly enough, many college students seem unaware of these basic strategies for writing success and end up resorting to disputing the grade they are given or complaining about how unfair their instructor is. Getting students to take ownership of and responsibility for producing quality writing will be a tremendous accomplishment that can be facilitated by implementing the Common Core writing standards as they were intended to be implemented, with lots of writing.

 Getting students to take ownership of and responsibility for producing quality writing will be a tremendous accomplishment.

Research Skills

Learning how to gather information and weigh evidence is an important skill that shows up in several places in the Common Core State Standards. This skill is best developed through what may be thought of as a form of research, where *research* means something more like a review or synthesis of the literature on a topic. The Key Design Considerations section of the ELA standards notes that research skills are intended to be blended into the standards as a whole. The writing anchor standards contain a specific standard devoted to research, and as a result, this standard appears at all levels in writing. References to research appear in the 6–12 speaking and listening standards, the reading standards for literacy in science and technical subjects 6–12, and the writing standards for literacy in history/social studies, science, and technical subjects 6–12.

More important perhaps is the fact that postsecondary courses are increasingly expecting students to be able to engage in the collection, synthesis, analysis, and summary of information from varied sources. This type of research requires a range of skills that goes far beyond simply collecting data or sources and reporting them. The notion of a research report as a verbatim collection of statements collated from several sources has long been obsolete (although many readers might recall the day when a research report consisted largely of copying passages from the encyclopedia verbatim, a practice that today would be labeled as plagiarism but was rewarded with an A back then).

College instructors keep upping the ante in terms of the research they expect students to be able to do independently, in part because student access to information has become so ubiquitous. Unfortunately, being able to access information does not necessarily translate into the ability to sort through, prioritize, validate, summarize without plagiarizing, and report succinctly the key findings in ways that add value through interpretation.

The Common Core State Standards create the potential opportunity to develop student research skills much more thoroughly over multiple grade levels and in multiple subject areas, and not just through a single twenty-page research paper written in eleventh or twelfth grade.

Speaking and Listening

The importance of speaking and listening has already been noted. These skills are common between college and careers to an even greater degree than are specific English language arts or mathematics knowledge and skills. Essentially everyone will need to be a proficient speaker and listener, whereas many will be able to get by with lesser competency in reading, writing, or mathematics. While it may be possible to think of a few careers where speaking and listening are not important, these are not areas of employment that will likely be growing in the future. The US workplace will continue to value communication proficiency highly. And while some of that communication may be in writing, much of it will be in the form of speaking and listening.

Students need more formal feedback on the quality and appropriateness of their speech in particular. The rules of formal speech are being bent and broken by popular culture, which is how language evolves and should not be the cause for any particular consternation. However, speech is context sensitive, and young people need to understand which types of speech are appropriate in which settings. For example, they need to know the following:

- How to communicate with adults who are older than they are, not with deference, but with sufficient interest and respect to cause the adult to want to engage in conversation or interaction with them when this is called for
- How to raise an issue to a superior or to a colleague without resorting to emotion or inappropriate language
- How to negotiate when they aren't getting what they want or feel they deserve
- How to compliment, praise, and dignify those with whom they are interacting
- How to deal with difficult people whose communication skills are not as good as their own
- How to use humor to relieve tension and to make communication more enjoyable

All of these are skills that are important in the workplace, society, and even college courses. None of these skills is developed through an approach that views speaking and listening as consisting solely of giving and following directions. Certainly this form of communication is important and is much easier to assess than many of the other aspects suggested previously, but limiting what is taught to procedural communication skills will send the wrong message to young people about the complexity of communication and the facility with language they will need for future success. It will insult their intelligence because many of them already know the importance of speaking and listening as a survival skill in their daily lives. Treating speaking and listening as complex, multidimensional, and critical for success will help young people be better prepared for college and careers.

There's an additional advantage to emphasizing speaking and listening. Many students with still-emerging literacy skills may thrive when given the opportunity to speak or listen. They may struggle more if reading and writing are the only means to demonstrate their competence. Being recognized as someone who is able to communicate well through speaking and listening can help validate many students whose literacy is still emerging and developing, and motivate them to improve their reading and writing as they then learn how to transfer their speaking and listening skills to the challenging tasks of reading and writing.

Integrating Mathematics into Science, Social Studies, and Technical Subjects

A final challenge to discuss, although many others remain unexamined, is getting mathematics integrated into science, social studies, and technical subjects. The ELA standards have the advantage of specifically adapting reading and writing standards to these subject areas, thereby calling out the importance of their being taught and learned outside of the English class. While this will be challenging to do, the ELA standards at least provide a general blueprint of expectations for teachers in other subjects.

The mathematics standards do not offer an analogous framework that tells teachers in subjects that could conceivably incorporate mathematics how they might proceed to incorporate the mathematics standards into their classes. This is unfortunate because the most important uses of mathematics in college and careers will, for the most part, be outside mathematics classes. Many college students in both two- and four-year programs struggle because they are unable to apply the mathematics they learned in math class to the science or economics or accounting class they are taking.

Science presents a particular case for the application and use of mathematics. Most science teachers do not have the time to reteach the measurement, proportional reasoning, number system, and algebraic content and concepts that are foundational to the study of science, but they must do so or end up watching their students struggle mightily. Standards for Success, for example, identified nine topical areas and twenty-eight specific standards that outline the mathematics that students need to know to be ready for college-level studies in the sciences. The Common Core State Standards mathematics standards authors also note a fact verified by college instructors: students will learn much of the mathematics they need for college success in middle school.

Some of this middle school math, such as proportional reasoning, basic statistical concepts and principles, and a set of foundational algebraic techniques, along with computational fluency and accuracy, becomes increasingly important in college courses in the social sciences as well as the sciences. Social science courses are making greater use of quantitative analytical methods and statistics as researchers in these disciplines apply a wider array of research methods made possible by computers and software programs that rely on quantitative analysis. Mathematics is a tool for understanding large and complex data sets, identifying patterns in human behavior or the content of documents, and solving complex problems in logical, step-by-step fashion. All students who go on to postsecondary education, even those who take little or no mathematics in college, are likely to be expected to apply much of the mathematics specified in the Common Core in the context of other subject areas. They will benefit from having prior experience doing so in their secondary school science and social studies classes, in particular.

> All students who go on to postsecondary education, even those who take little or no mathematics in college, are likely to encounter mathematics in the context of other subject areas.

A Key Role for Elementary School Teachers

Elementary school teachers may feel somewhat overlooked in parts of the discussion of how to teach the Common Core State Standards in ways that keep students on the path to college and career readiness. Although much of what is presented in this and previous chapters, particularly many of the elements of the four keys model, is applicable across all grade levels, elementary teachers will need to approach implementation somewhat differently from their secondary school counterparts. Elementary-level teachers can focus better on some Common Core standards than their secondary-level colleagues can. Beyond simply incorporating the standards, elementary teachers can develop specific foundational elements closely associated with postsecondary readiness. One of the most important is academic vocabulary.

Academic learning has its own vocabulary, and students who know this vocabulary have a significant advantage as they engage in more advanced learning. These words are used commonly by secondary and postsecondary instructors in lectures, appear in textbooks, and describe the specifics of assignments. When students understand these words and the concepts that underlie them, they are better prepared to engage in academic study. When they don't, they are at a fundamental disadvantage compared to their peers who do understand these words.

A basic set of academic vocabulary might entail three hundred to five hundred words. Figure 8.5 sets out some examples of verbs that have particular meanings in academic contexts, and all of them suggest complex, multistep processes that students should know how to execute with confidence when they encounter them, particularly in assignments. As you read them, think about how students will struggle if they have not mastered them.

Nouns are also important, and somewhat easier to teach. A few representative examples of nouns that students frequently run across in academic settings are in figure 8.6. Note that as with the verbs, these words have particular meanings in an academic context that may differ from their meanings in general use. Also, note that many of these words even

FIGURE 8.5 A SAMPLE OF VERBS IN THE ACADEMIC VOCABULARY

Analyze	Extract	Modify	Refer
Annotate	Foreshadow	Note	Rephrase
Anticipate	Frame	Outline	Review
Compare	Generate	Persuade	Show
Compile	Hypothesize	Portray	Specify
Define	Incorporate	Preclude	Suggest
Derive	Integrate	Presume	Validate
Discern	Locate	Prove	Verify
Excerpt	Model	Recall	

FIGURE 8.6 A SAMPLE OF NOUNS IN THE ACADEMIC VOCABULARY

Acronym	Effect	Relationship	Synonym
Analogy	Factor	Root	Theme
Argument	Genre	Sequence	Topic
Caption	Header	Significance	Trait
Characteristic	Intent	Simile	Viewpoint
Chronology	Irony	Strategy	
Detail	Method	Structure	
Diction	Passage	Symbol	

FIGURE 8.7 A SAMPLE OF ADJECTIVES AND ADVERBS IN THE ACADEMIC VOCABULARY

Arguably	Equivalent	Objective	Responsible
Authentic	Expository	Optional	Significant
Coherent	Figurative	Plausible	Specifically
Concise	Frequently	Possible	Subjective
Consistently	Indirect	Primarily	Succinct
Credible	Intermittent	Rarely	Typically
Credibly	Invariably	Regular	
Cumulative	Likely	Requisite	

mean different things in different academic contexts or subject areas. For example, *factor* is a verb in a mathematics class and a noun in a history class. *Passage* in an English class refers to an excerpt from text, while in a civics class it refers to the legislative process.

Adjectives and adverbs need to be learned as well. Figure 8.7 lists a few examples of adjectives and adverbs that students are unlikely to learn unless they are specifically taught them. Note that many more adverbs can be formed from academic nouns by adding "-ly" to them.

Teaching these words to students at a young age and using them throughout elementary and secondary school will help students be better prepared for academic work beyond high school and the terminology they will encounter in careers as well. The key is not to teach these words (and many more like them) through word lists, but to have students use them in their daily assignments and classwork so that they come to understand them in context and grasp their meaning fully. Doing so also means students are being given challenging work to do.

Here is a place where speaking and listening can play an important role as students use this vocabulary orally in context, an important way to consolidate understanding and retention. Some well-intentioned teachers substitute simpler, less precise forms of many of these words, for example, *think about* instead of *infer,* with the result that their students are never exposed to the key academic vocabulary they need for continued success. Even struggling readers can be taught academic vocabulary. In fact, these students in particular need to know these terms well.

A final reason for devoting time to teaching these specific words to all students in elementary school is the well-documented difference in vocabulary acquisition between students from low-income and high-income families. While high-quality preschools help close the gap somewhat, exposure to specialized academic vocabulary is not likely to occur outside the elementary school classroom for many students from lower-income households. Closing the achievement gap more generally begins with closing the language gap in very intentional ways, such as building academic vocabulary.

 Exposure to specialized academic vocabulary is not likely to occur outside the elementary school classroom for many students from lower-income households.

It is probably worth noting that instruction in these words should continue into secondary school as well. The goal is to introduce the words early in order to imbue them with as much meaning as possible through varied uses. However, secondary school courses should make even greater use of these terms and expect students to be able to define them and use them appropriately. This is another example of a skill that many high school teachers do not currently see as their responsibility to develop that will need to be addressed in secondary classrooms for the Common Core State Standards to lead to college and career readiness for more students.

The Challenge of the Common Core and College and Career Ready

This chapter has focused on the purpose and organization of the Common Core State Standards, some important characteristics of the standards, and select implementation issues, all through the lens of college and career readiness. Schools will surely face other challenges when implementing the standards beyond those enumerated here. One of the greatest challenges will be to have teachers understand how truly different in intent the standards are from most state standards with which they are familiar. The goal of getting all students ready to continue their education beyond high school is a new challenge level for schools, and the Common Core State Standards are the road map to achieving that ambitious goal. Doing so will require deeper student engagement and greater cognitive development sustained over multiple grade levels and subject areas.

Because much of the content identified in the standards is very similar to what is already being taught, the natural tendency will be for educators to assume that the Common Core State Standards are new wine in old bottles. In fact, when teachers were asked in early 2013 how much of their curriculum they would be changing as a result of the Common Core State Standards, two-thirds responded "none" or "a little." This point of view, however, overlooks many of the specific issues discussed here, all of which illustrate how the standards are designed to result in more students who are college and career ready. For this to occur, schools as organizations and educators as individuals must embrace much of what has been presented and discussed to this point. When this occurs, they will be ready to take teaching and learning to the level necessary to equip students for success in college and in the careers of tomorrow.

🌀 Awareness and Action Steps

- Review the results of the Reaching the Goal study (http://bit.ly/10uHqDs). What do the results suggest about the importance of skills that cut across multiple subject areas? Identify three to five such skills and determine how to focus on developing them across classes.
- Examine the verbs in figure 8.5, and determine the degree to which those concepts are taught and developed currently in all classes. Have each teacher pick three verbs on which to focus by first explaining why the verb is important to the subject area in question.
- Consult appendix A of the Common Core State Standards for guidance on developing student vocabulary. For additional suggestions, see *Bringing Words to Life: Robust Vocabulary Instruction* by Isabel Beck, Margaret McKeown, and Linda Kucan.
- Provide training on teaching the Common Core skills that are foundational to their subject area to teachers in subject areas outside English language arts and mathematics.

- Develop a plan for integrating key reading and writing skills into science and social studies classes in particular. Agree on a series of research papers at each grade level that develop and apply the literacy skills of the Common Core outside of English language arts courses.
- Reinstitute speech and debate if the program has been eliminated. If this is not feasible, build opportunities for speech and debate into English language arts courses, and expose all students to the principles and techniques of speech and debate.
- Build in time for teachers to grade student writing. Periodic late starts or early releases give teachers time for a range of activities to support students, such as individual consultations and study sessions. Teachers assigning writing should be able to use this time to grade papers, using effective techniques of the type described in the chapter.
- Consult appendix B in the ELA Common Core State Standards for examples of fiction and nonfiction texts appropriate at each grade level.
- Determine where and how the Common Core State Standards are currently being addressed in the curriculum. Conduct a course-level review using the CoursePathway system explained in the appendix.
- Have students create videos as a means to demonstrate speaking skills. Have students in the class listen to the videos as a way to improve their listening skills.
- Build greater emphasis on research projects into the school through annual events such as science fairs, heritage research displays, culminating projects, and public exhibitions of student work throughout the year.
- Organize your school's professional learning communities to focus on the instructional shifts necessitated by the Common Core. Focus specifically on literacy across the disciplines.
- Use the verbs chart in figure 8.3 to start a conversation with teachers outside of English and mathematics on how they develop these skills in the context of the Common Core State Standards. Examine how courses such as art and career technical education can contribute to Common Core mastery by all students.

CHAPTER 9

THE CONSORTIA ASSESSMENTS AND COLLEGE AND CAREER READINESS

Another unique aspect of the Common Core State Standards is that two separate assessment systems have been designed to measure a subset of the standards. They seek to provide information on student performance that can be used for multiple purposes, including college and career readiness. Designing and creating new assessments from scratch was a monumental undertaking made all the more challenging by the fact that they were developed before the standards were fully implemented.

While educators have begun to understand these assessments, particularly those who have a strong grasp of the Common Core State Standards, it's important to remember that these assessments will be a work in progress for a number of years to come, during which time many adjustments will be made and elements finalized. The purpose of this chapter is not to provide highly detailed descriptions of the assessments, because they will continue to evolve; moreover, their respective websites will be the best source of the most accurate and up-to-date information about specific elements and policies for each.

This chapter instead offers a high-level overview of the goals the assessments are designed to achieve, a general description of some of the key similarities and differences between the assessments in terms of philosophy and design, an explanation of the difference between fixed-form computer-based testing of the type the Partnership for the Assessment of Readiness for College and Careers (PARCC) will use and the computer-adaptive approach adopted by the Smarter Balanced Assessment Consortium (SBAC), a discussion of the trade-offs involved in two different ways of thinking about student performance on these assessments, and a consideration of how to prepare students to succeed on the assessments without allowing test preparation to become the driving force in a school.

The Goals of the Consortia Assessments

The assessments have been developed separately but in loose coordination by states banded together in consortia. The Partnership for the Assessment of Readiness for College and Careers (PARCC) and Smarter Balanced Assessment Consortium (SBAC) came into being as the result of a competition conducted by the US Department of Education in 2010. The competition had far-reaching ambitions and required the new assessments to accomplish multiple goals. These assessments were to replace No Child Left Behind (NCLB) tests and be administered in grades 3 through 8 and once at the high school level. They would need to accomplish the following:

1. Be aligned to college and career readiness standards
2. Measure the full range of knowledge and performance on these standards
3. Reflect classroom instructional practice
4. Support continuous student improvement
5. Provide timely information to determine educator and school effectiveness
6. Identify professional development goals
7. Improve instructional programs
8. Guide instruction

The intention of the competition was to develop assessments that could be used to measure student performance on any set of college and career standards, although it was reasonably clear that the intended target was the Common Core State Standards. The result would be that for the first time, the US educational system would have some consistency in the way student performance would be gauged in relation to key educational outcomes without creating a set of federal standards, curriculum, or assessments.

The eight stated goals of the assessment competition are clearly important. In fact, they represent all the elements necessary to have a quality assessment system. What is challenging is to get all of this information out of a single assessment. One of the cardinal rules of testing is that a test should not be used to measure and report in areas where it was not explicitly designed to do so. By specifying that the assessments were to be capable of measuring and reporting on so many different things, the US Department of Education created an immense challenge for the test designers. The teams constituted by the consortia to write the response to the competition in fact did agree to address all eight of the specified goals. In the process, they created a set of technical challenges and reporting demands that had never before been faced by test developers.

The notion that one test is going to address eight different goals tends to generate wildly unrealistic expectations. Little doubt exists that the experienced and highly professional staffs of the two consortia, along with expert technical advisory committees and world-class vendors, are producing probably the best tests of their kind ever created. However, the likelihood that any test will be able to address all the goals set for these assessments is low. Trade-offs are always a necessity in any assessment design. More goals can be met with more items, more item types, more time for testing, and more resources for scoring, training, and formative and interim assessment. However, states are seeking assessments that cost the least and can be administered in the shortest amount of time possible. They shy away from investments in assessment literacy for teachers that would enable teachers to interpret scores better and use data, and in teacher scoring of performance tasks, a powerful way to build educator understanding of what desired performance looks like. The inevitable result is a test that will most likely fall short of meeting one or more of the eight goal areas.

 The notion that one test is going to address eight different goals tends to generate wildly unrealistic expectations.

Of particular concern is goal 5, that the test results will be used to provide timely information to determine educator and school effectiveness. What this has meant in practice is that states that were awarded Race to the Top funds previously or have gotten NCLB waivers from the US Department of Education have been expected to devise teacher evaluation systems that take into account student performance. As a practical matter, the consortia assessments are likely candidates for generating information on student growth for inclusion in such evaluation systems.

While it may be entirely reasonable and appropriate in principle to consider student performance on high-quality tests as one component of teacher effectiveness, doing so in practice proves exceedingly challenging. Value-added and growth models (ways of measuring student achievement gains from year to year at a classroom level) raise serious technical challenges. It is likely to take a number of years to work out in practice the most feasible and effective methods for capturing student achievement information and applying it to the evaluation of individual teachers. The consortia assessments will need to demonstrate that they are valid measures for use in value-added or growth models for the purposes of teacher evaluation systems that require teachers to be evaluated, at least in part, based on student learning gains. This raises the bar for the consortia exams at the technical level.

These challenges should not be interpreted to mean that the tests are not going to yield good information. Instead, it is an observation designed to point out that additional data sources beyond the consortia assessments will be necessary and useful to address some of the goals specified by the US Department of Education. If the consortia assessments do nothing other than generate relatively common measurements of most of the Common Core State Standards, they should still be considered a success. If complementary measures, techniques, or sources are needed and necessary to achieve additional goals, this is not a bad thing.

The consortia assessments should be seen as a keystone element in what will ultimately become a system of assessments designed to gather data on a wide range of aspects related to the learning process and to student readiness for college and careers. This is a point taken up in more detail in the next chapter. The consortia assessments will be an important first step toward achieving the goals set forth by the US Department of Education. More work remains to be done, though, given the multidimensional nature of the eight stated goals and the high stakes associated with several of them.

Characteristics of Each Consortium's Assessment

The two consortia assessments differ in several important ways, but none more important than in their reliance on two distinctly different approaches to the use of computers to administer selected-response (multiple-choice) items. Each consortium will rely heavily on such items, although their tests will also include short-answer responses that are somewhat open-ended and require student written responses, as well as more complex performance tasks to be completed in the classroom over one or more class periods.

Computer Based versus Computer Adaptive

The primary difference in their use of computer delivery is that PARCC states have adopted a computer-*based* assessment, while the SBAC states have chosen a computer-*adaptive* approach. Although the approaches are similar in their aims, differences do exist in terms of the unit of learning that is being measured and what each score signifies regarding student content knowledge and mastery of standards within that unit of learning. Here is a brief, albeit oversimplified, explanation of those differences.

Computer-Based Assessment The PARCC model uses a computer platform to deliver what is known as a fixed-form exam. As the name implies, the items on a fixed-form exam do not vary across students taking that form, or version, of the test. In this approach, all students who take the test at a particular grade level or for the same conceptual category (e.g., algebra, geometry, functions at the high school level) answer the same test questions and see the same number of items. Multiple equivalent forms of the test are typically used in each administration; these forms may use the same items ordered differently on each form. Test items on a fixed-form test are a lot like familiar paper-and-pencil exams in which students bubble in answers, except that they select the answers online. As noted, PARCC will be including item types in addition to multiple choice. Examples include grid-ins (math problems in which students have no answer choices and must solve a problem and enter an answer) and fill-in-the-blank items in English language arts. However, the basic principle is the same: all students taking the same form of the test complete the same items.

Appropriately constructed fixed-form tests provide sufficiently precise estimates of medium or average student ability but provide increasingly less precise estimates for low- and high-performing students who are at the lower and upper ends of what measurement experts call the "ability distri-bution." Because fixed-form tests administer the same items to all students, they must contain a range that is easy and challenging enough for most students. Fixed-form tests may not have questions that reach the limits of what high-performing students know, and these students could find them-selves answering questions they find very easy. Similarly, lower-performing students may not be presented with many items that are easy enough for them to answer correctly while spending time on items they are not at all capable of answering correctly.

A frequent critique of fixed-form tests is that high-performing students may become bored and feel unchallenged by a test that is too easy, while low-performing students may be discouraged and unmotivated to take a test they feel is too difficult. When teachers see students disengage or struggle with a test, they tend to view the test as not valid or fair. Student frustration with diffi-cult items in particular has led critics to question the value of tests that include items that at least some students have little chance of answering correctly.

Computer-based fixed-form tests have several benefits, though. Scoring may not require the use of item response theory (IRT) methods, which are more difficult to understand and explain. Fixed-form tests are much more cost effective to develop and analyze than are adaptive tests. They do not require the large samples that computer-adaptive tests need to establish item characteristics and can therefore be administered to smaller num-bers of test takers and changed more frequently and easily. Examinees can receive their scores immediately upon test completion. These tests do a good job of describing student ability to respond to the range of content at a particular grade level. They are also the best method for end-of-course exams designed to measure what was taught in a particular course of study.

Computer-Adaptive Tests A computer-adaptive test (CAT), the method selected by the Smarter Balanced consortium, has its own advantages and drawbacks. Because it adapts, it seeks to select items throughout the test at an appropriate level of difficulty for each student taking the test. A CAT typically begins with an item of average or slightly lower than average dif-ficulty. Students who answer this initial item correctly are given increasingly difficult items until they begin to enter incorrect responses. Similarly, if students answer the initial item incorrectly, they see items of decreasing difficulty until they begin to respond correctly. The test continues until a stopping criterion is met, which can be after a specified number of items, when a predetermined level of precision in the student's score is reached, or when content coverage is sufficient to meet test specifications.

In order for the test to proceed beyond the first item, each item is scored immediately in real time. This means test results are available on completion of the test, as with a fixed-form test. A CAT model takes into account several factors, including student ability, item characteristics that include difficulty of the item, and sometimes discrimination (the extent to which the item can differentiate students of different ability levels) and guessing. Because of these complexities in item selection and score reporting and interpretation, CAT models are often not well understood by those outside the measurement community.

Because CAT tests do not have students spend time answering items that are too easy or too difficult, they may contain fewer items (although the Smarter Balanced test is likely to have about the same number of items as the PARCC test). Students may show increased engagement because the items they encounter are challenging but not too difficult to answer. The scores can be more precise estimates of ability than fixed-form tests that can contain more items, and score precision is the same regardless of where a student falls on the ability distribution.

Drawbacks of CAT include increased complexity and cost of test design, development, and scoring. Explaining computer-adaptive testing to educators, policymakers, and parents is more difficult than explaining fixed-form models, particularly if the discussion turns to the algorithm used to select items, how item characteristics are used to determine when enough information has been gathered on a particular test taker, or how results can be interpreted comparably when students are answering different questions, which suggests to some they are not being tested on the same content. Computer-adaptive tests require extensive information about the difficulty of each item, so continuous large-scale piloting is necessary to refresh and expand the item pool. Also, because most students are concentrated near the midpoint on the ability continuum, items at this level can be selected more often by the CAT algorithm, which can overexpose these items, leading to greater familiarity and the ability to teach to them. Finally, because no students are likely to see the same items at the same time, the likelihood of student cheating is decreased.

Because the Smarter Balanced test asks questions about the content to which students seem likely to be able to respond, it includes for the small number of students who need it test content from prior or subsequent grade levels or courses. PARCC does not add off-grade-level items of this type and tests grade-level content only. This is not necessarily a significant issue in practice, but it is one that comes up when policymakers compare the two assessments, particularly if the intent is to use test results for teacher evaluation. The SBAC approach would include some content not taught by the grade-level teacher, a potential problem for determining student growth in the teacher's classroom.

Some policymakers have more difficulty understanding and accepting the results from computer-adaptive tests because they do not like the idea of each student seeing potentially different items. And some may not like the idea of out-of-grade-level items because this leads to the testing of content taught by other teachers and content students have learned outside school altogether. They want to know what a teacher at a particular grade level can be held accountable for having taught and their students having learned. If they are from states with end-of-course testing systems, they question how well the test is aligned with the content taught just in a particular course.

Grade or Course Level versus Learning Progressions

A second important difference is in the way that each consortium thinks about how its exam is the concept of a learning progression—in other words, the idea that content progresses continuously from grade level to grade level and that students keep accumulating new knowledge and skills in a sequential, linked fashion. While both consortia are in agreement that tests administered at grades 3 to 8 represent the cumulative content taught up through those grades, the two consortia have somewhat different views of what they are testing at grade levels and particularly at the high school level.

Smarter Balanced tests are based on the assumption that the Common Core State Standards represent a learning progression. Therefore, Smarter Balanced tests will be given once at each grade level from third to eighth, and then once in high school at grade 11. The third- through eighth-grade tests can include out-of-grade-level content for some students, as noted previously. The eleventh-grade test is designed to assess what has been taught through the first three years of high school cumulatively.

 Smarter Balanced tests are based on the assumption that the Common Core State Standards represent a learning progression.

The PARCC philosophy is to test at the end of each course of study. At the elementary and middle school levels, this means limiting items to content taught at a grade level. At the high school level, tested content is functionally equivalent to what is taught in a specified high school course.

An end-of-course approach has the advantage of allowing student assessments to be matched to courses actually taken. The challenge is the greater variation that occurs in high school course-taking patterns and course content, which makes it more difficult to ascertain what should be assessed for all students and when.

This means that at the high school level, PARCC administers exams aligned with select English and mathematics courses at the end of each of the first three years of high school. This approach solves some problems, particularly in mathematics, where students often take courses out of grade-level sequence, and in English language arts as well, where a wide variety of courses can be used to meet requirements.

The plan as of early 2013 was to include course-based tests in algebra 1, geometry and algebra 2, as well as equivalent exams for integrated courses mathematics 1, 2, and 3. For the first three years of PARCC, the determination of college and career readiness in mathematics will rely on an enhanced version of the assessment taken in one of two courses assumed to be at the college and career readiness level, algebra 2 or mathematics 3. This "enhancing" is achieved by incorporating two additional performance-based tasks designed to measure key concepts and skills from earlier high school mathematics courses.

Performance Tasks: Why Include Them?

Each consortium's assessment also includes performance tasks, which are longer, more complex work products that students create in the classroom. Examples include research papers or mathematics problems requiring multiple steps and the use of data. Performance tasks take longer to complete and are more challenging to score, but they have the advantage of assessing standards that cannot be gauged with computer-delivered items alone. A performance task can be accompanied by selected-response items. Students complete the performance task separately and then answer multiple-choice questions, thus allowing testing of more Common Core standards as well. At least one of the consortia, Smarter Balanced, intends to couple these multiple-choice-type items with the tasks and combine the results from the performance task and its attendant multiple-choice items to generate one overall score for the task.

Performance tasks pose challenges for the consortia:

- They take more time, and they are more expensive to develop and difficult to field-test when compared to traditional test items.

- They must be replaced regularly, in most cases yearly.
- They must be administered in the classroom and can take up to several class periods, which can cause problems when students are absent for one of the periods.
- They can be more challenging to score, although it is possible to achieve high reliabilities with proper scorer training and monitoring.
- Teachers can inadvertently change the conditions of administration or supports provided to students.
- The results from the performance task must be combined with the score on the on-demand portion of the test, resulting in another set of technical and interpretive challenges.

So why include them? The Common Core State Standards contain a number of skills that would be difficult to impossible to assess any other way. They require learning behaviors that are more complex cognitively and help address standards that cannot easily be parsed into discrete elements to be tested separately. For example, the standards expect students to:

- Conduct research and synthesize information
- Develop and evaluate claims
- Engage in critical reading and analysis
- Communicate ideas in writing, speaking, and by responding
- Plan, evaluate, and refine solution strategies
- Design and use mathematical models
- Explain, justify, and critique mathematical reasoning

Performance tasks are also important for what they signal about the type of teaching and learning that is desired. The advantage of selected-response items is that they can break down complex bodies of content into a series of distinct and manageable components and skills, each of which can then be taught and tested discretely. The problem is when this seeming advantage leads to a style of teaching in which all knowledge is reduced to disconnected bits of information or isolated skills. Not only is this way of teaching extremely inefficient because not everything can ever be covered this way, it is also runs counter to the way that students learn. This is particularly true when it comes to the kinds of skills necessary for college and career readiness. Including performance tasks as components in the consortia assessments signals the importance of instruction that goes to higher levels of cognitive challenge and that causes students to integrate and apply all the bits of knowledge and skill they have acquired to some larger purpose and meaning.

Including performance tasks as components in the consortia assessments signals the importance of instruction that goes to higher levels of cognitive challenge.

Score Reporting

Each consortium plans to combine the scores from the performance task with the scores from the computer-delivered test. The specifics of how the two types of scores will be combined and weighted is still being finalized as of spring 2013. Plans call for scores to be reported in a series of categories, called "achievement levels." Each level describes a range of performance and is designed to give policymakers, educators, parents, and test takers a general idea of how students are doing as a group. Achievement levels are not the same as scores. Student scores place them into a category, or level, of achievement.

The PARCC model has five achievement levels: minimal, partial, moderate, strong, and distinguished. The Smarter Balanced model has four: minimal, understanding, adequate, and thorough. The PARCC consortium set both college readiness and career readiness at the same level—a score of 4 on its five-level scale. At this level, students are expected to have a "strong command of the knowledge, skills, and practices embodied by the Common Core State Standards for English language arts/literacy assessed at grade 11." Smarter Balanced had not made a final determination as of the spring of 2013 whether it will have one performance level for both college and career readiness or two separate levels, and which level will represent college and career readiness. The fact that the two consortia have different numbers of achievement levels will pose a challenge in interpreting the meaning of *college and career ready* when comparing performance on consortia exams across states and between students from different consortia states.

The use of college and career readiness achievement levels in the educational policy arena is both convenient and potentially controversial. Making high-stakes decisions about students based on a single score or set of scores raises a host of issues. This practice will be even more controversial if scores are used to place students into remedial education programs because it risks improper placements, something that is already occurring at an alarming rate when decisions are made based on a single placement test. The fact that each consortium may be using a slightly different achievement-level model potentially adds to the challenge of determining

9

THE CONSORTIA ASSESS-
MENTS AND COLLEGE
AND CAREER READINESS

if valid decisions will be made about individual students' readiness for college and careers.

Additional Elements

Several additional elements are reported but not included in the overall score derived from the computer test and the performance task. The PARCC states that it will administer a speaking and listening task, which will be scored at the classroom level. The results will be available for use by teachers, schools, and states for formative purposes and will not be included or combined with the English language arts and mathematics scores. Similarly, Smarter Balanced will include a listening assessment composed of computer-adaptive multiple-choice and short-answer items, and it plans to develop a speaking measure at some point in the future.

This limited low-stakes inclusion of speaking and listening is perhaps understandable. Speaking and listening can be devilishly difficult to assess from a technical perspective. Technical complexity issues related to speaking and listening create a cascading series of problems, and the consortia appear understandably cautious in taking on these challenges. While most can be addressed by having teachers score students on the spot using scoring guides, which PARCC intends to do, not all states are necessarily comfortable asking teachers to take on this role.

Setting College and Career Readiness Levels

Chapter 2 introduced a definition of *college- and career-ready students* as those who can learn successfully beyond high school in a formal learning setting. This broad definition opens the door to more students reaching readiness because the specific knowledge and skills that students need are determined to some degree by the postsecondary environments and programs in which they wish to participate. This allows a wider range of students to potentially qualify for a program of study while not necessarily being ready for every program.

The issue is how to set performance levels and criteria that indicate readiness. Should all students have to meet the same standards to be deemed ready, or should individuals be able to compensate for weaknesses in some areas with strengths in others, if those strength areas align with the expectations of the programs they seek to enter and they possess strong foundational knowledge? Both methods can be used if one is at the system level and the other at the student and program level.

The Smarter Balanced and PARCC assessments propose using the results from tests in English language arts/literacy and mathematics as the primary arbiters of college and career readiness. While no plans are underway to use test results for admissions decisions, states are committing to using the scores to determine students who will be exempt from having to take remedial courses in math or English..

Conjunctive versus Compensatory Standard Setting In the assessment world, two basic approaches are commonly used to determine if someone meets a standard when multiple criteria or performance standards are being used to make the determination (as will be the case when the consortia assessments are fully implemented on their own or in combination with other state-specific measures). A *conjunctive* system requires students to meet a defined level of performance on all measures. A *compensatory* system allows for some variation in scores across measures (table 9.1).

TABLE 9.1 CONJUNCTIVE VERSUS COMPENSATORY SYSTEMS

Conjunctive System	Compensatory System
Students are required to meet a defined level on all applicable measures.	Students are allowed some variation in scores across measures.
Fewer students reach the required level on all measures.	More students meet the overall standard.
Best for making statements about performance on the systems level.	Less effective at generating system-level performance information.
Less effective when applied to individual students.	Best for allowing individual students to progress in areas of strength while still continuing to address areas in need of improvement.
Assumes that all students need to do all things equally well to be recognized as being college and career ready.	Based on the belief that college- and career-ready knowledge and skills vary somewhat among students.
Requires students to devote more time to certain subjects regardless of their future interests.	Takes into account future interests of the student.
Fewer exceptions are made for individual students.	Students have more ways to show readiness.
Students know areas of weakness they need to improve to meet the standard.	Lets students focus on and improve strengths as well as work on weaknesses as a means to demonstrate readiness.

TABLE 9.2   EXAMPLE OF A CONJUNCTIVE APPROACH: COLLEGE READINESS BENCHMARKS BY SUBJECT

Subject	Percentage
English	67
Reading	52
Mathematics	46
Science	31
All four subjects	25

Source: The Condition of College and Career Readiness 2012 (Iowa City, IA: ACT).

If a state follows a conjunctive approach and requires students to meet specified performance levels on several measures, then fewer students overall will reach the required level to be deemed ready. Table 9.2 presents an example of what a conjunctive approach looks like. The ACT computes its annual determination of the number of students nationally who are college ready by setting a cut point on each of its four tests (English, reading, mathematics, and science) and then determining how many meet all four. In 2012, 67 percent of students met the readiness standard in English, 52 percent in reading, 46 percent in math, and 31 percent in science. Under a conjunctive system, no more than 31 percent could possibly meet the standard because this is the number who met the standard in the area where the lowest percentage met it, science. The actual figure is 25 percent because 6 percent of students who met the science standard failed to meet one of the other three standards.

The net result is that fewer students achieve the overall standard when a conjunctive approach is taken. The conjunctive approach works best when making a broad generalization about the performance of a whole group, as in the example. It is less effective when it is applied to individual students, some of whom may fail to reach the required performance level on only one of the exams and therefore not meet the overall standard but still be capable of succeeding in a particular program of study or major in college. This is a problem because for some students, falling short on one of four measures may not have a significant practical effect on the likelihood of their subsequent success.

A compensatory approach allows some flexibility. A student could use stronger performance on one measure to compensate for a score that fell below the standard on another but above a specified minimum. The advantage of this approach is that more students are going to meet the overall standard. The disadvantage is that individual students may have more overall variation in their knowledge and skill levels than students who are declared to meet the standard on all measures. The compensatory approach does not generate information about the knowledge and skills of groups of student that is as easy to interpret as does a conjunctive model.

The strengths and weaknesses of conjunctive and compensatory methods are important to understand. One assumes that all students need to do all things equally well to be recognized as being college and career ready. The other is based on the belief that a college- and career-ready student is someone whose skills may vary within a defined range, but can compensate for weakness in some areas with strengths in others.

This is a critical distinction because it influences a whole range of decisions about how to organize instruction for students, particularly those who are struggling. The conjunctive model suggests that interventions focus primarily on areas of student weakness, regardless of their future interests. A compensatory approach acknowledges student strengths and allows students to continue building on them while not ignoring their areas of weakness.

Trade-Offs between Conjunctive and Compensatory If *college readiness* is defined simply as the ability to enter a four-year university without the need for remediation, then a conjunctive approach is probably a good way to go. That's because students are expected to be ready for the full range of general education courses across multiple disciplines. They need to be proficient in the uses and applications of English and mathematics to science, social sciences, and related academic areas because they will take courses in all of those areas to meet their breadth requirements. The assumption is that a sufficiently high score on English and math exams means they are ready for all of these courses.

Students going on to postsecondary studies in programs that do not require the full range of academic disciplinary knowledge may have more room for variation in readiness measures, particularly test scores. This may also be true for students who are very clear about the college major they wish to pursue. While all students need a foundation of academic knowledge and learning skills, a student entering a program with an emphasis on basic numeracy, such as bookkeeping, may not need the same mathematical knowledge as a student entering a preengineering program, even though both programs require quantitative skills. College majors have long taken this into account to some degree, making exceptions for students with deficiencies in one area if they show greater strengths in another.

For example, a student pursuing a medical records technician certificate or associate degree will benefit from much stronger and more specialized reading and vocabulary skills than a student in an automotive technician program that emphasizes graphical information, schematics, and instructional manuals. Both need a foundational level of literacy, but the precise reading skills each needs vary, and the scores they need to achieve on any particular set of measures in order to indicate readiness will likely be different.

Herein lies a significant challenge when implementing the Common Core State Standards or any other set of college and career readiness criteria: Should college and career readiness be defined as one high, consistent level of performance that all students need to reach—knowing that not all students will reach it and that many of those who don't will still be perfectly capable of succeeding in postsecondary education somewhere—or should readiness be designated in terms of performance ranges that allow students to compensate for weaknesses in one area with strengths in another, based on the specific types of postsecondary programs to which they aspire? Clearly the manner in which college and career readiness is defined affects the way scores are interpreted and how readiness is put into practice operationally, particularly in terms of remedial course placement.

> The manner in which college and career readiness is defined affects the way scores are interpreted and how readiness is put into practice operationally, particularly in terms of remedial course placement.

Each approach has benefits and drawbacks. If the scores designating college and career readiness are set at a uniform level, fewer decisions have to be made about individual students. A glance at a score tells students and teachers who meets the readiness standard and who doesn't. Students know where they need to devote more time and energy to meet the standard. The problem with this approach arises when significant numbers of students fail to reach that score level in one area, particularly if most of them are very close to reaching it. Should these students be deemed not to be college and career ready and in need of remediation? Political pressure, if nothing else, will be strong to find an accommodation for them. This has been the case when high school graduation tests have resulted in many students falling just short of meeting the standard. The most common solution has been simply to lower the required scores or offer alternatives to the state test.

If students are allowed to compensate within a given range for a lower score in one area with a higher score in another, then more decisions need to be made about how the strengths and weaknesses of individual students align with their goals. Students' academic aspirations come into play to a greater degree. The feedback students receive is in relation not just to their cut score, but to their postsecondary goals as well. Doing so will require more and better information about the knowledge and skills students actually need to succeed in specific postsecondary programs of study.

The compensatory model can also be problematic for students who have no sense of what their future might be and therefore cannot connect their scores with any postsecondary program. This is a major challenge that schools should be addressing by having students explore and broaden their vision of the postsecondary and career options open to them. The only way to avoid having students aspire to less challenging futures is to get them motivated about pursuing options that require greater educational attainment. Even with such experiences, not all students will be able to articulate a goal. For these students, a conjunctive set of requirements may help them keep all of their options open. The conjunctive approach makes sense here because it prepares students better for the full range of general education courses in multiple subject areas.

One danger of a purely compensatory approach without specifying a foundational level that all students must meet in all subject areas is that some schools may be tempted to track students with lower scores in, say, math into career options requiring less math without necessarily challenging students to strive first to improve their math performance. Regardless of whether scoring is conjunctive or compensatory, all students should have the opportunity to learn all of the Common Core State Standards.

If the goal is to ensure that as many students as possible have the best opportunity to succeed in postsecondary education, it may be necessary to use elements of both conjunctive and compensatory models depending on student interests and aspirations. Doing so will keep the focus on what students can conceivably do, not only on what they cannot do. Readiness will be a function of knowledge and skill at a foundational level and in relation to specific postsecondary goals, interests, and aspirations.

Preparing for the Consortia Assessments

There is no magic way to prepare all students for the consortia assessments. Intensive, short-term test preparation does not appear to be a very effective method on which to rely, particularly if the goal is deeper learning and continuous improvement in student test scores. The Common Core State Standards create a framework that spans the grades and helps educators develop a more integrated view of what students should be learning. This type of structure is conducive to skill development over time and helps avoid problems that occur when students are taught one topic after another across grade levels without connections, repeat material from one grade to the next for no good reason or, worse yet, have no opportunity to learn some material in the first place. The first step in preparing for the consortia assessments will be carefully and thoughtfully aligning curriculum across grade levels, a process that has been explored in previous chapters. No amount of test preparation will overcome curriculum and instruction not aligned with the standards.

 No amount of test preparation will overcome curriculum and instruction not aligned with the standards.

The Common Core State Standards are also designed around the notion of the application of knowledge in useful and sophisticated ways. Not only is it a good idea from the point of learning theory to apply knowledge in meaningful ways, but such an approach supports greater integration of test preparation into teaching and learning. The tasks, assignments, and activities students do to apply what they are learning need to be carefully designed—not to mimic test questions, but to enable learners to deepen understanding, enhance retention, and create connections among key concepts and linking ideas while also mastering academic nomenclature and factual information.

Every learning activity has meaning and value. Selecting each carefully and deliberately will help students deepen their understanding of the content they are learning and the structure of the subject areas they are studying. As a result, students will retain what they are learning and be better prepared for the consortia exams.

If schools and teachers begin with a formula that organizes instruction specifically around the structure of the Common Core State Standards and does not simply view the standards as a checklist to be taught in a sequence and crammed for a month before the test, students will have the opportunity to absorb, organize, and consolidate the knowledge and skills contained in the Common Core. To do this, teachers can make use of the extensive interim and formative assessment resources that the consortia will make available that will integrate assessment into instruction and provide timely feedback on student progress on the standards. Interim assessments are mini-versions of the final, summative assessment that help teachers (and students) know how well students are likely to perform on the summative test. Formative assessments provide insight into what students understand, what they don't understand, and why, and they thereby help shape instruction.

Many schools will begin to prepare for the consortia assessments by learning how to use and integrate interim and formative assessments. These types of measures create some room for teachers to try out different approaches to see what is working and what isn't. The data generated can help hone instruction and let students know where they stand. The danger is if teaching and learning become completely focused on formative and interim assessment at the expense of developing a deeper understanding of material. Skill building is clearly important, but it should occur within the broader context of students' gaining insight into the subject areas they are learning.

Interim assessment tests the same or similar material as will be included in the consortia summative assessment, but in a low-stakes way to give students and teachers more specific information on where students stand along the learning progressions and how well they are proceeding toward end-of-course goals. Interim assessments use items like those on the summative assessment and yield reports that are similar in format, organization, and information to those generated by the summative assessments. Interim assessments help teachers make longer-range instructional decisions about what students still need to master and on the performance of the class as a whole.

Formative assessments can be thought of as ways to gauge student understanding and knowledge on a more regular and frequent basis, something many teachers already do informally and formally through methods such as teacher-developed tests, assignments, projects, and activities. While formative assessment may contribute to course grades, its purpose relative to the consortia assessments is to give teachers information that helps them inform their own instruction, to see if it is on track and aligned with the standards, and also to let teachers and students know where students stand in terms of their understanding and mastery of the standards.

The consortia provide extensive interim and formative assessment resources, including instruments, materials, and professional development opportunities, but teachers need support and encouragement to organize their classrooms around a combination of high-quality formative assessments and carefully selected and administered interim assessments. The danger is that the interim assessments in particular could be overadministered to such a degree that all teaching degenerates into skills instruction in areas where students do poorly on interim assessments. Class then becomes nothing more than continuous assessment-driven test preparation. This is not a formula likely to work given the cognitive complexity of the Common Core State Standards and the consortia assessments.

Skillful teachers will use interim assessment judiciously and in combination with consortia-developed formative assessments and their own measures to gain insight into student understanding and mastery of relevant Common Core State Standards within the overall context of their course or grade level. This broader understanding allows focused basic skill instruction when necessary, but also encourages teaching bigger concepts and ideas and integrating knowledge through more complex and meaningful assignments that cause students to apply what they know.

The Challenge Remaining

The consortia assessments clearly represent an ambitious attempt to measure a complex set of standards that is designed to lead students to be college and career ready. They will seek to achieve this goal through the use of slightly different approaches. In doing so, they will yield information on how best to determine student performance on the Common Core State Standards and toward college and career readiness. Consortium states will then need to decide how to use test results for a variety of purposes.

A great deal remains to be done over the next several years to complete and implement these assessments and determine how well suited they are to meet the purposes they were created to address (visit the consortia websites or the book's website to get up-to-date information). However, regardless of how the consortia decide to resolve some of the specific decisions still before them, this chapter effectively outlines their operational approaches and the major challenges they face. The goal is to provide readers with the kind of general understanding necessary to spot issues and know what kinds of questions to ask as implementation goes forward.

Whether one assessment system, however well conceived and designed it is, will be able to meet the various needs of multiple constituencies remains to be seen. These constituencies include students and parents, teachers, principals, superintendents, boards of education, state education personnel, legislators and governors, and the US Department of Education. The consortia are clearly making a valiant effort to do so using all the tools at their disposal. The next chapter presents a different potential framework. Rather than a single assessment system that seeks to be all things to all people, it explores the notion of a system of assessments that would acquire information from a wider range of sources to address state goals.

🌀 Awareness and Action Steps

- Download and review *Coming Together to Raise Achievement: New Assessments for the Common Core State Standards* (http://bit.ly/11wiab3).
- Familiarize yourself with the performance-level descriptors your consortium uses. Once everyone in the school has a shared understanding of the performance levels, begin to determine the likely distribution of students in the school among the performance levels.
- Look at the Common Core State Standards across grade levels to become more familiar with how they progress. Notice where prior learnings shape expectations at a subsequent grade level. Examine how well courses in the school take into account prior and subsequent knowledge and skill development.
- Determine how familiar teachers in the school are with performance tasks. Many examples of performance tasks can be found online. Appendix B of the English Language Arts Common Core State Standards contains examples at all grade levels, including college and career ready. To foster familiarity, have all teachers in a subject area score a common performance task, and then compare their results.
- If the data are available, compare how many students in your school do well on measures that are likely to align with the consortia assessments, such as ACT/SAT and state tests. Assume that student scores on assessment consortia will be lower than these. This can serve as a rough predictor of how students in the school will perform initially at the college and career readiness level on the consortia assessments.
- Discuss whether you favor a conjunctive or compensatory approach to granting high school diplomas. Should all students have to meet the same standards to earn a diploma, or should some students be able to compensate with strengths in some areas if they fell short in others, assuming they have a strong foundational knowledge base?
- Review your school's strategy for preparing for your consortium's assessment. Is the emphasis on short-term test prep? What role will formative and interim assessment play in guiding instruction and diagnosing student needs?

- The performance tasks of the both consortia include on-demand writing and revision within fixed periods of time. Build on-demand writing activities into in-class assignments to help reduce anxiety or time management issues when students encounter the formal writing tasks on the assessments.
- Help teachers become more assessment literate, particularly in their ability to use and interpret formative assessment information that provides them with insight into student understanding at higher levels of aggregation than individual standards. Are students comprehending the standards at a conceptual level as well as at a content level?

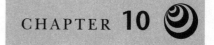
FROM AN ASSESSMENT SYSTEM
TO A SYSTEM OF ASSESSMENTS

This chapter makes the case for the use of multiple assessment measures and a wider array of data sources for determinations of student college and career readiness and for a range of other purposes as well. A multidimensional system of assessments within a state yields data that can be used at all levels, from the statehouse to the schoolhouse. Such a system will be more consistent with the model of college and career readiness presented in earlier chapters, which emphasizes the wide range of aspects that need to be developed in students for them to be ready to succeed in college and careers.

More complex and varied data can yield improved insight into the degree of overall student readiness. Students can also be afforded alternative means to demonstrate readiness. A grade point average can still generate useful information in combination with other sources, although its role is becoming somewhat limited as more students have GPAs that approach or exceed 4.0. An increasing number of states administer college entrance examinations to all students. The ACT, with its EPAS system of EXPLORE/PLAN/ACT, and College Board, through its Pathway system consisting of ReadiStep, the PSAT, and the SAT, provide an overall judgment in relation to a score cut point and nationally normed comparative information on student readiness for college and careers. An increasing number of students complete college-level work in high school through Advanced Placement or International Baccalaureate tests or from college courses taken while in high school through concurrent or dual-enrollment programs. A few states have instituted other testing requirements as well. In short, a range of information is already being collected, but most of it is not yet being integrated and reported in complementary ways that create a valid and complete picture of college and career readiness.

Results from the consortia assessments are now being added to the mix, including performance tasks that require more complex and extensive writing and other skills, such as problem solving. This information can offer additional insight into readiness. Evidence strongly suggests that skills such as being able to write a research paper independently are highly indicative of potential preparedness for a wide range of postsecondary programs. Knowing more about how well students write research papers is an example of additional evidence that is highly useful when making readiness determinations and offers students an alternative way to demonstrate readiness. Valuing this type of more complex information that a student work product generates also clearly signals to students the importance of developing the academic skills necessary to produce quality products.

Many schools throughout the country already espouse a philosophy of learning that can be measured only through more complex performance assessments. Schools such as the Aspire and Envision charters ask students to complete semester- and year-long projects that require integrating a broad range of skills and knowledge. The New York Performance Standards Consortium consists of schools that build instruction around performance tasks. The Coalition of Essential Schools has a long tradition stretching back to the mid-1980s of juried reviews of student work products and projects. Deborah Meier and her colleagues at Central Park East Secondary School, for example, expected students to produce highly complex and challenging graduation portfolios. Many other schools have long histories of using performance tasks. In addition, a number of states have instituted requirements for culminating projects or other types of performance demonstrations as required elements for high school graduation. Massachusetts, Washington State, and Oregon, for example, allowed students to submit collections of evidence in place of scores on high school exit exams. In other words, complex assessment is not entirely new or novel, and many schools throughout the nation can already serve as laboratories or demonstration sites for those interested in implementing tasks in their schools and for states looking to adopt multiple routes for students to demonstrate necessary knowledge and skills.

As new tests are implemented and current state tests are reviewed and revised, the opportunity exists to move away from an assessment system composed of often overlapping, redundant, or disconnected scores or reports and toward a *system of assessments* model that yields information that addresses state accountability requirements and also provides students, teachers, schools, and postsecondary education institutions with performance data to inform a range of decisions that leads to ongoing improvement. Rarely is it possible to achieve this goal with a single test or even multiple measures when such measures overlap with one another on what they test.

While the Common Core State Standards do not specify everything that is necessary for postsecondary readiness and success, they do include many standards that are cognitively complex and critical for success in college and careers. The consortia assessment developers readily admit that their tests do not capture every factor necessary for college and career readiness because they test only English and mathematics. However, even in these two subject areas, consortia assessments will not be able to assess some Common Core standards. Following are some examples of concepts contained in the standards, explicitly or implicitly, that are not well addressed by the consortia assessments in their current configuration and that require assessment beyond what the consortia exams will be able to offer:

- Conducting research and synthesizing information
- Developing and evaluating claims
- Reading critically and analyzing complex texts
- Communicating ideas through writing, speaking, and responding
- Planning, evaluating, and refining solution strategies
- Designing and using mathematical models
- Explaining, justifying, and critiquing mathematical reasoning

A number of states that want to provide students, teachers, schools, and postsecondary programs with the information they need to determine college and career readiness levels for students are considering a system of assessment approach. For example, the Innovation Lab Network, sponsored by the Council of Chief State School Officers, is a group of ten states committed to a series of educational reforms to support, supplement, and at times go beyond the Common Core State Standards. One of their initiatives is the "Consortium-Plus" model of assessment in which states commit to develop additional measures beyond the common core. Kentucky is perhaps the best example—as of the spring of 2013—of a state that has taken steps toward developing a more comprehensive set of measures that moves the state toward a system of assessments model.

While some may disagree with specific elements of the Kentucky model or question the overall amount of assessment that is going on in the state, the important point is that the model has been developed to meet the needs of the Kentucky educational system. The idea behind a system of assessments approach is that each state that adopts such a strategy will likely have a different mix of measures based on state goals, priorities, and traditions. Some states might opt for more classroom-based assessment, demonstrations, and performance tasks aligned with a competency grading system, while others might add data points and measures that would yield high-quality information for teacher evaluation and instructional improvement, along with other important purposes. The system of assessments approach allows each state to craft the set of measures necessary for its schools to demonstrate performance in relation to key state goals while addressing school-level needs and contributing to college and career readiness determinations. Table 10.1 shows Kentucky's system of assessments.

A carefully designed system of assessments takes into account the varied needs of all the constituents who use assessment data: teachers, principals, superintendents, and boards of education; college and university officials and administrators in proprietary training programs; state education department staff, legislators, and governors; staff at the US Department of Education and in Congress; members of education advocacy groups; parents; the business community; and many others. The system of assessments approach collates information from enough different sources to address a wider range of needs than does rating schools as succeeding or failing based on one set of test scores. The system does so in a way that results in a more holistic picture of students, schools, and educational systems that does not waste or duplicate information or effort but also does not use a single source of data inappropriately. This method also allows a wider range of students to demonstrate what they know and can do by means of additional options and methods.

TABLE 10.1 SYSTEM OF ASSESSMENTS
FOR THE STATE OF KENTUCKY

Kentucky System of Assessments	Grade Level	Purpose of Exams
Assessing Comprehension and Communication in English State-to-State (ACCESS)	K–12	English language proficiency
ACT	10–11	College readiness
ACT QualityCore	10–12	End of course
ACT Work Keys (Applied Math, Locating Information, and Reading for Information)	12	Career readiness
Armed Services Vocational Aptitude Battery (ASVAB)	10–12	Career readiness
COMPASS	12	College placement assessment
EXPLORE	8	College readiness assessment
Industry Certificate Assessments	9–12	Career readiness
Kentucky Occupational Skills Standards Assessment (KOSSA)	10–12	Career readiness
Kentucky Performance Rating for Educational Progress (K-PREP)	3–8	Kentucky Core Academic Standards
Kentucky Online Testing (KYOTE)	12	College readiness
PLAN	10	College readiness

> The system of assessments approach collates information from enough different sources to address a wider range of needs than does rating schools as succeeding or failing.

For example, using test scores to determine where individual students fall on a performance-level system (e.g., approaches, meets, exceeds) requires a great deal of attention to the stakes associated with the decisions. As the stakes get higher, more information is needed. For example, if scores are going to be used to make determinations about graduation, remediation, placement, financial aid, or admissions, more than a single test score should be factored into the equation. Additional sources of information on the knowledge and skills associated with readiness and success help reduce classification errors, which occur when a student who is ready is labeled not ready or vice versa. A system of assessments can provide more

10

FROM AN ASSESSMENT SYSTEM TO A SYSTEM OF ASSESSMENTS

valid and reliable information for a variety of purposes, including high-stakes decisions about individual students.

A system of assessments can derive information on college and career readiness from a wide range of potential sources. For example, tests or end-of-course exams in subject areas other than reading, writing, and math yield better insight into breadth of knowledge. Surveys of student learning skills and techniques reveal whether students are becoming lifelong learners. Inventories of student knowledge about the college selection and application process, financial aid, and matriculation demonstrate the degree to which students are learning about the transition process.

Performance Tasks: Key Element in a System of Assessments

One additional source of information is the performance task, which comes in a wide variety of shapes and sizes. Administered in the classroom, these tasks can vary dramatically in length and complexity. They can take anywhere from a period to a semester to complete and have the potential to yield information that standardized tests do not. Performance tasks are not necessarily the same as teacher-generated assignments. Task quality is generally more tightly controlled by identifying relevant content, specifying the conditions for administration, designating the scaffolding or support available to students, standardizing the scoring process, and controlling how results are reported. Additional quality control can be achieved through the use of moderation processes in which selected tasks are rescored by someone other than the teacher, and the moderation scores are then used to help teachers score more reliably in the future.

Information from classroom-based performances is used more frequently than standardized tests in a number of educational systems around the world. For example, the states of Queensland and Victoria in Australia and schools in the International Baccalaureate Diploma Programme have invested in developing educator skills as classroom-based performance assessors. They devote resources to training teachers to develop quality assessments at the classroom level, then expect teachers to incorporate complex assignments and projects into their courses, and then assess student work appropriately and accurately. It is not uncommon for students to write essays or give presentations and have them scored by their teachers or members of expert panels who use scoring guides. Much of this assessment occurs at the end of courses as well as at the culmination of studies at designated levels.

This type of assessment can take place because educators have acquired over time very similar ideas and explanations of what adequate performance on these papers and tasks looks like. In nations as varied as the Netherlands and Singapore, teachers share mental models of student performance that allow them to administer performance tasks with consistency and to judge student performance reliably. These mental models are developed from the earliest stages of teacher preparation and induction and are reinforced by high-quality in-course assessments and grading practices that also use scoring guides closely aligned with teachers' mental models of adequate student performance. In this fashion, teachers can score performance tasks efficiently and effectively.

Range of Performance Task Types

The types of performance tasks or measures that are useful in a system of assessments can cover a wide span (figure 10.1). At one end are simple assignments that can be completed in a portion of a class period. Exhibits 10.1 and 10.2 contain examples of tasks that simply require students to write several paragraphs. These exhibits are tasks created by PARCC and SBAC, respectively, in preparation for their consortia assessments. Other short performance tasks may ask students to take information that is given and interpret it, reorganize data and draw diagrams that explain relationships, or classify and categorize objects or data into like and

FIGURE 10.1 CONTINUUM OF ASSESSMENT FOR DEEPER LEARNING

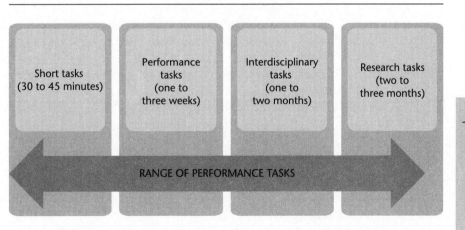

Short tasks (30 to 45 minutes)

Performance tasks (one to three weeks)

Interdisciplinary tasks (one to two months)

Research tasks (two to three months)

RANGE OF PERFORMANCE TASKS

Exhibit 10.1   Short Performance Task

Grade 10 Prose Constructed Response

Use what you have learned from reading "Daedalus and Icarus" by Ovid and "To a Friend Whose Work Has Come to Triumph" by Anne Sexton to write an essay that provides an analysis of how Sexton transforms "Daedalus and Icarus."

As a starting point, you may want to consider what is emphasized, absent, or different in the two texts, but feel free to develop your own focus for analysis.

Develop your essay by providing textual evidence from both texts. Be sure to follow the conventions of standard English.

"Grade 10 Prose Constructed Response—Sample #1 from Literary Analysis Task." *Parcconline.org.* Partnership for Assessment of Readiness for College and Careers, n.d. Web. 18 June 2013. (http://www.parcconline.org/samples/english-language-artsliteracy /grade-10-prose-constructed-response%E2%80%94sample-1-literary-analysis).

 Exhibit 10.2   Short Performance Task

Grade 6 Writing Task – Cell Phones

Read the text and complete the task that follows it.

Cell Phones in School—Yes or No?

Cell phones are convenient and fun to have. However, there are arguments about whether or not they belong in schools. Parents, students, and teachers all have different points of view. Some say that to forbid them completely is to ignore some of the educational advantages of having cell phones in the classroom. On the other hand, cell phones can interrupt classroom activities and some uses are definitely unacceptable. Parents, students, and teachers need to think carefully about the effects of having cell phones in school.

Some of the reasons to support cell phones in school are as follows:

- Students can take pictures of class projects to e-mail or show to parents.
- Students can text-message missed assignments to friends that are absent.
- Many cell phones have calculators or Internet access that could be used for assignments.
- If students are slow to copy notes from the board, they can take pictures of the missed notes and view them later.
- During study halls, students can listen to music through cell phones.

- Parents can get in touch with their children and know where they are at all times.
- Students can contact parents in case of emergencies.

Some of the reasons to forbid cell phones in school are as follows:

- Students might send test answers to friends or use the Internet to cheat during an exam.
- Students might record teachers or other students without their knowledge. No one wants to be recorded without giving consent.
- Cell phones can interrupt classroom activities.
- Cell phones can be used to text during class as a way of passing notes and wasting time.

Based on what you read in the text, do you think cell phones should be allowed in schools? Using the lists provided in the text, write a paragraph arguing why your position is more reasonable than the opposing position.

unlike groups. Even simple tasks can assess knowledge and skills that cannot be gauged well with multiple-choice items. Teachers often devise these types of tasks themselves, pull them from curriculum materials, or access them online. They are generally closely tied to the content at hand and require only modest extrapolation and application of terms, ideas, and concepts being learned in class. An example of this type of task might be one in which students are asked to write a new ending to a story using a different literary style. A math-oriented in-class, single-period tasks might provide students with a list of prices at local gas stations and ask them to determine which was the best value from a cost-benefit perspective, taking into account variables such as time to travel to the station, gas costs of driving there, proximity to other stops that must be made while getting gas, and other salient factors.

Next along the continuum of performance tasks are those that require at least some out-of-class work. These are incrementally more complicated because the teacher has to verify that all the work produced is the student's own. For example, students might be required to access information from US Census databases to answer specific questions about local conditions. The task could measure ELA knowledge and skills, math knowledge and skills, or a combination of the two. Part of the requirement would be a draft and then a final version with edits and revisions. Tasks of this type are

◎ Exhibit 10.3　One- to Three-Week Performance Task with In-Class and Out-of-Class Work

A Modest Solution: Writing Satire about Current Events

Students write a satire in the form of Jonathan Swift's essay, "A Modest Proposal." Students first research a real-world problem that interests them to learn about its causes and possible solutions. For their proposal, they create a persona who offers an overt, absurd solution while also communicating a covert, but real, solution proposed by the student.

© CCR Consulting Group 2013

increasingly available from both commercial sources and online task banks. Although some are teacher developed and not necessarily reviewed for their content validity or other psychometric properties, a growing number of such tasks have been carefully designed and thoroughly vetted to ensure they measure what they purport to measure and can be scored reliably. Exhibit 10.3 presents an example of a ThinkReady task that requires students to work in class and out of class to collect information and conduct research on a topic of interest and produce multiple drafts.

In another performance task example, students in middle school math might be asked to use information about traffic volumes and flow to identify the best routes to take to get to various destinations and then to make recommendations on how to improve traffic flow overall or where to site a new hospital so that it is accessible but not in an area of high congestion. The first part might be completed in class individually, while the second might require additional work outside class followed by group work in class. Scoring might include a component score for correct use of mathematics, a second for problem-solving techniques, and a third for thoroughness of proposed solution.

A third example is a type of task that is longer in duration and may take up to a third of a semester. This is really best described as a project. Often it is the student who defines the focus of the project and is responsible for organizing the task and locating all the necessary information to complete it. The student may be expected to follow a particular outline or to address a range of requirements in the process of completing the project. The project may be judged by the teacher alone or in conjunction with someone who has expertise in the subject area in which the project is focused. Exhibit 10.4 contains an example of an interdisciplinary task from Envision Schools requiring students to integrate knowledge from several subject areas.

Exhibit 10.4   One- to Two-Month Interdisciplinary Task

Disaster in the Gulf Project

In response to the April 2010 BP Deepwater Horizon oil drilling rig accident, seniors at Envision Schools explore effects and impact through Disaster in the Gulf, an inter-disciplinary project:

- AP Government: Produce a research paper about our government's role in respond-ing to such a disaster, including the role of federal agencies and our national emer-gency management system.
- World Literature: Write a three- to four-minute speech using rhetorical skills and deliver the speech at a simulated congressional hearing.
- AP Environmental Science: Explore the environmental impact of the oil spill. Consider different methodologies of cleaning the affected areas, along with the social, economic, and environmental impact of the oil and cleaning.
- Advanced Visual Arts: Create sculptures and other art forms from petroleum-based materials.

This project takes place over nine weeks and is reviewed by the subject area teacher using a rubric from the College Success Student Performance Assessment System.

Reprinted by permission of Envision Schools. All rights reserved, 2010.

For this type of project, a student or team of students undertakes an investigation of some sort, such as locally sourced foods. The investigation requires them to conduct research on a number of topics:

- Where food they eat comes from
- What proportion of the price represents transportation
- How dependent they are on other parts of the country for their food and what would happen to local food supplies if the national transpor-tation system were disrupted for a week or a month
- What choices they could make if they wished to eat more locally pro-duced food, what the economic implications of doing so would be, and whether doing so could cause unintended economic consequence in other parts of the country

The project is presented to the class and scored by the teacher using a guide that included ratings of the use of mathematics and economics content knowledge; the quality of argumentation; the appropriateness of

◑ Exhibit 10.5   Four-Month Research Task

The extended essay is an independent, self-directed piece of research that takes place over the course of a semester, culminating in a four-thousand-word paper. As a required component, it provides:

- Practical preparation for the kinds of undergraduate research required at tertiary level
- An opportunity for students to engage in an in-depth study of a topic of interest within a chosen subject

Emphasis is placed on the research process:

- Formulating an appropriate research question
- Engaging in a personal exploration of the topic
- Communicating ideas
- Developing an argument

Participation in this process develops the capacity to:

- Analyze
- Synthesize
- Evaluate knowledge

information sources cited and referenced; the quality and logic of the conclusions reached; and overall precision, accuracy, and attention to detail.

Finally, a fourth type of performance assessment is really more like a culminating examination in which skills acquired over multiple years are applied to a large, complex problem. The prompt may be standardized and developed externally, as in the case of the International Baccalaureate Diploma extended essay requirements example in exhibit 10.5, or may be generated at the school site or by the teacher, in the case of a culminating project undertaken to meet graduation requirements. This type of task takes the form of a paper that is scored with a common scoring guide. This task has elements of the interdisciplinary task but is distinguished primarily by the longer period of time over which it takes place (up to a semester), combined with the higher level of rigor that comes from the external scoring. The extended essay reflects the types of assessments used in many other countries to gain greater insight into student thinking skills and content understanding and mastery.

Students are supported throughout the process with advice and guidance from a supervisor (usually a teacher at the school). Performance tasks can generate insight into other aspects of student learning skills and strategies. For example, teachers can report on student ability to sustain effort when confronted with difficult tasks; to manage time to complete complex, multistep assignments; and to work with others to improve both individual and group performance. This evidence of readiness for postsecondary educational opportunities and career pathways can be used in combination with scores on English and math tests to allow students with a lower score in, say, math, to compensate with strong evidence of effective study habits, good collaborative skills, and the ability to seek help from instructors. This more varied information can come from performance tasks, where teachers observe the learning skills, techniques, and strategies students employ. Scoring guides can rate these types of learning skills along with content knowledge. Such performance task scores can be used to identify students with postsecondary potential who may be struggling academically but respond well to performance tasks as a means of expressing their learning skills, thus showing their greater potential for success in a postsecondary program that require the ability to learn independently and seek help when needed.

How a System of Assessments Addresses a Wider Range of Standards

The Common Core State Standards include many areas that are crucial for postsecondary readiness and success but cannot easily be assessed with the types of methods being used by the consortia assessments (the list near the start of this chapter contains examples). These standards and others are candidates for the range of performance tasks just described. It's easy to think of extended activities that would cause students to demonstrate the more complex cognitive skill sets these standards are attempting to develop. This could be accomplished through structured tasks that require the application of content knowledge and problem-solving skills to a defined problem, such as choosing among several proposed plans to improve local economic development, or they could be much more open-ended, such as requiring students to identify an issue or topic, explain their choice, and then indicate which standards the project will address. Students would be challenged to formulate the problem and then present their interpretation and potential solution.

This type of more active engagement with content not only helps students understand what they have been taught and to integrate their knowledge; it also develops cognitive skills and learning strategies that help them to be successful with new content. When the focus of schooling is on one test, no matter how good that test is, classroom instruction and learning naturally gravitate toward what is on the test. Aligning instruction with a test is not automatically a bad thing, but it can become problematic when the test does not or cannot address all of the standards that are supposed to frame overall curriculum and instruction. Widening the range of assessment types and integrating assessment more fully into classroom practice helps ensure that the full range of standards, including the complex and intellectually demanding ones, are properly valued and evaluated.

 Aligning instruction with a test is not automatically a bad thing, but it can become problematic.

A system-of-assessments approach opens the door to a much wider array of measurement instruments and approaches and of opportunities for students to become involved in and take ownership of the work they are doing. Currently states limit their assessment options because almost all measures are viewed through the lens of accountability purposes and the technical requirements of high-stakes testing. These requirements generally end up emphasizing reliability over validity. In other words, instruments that yield the same results over repeated administrations are valued more highly, even if what the instrument measures is not necessarily the most accurate representation of the learning or behavior that is of interest in the first place. Reliability is important because people tend to find unreliable measures to be unfair. However, validity is also important, and it is strengthened by using appropriate means to measure what is important.

A system of assessments would be necessary and useful even if the consortia assessments tested all of the Common Core State Standards perfectly because it would allow more students to demonstrate their knowledge and skills in different ways. However, they do not and cannot capture information from some of the most important standards and other key college and career readiness variables. Therefore, states that wish to ensure that students, teachers, schools, and postsecondary programs have the right kinds of evidence necessary to determine college and career readiness will want to consider moving toward a system of assessments. Such an approach can open the door to student profiles that generate more comprehensive portraits of student performance across a wider range of relevant factors and variables and that enable more students to meet standard. This helps reduce the probability of lowering standards due to pressure that results from many students doing poorly on one test or measure.

Moving toward Student Profiles

A student profile is a way to compile and report all the data on student performance on key factors that a system of assessments generates longitudinally across multiple grade levels.

Benefits of a Profile Approach

A profile approach supports a compensatory measurement system where information on strengths in some areas can help compensate for areas of weaknesses in others. A profile places individual test scores and other measures of student knowledge and skill into context and permits better judgments about student readiness in relation to aspirations and goals. A profile can paint a better picture of the match between student knowledge and skills and the postsecondary program or career goal to which they aspire. The profile also validates a wider range of learning skills and techniques by permitting learners to demonstrate their abilities through a wider range of options.

Gathering and reporting information in this fashion leads to a fuller portrait of the knowledge, skills, and dispositions students need to succeed after high school. The profile provides students with information on the degree to which they are ready to pursue their postsecondary goals and also signals to teachers and schools a wider range of areas where student readiness needs to be addressed. While much of this information would be less useful for high-stakes accountability purposes, it is absolutely essential for students to have as they seek to become ready for college and careers. However, some of the indicators in a profile would also have potential use for statewide accountability purposes. For example, knowing something about student aspirations could be a key statewide indicator, and schools could be encouraged to raise student goals and aspirations. The net effect would be better data for the student, the school, and the state and more students seeking to increase their achievement by taking on more challenging material.

Considerable evidence suggests that students can make great strides toward overcoming specific skill deficiencies or weaknesses if they are highly motivated to succeed in a particular field, the skill itself is not critical to success in that area, and they possess learning techniques and strategies that enable them to acquire those skills. Knowing something about their motivation and willingness to work hard helps postsecondary programs identify students who can succeed with targeted support. Conversely, students who get decent grades but do not demonstrate any other characteristics associated with the likelihood of succeeding in college are at greater risk of failure and should be encouraged to develop more of the skills and behaviors associated with college readiness and success.

What Might Comprise a Profile

What information would states, schools, and teachers put into a profile so that it might inform students about their readiness, while also helping schools know how effective they are in preparing their students, while also enabling states to have a better sense of how well their schools are working? Bear in mind that the four keys model identifies forty-one indicators of college and career readiness. Ideally, measures of all of these would be included in a profile. However, as a practical matter, assembling information that addresses perhaps a dozen key factors would be a tremendous advancement over current approaches that gather overlapping and redundant information about English and math proficiency from several sources.

The following description is meant to be illustrative only and is not sufficiently detailed to serve as a blueprint for a profile system. Clearly some of these sources need further development, and some would be appropriate only to use as supplemental information, not as the sole source of a decision about a student's readiness. Work continues on identifying measures that can contribute to functional student profiles that combine multiple data sources in ways that yield greater insight into the probability that a student will succeed in postsecondary education in a designated program of study or in general education courses.

An example profile could have the following types of measures in it:

- Common Core State Standards consortia exams
- Grade point average (cumulative and disaggregated by subject)
- Admissions tests (e.g., SAT, ACT) or sequence of Common Core or admissions-aligned tests (e.g., EPAS, Aspire, Pathways)
- Classroom-administered performance tasks (e.g., research papers)
- Oral presentation beyond consortia requirements, scored discussion
- Teacher rating of student note-taking skills, ability to follow directions, persistence with challenging tasks, and other evidence of learning skills and ownership of learning

- Student self-report on effort used to complete an activity; and student self-report of goals and actions taken to achieve personal goals
- Student self-report of aspirations and goals
- Student postsecondary plans

The list in table 10.2 ranges from highly rigorous tests to self-reports. Many psychometricians might cringe when they see all of these measures combined in this way because it is very difficult to make them comparable and interpret what they mean as a whole. Clearly the data will need to be combined and reported in different ways based on the types of decisions being made. The advantage of a profile approach, regardless of the precise measures selected to comprise it, is that students receive clear guidance about where they stand in relation to college and career readiness, and they are then able to act to change their behavior consistent with their goals. Furthermore, a wider range of behavior and skills is valued, including student goals, aspirations, and postsecondary plans. In this way, student ownership of learning is strengthened. Furthermore, schools and postsecondary institutions get much more actionable information that can be used to improve student success, while the state gets a truer picture of how well schools are preparing students for college and careers.

As a practical matter, a profile system can be implemented in stages, with new data sources added periodically as the system is able to generate

TABLE 10.2   EXAMPLES OF STUDENT PROFILE MEASURES

Type of Measure	Ways to Measure
Math, ELA knowledge and skills	Consortia exams
Other subject areas	State exams
Grade point average	Cumulative and disaggregated by subject
Admissions exams	SAT, ACT
Performance task	Classroom-administered research paper
Speaking	Consortia exams, classroom activities
Listening	Consortia exams, classroom activities
Goal focus	Student goal plan
Aspirations	Student self-report
Postsecondary plans	Student plans for postsecondary education

evidence, confirm its validity and reliability, and ensure the consumers of new measures understand them and are able to act on them. What is somewhat worrisome currently is the tendency of many states in the assessment consortia to want to reduce the amount of information being gathered by cutting to the minimum the time devoted to testing and then making score reports as simple as possible by collapsing reporting categories. This is the opposite of a profile approach. While issues of time and expense are by no means trivial, generating more student performance data is critical—to students, teachers, schools, and states. Profiles can provide the continuity and depth necessary to understand student performance and readiness for the next level. Saving a few dollars per student by slashing the amount of useful and actionable information that is gathered from large-scale assessments and other measures is akin to eliminating blood tests from physical examinations in favor of taking blood pressure and temperature only. The cost savings are nowhere near commensurate with the lost opportunity to address serious problems early and in a cost-effective fashion.

Education is lagging far behind other sectors of the economy that are redesigning and reinventing themselves around comprehensive, multidimensional, real-time data systems. Although the consortia assessments will be a step forward in many respects, they still report only on a subset of readiness knowledge and skills in English and mathematics. Almost all other dimensions of learning outside of content acquisition in these two subject areas and some cognitive processes in English and mathematics continue to be largely neglected or ignored entirely as potential sources of supplementary information to explain why students are succeeding or struggling. Profiles offer the potential to combine information and add new sources to reveal a fuller picture of the learner.

Systems of assessments are imperative to understanding student college and career readiness better because readiness is such a multifaceted phenomenon. Classroom-based assessments can also contribute data to such a system if they are of high quality. Teacher-generated grades that capture student performance in the classroom along multiple dimensions that are clearly specified can be valuable sources of unique information and insight, along with external exams, performance tasks, student self-reports, and other measures that combine in a system-of-assessment approach that is complex, valid, and valuable.

If US schools and teachers are to be judged on their performance and if high-stakes decisions are to be made based on performance, then more information from a wider range of highly valid sources is necessary. Without such a system, schools will adapt practices based to whatever college and career readiness indicator a state adopts. If the measure is number of students taking AP courses, then students will be funneled into these courses regardless of their readiness. If it is the number of students who apply directly to college from high school, then colleges will be flooded with applications from students who are in no way ready to succeed. If it is ACT or SAT scores, test preparation programs will proliferate.

The answer is not to be found in seeking the single magic bullet measure that tells whether a student is college and career ready and can also be used to judge a school. Instead, a complex approach that better reflects the reality of the process is called for. College and career readiness consists of a constellation of knowledge and skills. Developing and measuring it properly will require data from a host of sources. Getting a more complex model in place may take patience and the gradual addition of one new measure at a time. A commitment to such an approach can result in educators engaging more actively in the use and integration of a range of assessment practices in their classrooms. This can ultimately lead to improved student learning and achievement, to colleges making better determinations about the help and support incoming students need in order to succeed, and to states making better judgments about how and in what ways schools are successful or unsuccessful in getting students ready for college and careers.

The preceding chapters have presented a comprehensive overview of a series of interlocking issues with which schools need grapple:

- College and career readiness as the focal point of the school's instructional program for all students
- An acknowledgment that college and career readiness is more complex than how it's currently conceived
- A commitment to developing readiness in four key areas and addressing the forty-one factors identified as important to college and career readiness
- The importance and value of deeper learning as a tool for both college and career readiness and Common Core State Standards mastery
- A deeper and more complete understanding of the nature of those standards and the steps that need to be taken if they are to become vehicles for college and career readiness
- The ways in which the standards will be assessed and the strengths and limitations of those assessments
- An approach to using a wider range of indicators to determine readiness in relation to student aspirations and goals and state accountability needs.

While educators should rightly be focused on current challenges posed by the Common Core State Standards and consortia assessments and the need to get many more students ready for college and careers, the next chapter takes a look forward to preview new challenges and opportunities and offer conjectures on where all of the current issues examined here may be heading next.

🌀 Awareness and Action Steps

- Review the list of Common Core standards near the start of the chapter. Think about ways that these could be assessed either at the classroom level or by an external method.
- See the Innovation Lab Network for examples of states that are going beyond the consortia assessments with additional assessments (http://bit.ly/19OkfHx).
- For a better understanding of the research base underlying performance assessment, read and discuss Paul Black and Dylan Wiliam's *Inside the Black Box: Raising Standards through Classroom Assessment*. A summary is available at http://bit.ly/15kuRqF.
- See the International Baccalaureate Diploma Programme Assessment Principles and Practice for an overview of how a combination of assessments, internal and external, can be used to gain greater insight into a wider range of student knowledge and skills (http://bit.ly/11JHxoV).
- Examine the example performance tasks that represent points along the continuum presented in figure 10.1. Which kind of tasks along the continuum are used in classrooms in your school? What would have to occur for your school to the next type of task on the continuum?
- Create a hypothetical student profile. What would it have in it? What additional information on student knowledge, skills, and abilities is readily available to include when making important decisions about student readiness? How can available information help students make better decisions about possible goals?
- Give students opportunities to build portfolios of work across multiple grade levels. Portfolios can be constructed on public spaces such as Google and can embed material created on YouTube, Prezi, SlideRocket, and Screenr, in addition to scanned student work products.
- Review the Raikes Foundation inventory of social-emotional learning assessment tools (http://bit.ly/13ZbSlO).
- Gauge your students' families' current comfort levels with student performance data. Do you think a more comprehensive profile would be welcome or confusing? What kinds of conversations and awareness raising need to accompany an expansion into a profile-based system of assessments?

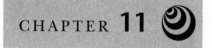

CHAPTER **11**

WHERE TO FROM HERE?

The arrival of our first grandchild a year and a half ago sparked an ongoing conversation in our family about what it will mean for her to be college and career ready. Admittedly this may not be a topic that all new parents and grandparents discuss. However, it is important to consider looming changes in education even if it is impossible to know for certain how events will unfold over the next eighteen years. Some questions of importance include the following:

- How will a college education look different?
- Will the Common Core State Standards still exist?
- Will the consortia assessments be important?

- Will students be judged more on their subject matter competency than on seat time as measured by Carnegie units?
- Will online learning be the norm and classroom-based instruction the exception?

These and many other issues stand as major unknowns for the future of college and career readiness. The one certainty is that education will look very different than it does now in both the secondary and postsecondary arenas.

This chapter explores these and related issues to gain some insight into how teaching and learning might change in the foreseeable future, particularly around the interface of high school and postsecondary education, and what this might mean for the enterprise of education generally and for the Common Core State Standards and the consortia assessments specifically. To do this also requires at least touching on how instruction in college might change. Whole books have been written on this subject, and this brief discussion only highlights some of the key issues to illustrate their potential effect on the notion of college and career readiness.

Clearly issues of cost will drive the emergence of new approaches to the delivery of a postsecondary education, many of which will likely be built around competency models in which students move through programs at the rate they demonstrate mastery of defined knowledge and skills. "Badges" and "stackable certificates," indicators of competence in specific areas, are already emerging as models in which competency is the defining criterion. The line between high school and college is already blurring as secondary students have more options for collecting college credits, a trend that is likely to increase with the ability to demonstrate competency independent of the context in which it was acquired.

Career readiness is growing in importance as far more occupations require certificates that can be obtained only with education or training after high school. Our family wonders, What kind of careers will be available to our granddaughter? Will she need to accumulate degrees and certificates, or will she have to demonstrate competencies? Online learning, the other great unpredictable factor in the evolution of postsecondary education, will demand more of students, particularly the need for them to take more direct ownership of their learning and responsibility for managing the learning process. How should we go about preparing our granddaughter now for a postsecondary education that may be different in so many ways from what her parents and grandparents experienced?

A host of other issues will also be playing out at the K–12 level, particularly over the next five or so years. During that time, the impact and long-term prospects for the Common Core State Standards will become clearer. If they emerge as true national standards, issues about how they will they be maintained, revised, updated, and improved and who "owns" them will become much more important and pressing.

The consortia assessments face the challenge of surviving beyond the initial federal funding they have received. To do so, they must deal with complex questions regarding how will they will be managed, whether or to what degree they need to be consistent across consortia and states, and whether or how many individual states will begin to diverge from the current two consortia by adding or subtracting elements. While work is already well underway to address these and related issues regarding the future of the consortia, the dynamic landscape of ever-shifting state education policy priorities, goals, and players may upend even the most carefully crafted consortia transition plans.

If US schools adopt and deeply implement a set of common content and instructional practices, the possibility for high-quality instructional material derived from research on specific standards increases. New technologically based systems offer the potential for dramatic increases in individualization (selecting the topics each student needs to learn individually from among the Common Core State Standards) and personalization (relating the Common Core to each student's personal interests and aspirations). If colleges become more competency friendly, the nascent movement toward competency-based learning in secondary schools may blossom and offer the first real challenge to the time-based measure of student achievement, the Carnegie unit, in a hundred years. These issues and many others will influence the co-evolution of elementary and secondary education in tandem with postsecondary education. This interactive process, where changes in one influence and generate changes in the other, will lead to faster evolution and, at times, more disruptive change than in any period since the early 1900s, when industrialization and rapid immigration exerted a similar transformative effect on elementary and secondary schooling and its relationship to college and the workplace.

What Will "Ready" Mean?

The current definition of *readiness* offered in chapter 2 is built around students being able to succeed in credit-bearing, entry-level college courses without the need for remediation, particularly in relation to their area of interest. It is a definition that does not take into account institutional variation in the nature and challenge level of entry-level courses or in the range of potential student interests. This definition is useful because it expresses well the need for alignment between high school preparation programs and college expectations. It does not, though, go so far as to suggest that students need dramatically different knowledge and skill sets for each of the thousands of programs of study available in the nearly four thousand postsecondary institutions in the United States.

It does mean that readiness can be better defined and assessed, and then aligned with college and program types. Research on college readiness is beginning to provide much more detailed profiles and descriptions of readiness at the level of programs of study. These findings can be used to determine better where individual students stand in relation to their aspirations and the expectations they will face in college and job training programs. As this line of research continues to mature, students will be able to think of readiness in terms of four or five levels of knowledge and skill cross-referenced against a dozen or more pathways that comprise groups of occupations, careers, or college majors. While this model requires significantly more information than a single score on an admissions test or state exam or a grade point average currently provides, its effects will be powerful and will help to increase first-year college success rates and speed time to degree completion. Doing so will reduce student debt, a key goal in the immediate future, and will also allow postsecondary programs to be held more accountable for the decisions they make to admit students and the support they provide those they admit.

It's worth noting that none of this is meant to suggest that all students should not be provided the opportunity to learn all of the Common Core State Standards. A challenging program of study is key for all students to develop a strong core knowledge and skill set. Given the opportunity to learn the Common Core, some students will excel in one or more areas and perhaps not fare quite as well in others. These students should be allowed to begin their postsecondary education without penalty if their areas of strength align with their career aspirations and the postsecondary programs they are entering. This is particularly true when students also possess the strong motivation and self-management skills that can help them overcome skill deficits in selected areas.

This section turns now to several other dimensions of how the notion of readiness may evolve. It begins by positing that more data will be available on more dimensions of readiness and then presents a more in-depth discussion of competency models and their implications for specifying and assessing readiness. While the notion of competency-based approaches may not be brand new, the large-scale use of competencies to determine college and career readiness, explored briefly in the 1990s, may soon become more commonplace.

Increased Use of Data

Readiness in the future is likely to be much more data driven. Pretty much every other area in the economy and the society is using more data to make decisions. Whether it's supermarkets or insurance companies learning about consumer preferences and behaviors, or political campaigns using crowdsourcing and demographic analyses, data on individuals and groups are becoming more sophisticated and ubiquitous as tools to make decisions about how organizations can best achieve their goals, whether those goals are turning a profit or electing a candidate. While the ways in which data are collected and used certainly raise a host of issues, these practices are likely here to stay. Much can be learned about how data are used in other sectors to better meet individual needs and achieve organizational goals simultaneously.

 Readiness in the future is likely to be much more data driven.

If it's possible to know so much about people's shopping habits, why isn't it possible to know more about what students know, how they learn, and what they're interested in? The field of education is moving in this direction, but slowly, in fits and starts, and with the burden of legacy data systems that limit the type and amount of information that can be collected and how it can be used. The reality is that for all the information schools collect about students currently, teachers actually know very little about what each individual student knows and doesn't know and how best to get all students to learn more. Unfortunately, most of the proposed augmentations in data collection are going to result in more information about the same few areas where most data are currently being collected.

In the future, schools will likely gather more information on a wider range of student attributes, including behaviors, aspirations, challenges, and interests. This information will help students and colleges make better decisions about how prepared students are generally and for specific majors or programs. This information will eventually tell students how ready they are for particular types of colleges and for specific programs of study at those types of colleges.

Students will not prepare for "college." Instead, they will give more thought earlier to their interests and goals, and they will have much more information about the postsecondary options that align with those interests and goals. Student ownership of learning, emphasized throughout this book, will be a key component in a new model that is more interactive with and adaptive to the individual. Rather than simply taking a prescribed set of courses, students will pay closer attention to the competencies they are developing and how those relate to their aspirations and goals.

The danger, of course, is that schools will prescribe particular futures for groups of students based on assumptions of what they are capable of doing or achieving. This is now a widespread practice, and the goal with the implementation of any new data system or set of indicators should always be that it decreases social sorting and creates new opportunities for students rather than limits them. The fact is that the changing reality of the US economy and its need for more highly skilled workers should give schools far fewer incentives or excuses in the future to group students inappropriately or encourage some students to adopt lower goals than others. The introduction of adaptive systems to determine readiness need not result in the perpetuation of the worst aspects of the institutionalized social stratification that has been the legacy of tracking, poor counseling, and notions of ability. These practices have characterized far too many US high schools for far too long. Introducing more data and options to students and supporting and encouraging them to aim higher can be done in ways that get them to develop higher aspirations. Fear of social sorting as an inevitable outcome should not deter us from collecting more information that students, parents, and teachers alike can use to explore the range of possible futures available to students and for students to see what they need to do to be prepared to pursue the future of their choice. In fact, the only way to counteract social sorting effectively is to provide students with real options, opportunities, and visions of possible futures.

Competency Models

Competencies as a means to determine college readiness have been gradually gaining momentum and credibility since the first competency-based college admission systems were piloted in the early 1990s in Oregon, Wisconsin, Georgia, and, on a more limited scale, elsewhere. A proficiency approach to admissions details the knowledge and skills colleges expect of entering students that can be assessed or recorded and reported. If more students are to become college and career ready, K–12 education will likely need to use competency or proficiency principles for at least some students, if not all.

Competency-based approaches differ from mastery learning and other skill-based models because competencies are larger collections of skills. Rather than consisting of dozens of fine-grained bits of knowledge—the declarative knowledge level—a competency model focuses at the procedural and conditional levels, where students apply knowledge in integrated and sophisticated ways. Competencies are generally better measures of readiness because they align more closely with the actual tasks that students will need to be able to perform in college and careers. They also create a framework for the development of curriculum models, specific courses, individualized plans of study, progress monitoring, and assessments, both performance based and traditional, that, when combined into a system, let students demonstrate proficiency on key competencies.

Learning progressions support competency-based models because they allow the teaching and assessment of larger constellations of knowledge and skill that have to develop across grade levels. A learning progressions model also supports the use of a novice-expert continuum to report performance as students progress from novices toward emerging experts in their content knowledge, in their cognitive development, and as strategic learners. Key competencies can be more complex in nature, can take longer to develop fully, and can be demonstrated at different points in time through a variety of tasks and methods that capture student expertise more validly.

Competency Models and Key Readiness Proficiencies At the heart of the competency approach is the idea that key knowledge and skills must be identified, taught, mastered, and demonstrated rather than determining college eligibility on the basis of high school titles, grade point average, and admissions tests, each of which has significant limitations in its ability to gauge competence. Reading and writing skills, in particular, can manifest through a range of projects and products, such as the ability to analyze literature, read informational texts, conduct research reviews, and write expository papers. Mathematics proficiency requirements can require students to demonstrate understanding of mathematical concepts, as well as content, by applying mathematics to other subject areas, such as science and social sciences, with tasks and assessments in those subject areas.

A competency approach as applied to postsecondary readiness first identifies what students need to know and be able to do to succeed after high school and then assesses key knowledge and skills as directly as possible to determine if student performances are at the level of postsecondary readiness. The consortia assessments will have a college readiness level and a career readiness level (this may be the same or different, depending on the final decisions of the consortia) that provide some overall insight into student competence in the math and English tested. Proficiency evidence can come from additional sources beyond the consortia exams, for example, classroom assignments, tests, performance tasks, demonstrations, projects, and presentations.

One development that encourages wider use of competency or proficiency-based admissions models is that research is offering a much better understanding of the nature and content of college courses and the expectations of college instructors. This research includes examples of college courses that high schools can use to develop proficiency models, what are called reference courses. (See the appendix for examples of reference courses in the ReadinessConnect section.)

Schools can refer to sets of validated college readiness proficiencies as they develop their competency- or proficiency-based programs. The Common Core State Standards offer the latest and most refined version of college- and career-readiness competencies, and other sets exist as well. Schools have these available as points of reference that help inform the design and sequencing of instructional programs focused on key knowledge and skill acquisition and demonstration.

With the emergence of all the components necessary for a competency approach that is compatible with postsecondary readiness, proficiency-based college admissions may become more feasible in the near future. A first small step in this direction occurred when in 2013 the US Department of Education allowed course credits earned through competency-based grades, not just seat time, to fulfill eligibility requirements for federal student aid. Widespread adoption of proficiency-based admission systems by postsecondary institutions will promote and support such approaches to grading in secondary schools. One advantage is that an individual teacher can allow those students capable of demonstrating proficiency earlier in the course to do so and complete the course and then devote more time and energy to assisting students who need more help. Another potential advantage is that some students may be able to "test out" of courses more easily by demonstrating competency, thus helping to reduce class size somewhat or accelerate time to graduation. When and if this happens, the stage is set for dramatic changes not only in instruction and assessment but in the design of secondary programs more generally. When competency becomes the dominant way of determining knowledge and skills, students can learn what they need to know and demonstrate their learning in many different ways. They can move through the curriculum more at their own pace. They can seek help when they need it, but also take far more owner-ship of their own learning.

Competency Models, Certificates, and Postsecondary Education Although colleges have not forgotten or abandoned the importance of intellectual development, they find themselves caught in a marketing dilemma whereby the only way to get students (and their parents) to pay rapidly increasing tuition rates is to emphasize the economic value of a college education over its ability to expand students' thinking strategies and worldviews. In doing so, colleges stress how their programs develop marketable skills, connect students with workplace opportunities, and lead to employment directly after graduation. In other words, they have been forced to emphasize the instrumental value of a college education.

Whatever the downsides of this bargain that colleges are making with students, the increase in instrumentality does set the stage for greater speci-fication of key skills and the direct assessment of them. Once this begins to occur on a large scale in colleges and universities, the next step is likely to be the awarding of certificates in specific skill areas in addition to (and perhaps eventually in place of) a bachelor's degree. For example, a student who completes several complex problems successfully in several classes and then submits an integrative project addressing a range of problem types might receive a certificate in problem solving. Students who complete mul-tiple literature syntheses and research projects might receive a research certificate. In the sciences, such certificates could demonstrate mastery of specific skills, such as sequencing DNA or interpreting geological data.

Currently, programs leading to certificates are commonly offered at the postbaccalaureate level. They are used most often by workers to update skills and qualify for new jobs in numerous professional areas. The cred-its are often awarded through university extension offices and may apply toward a master's degree as well. The big shift would be for the certificate concept to permeate undergraduate education as well and become a com-ponent of or a replacement for a bachelor's degree. Undergraduate cer-tificates are a concept quite distinct from these postgraduate certificates or the occupational certificates offered at community colleges.

The undergraduate certificates would be awarded for intellectual and knowledge skill sets in particular topical areas within bachelor's degree majors. If this were to happen, undergraduate students would have mul-tiple focal points for their education, working to acquire as many relevant certificates as possible on the way to the bachelor's degree. Taken to its logical extension, a bachelor's degree would be awarded based entirely on certificates. The concept of "stackable certificates" presents a vision of how an undergraduate education could come to comprise a series of certificates, each signifying a key skill set, collected after taking three or four courses and then demonstrating competence on tests, projects, or culminating projects in order to earn each of perhaps a dozen certificates.

Students in majors with less direct ties to jobs could conceivably earn certificates in areas such as oral communication, which would reflect their ability to engage in informed discussion and argumentation, and make presentations to groups. Such a skill could be valued by employers seeking individuals who are able to communicate effectively internally with work groups and externally with clients. An individual with strong, demonstrated communication skills could then be taught the specifics of the company's line of work. Writing is another one of these communication skills for which a competency certificate would be extremely valuable and marketable. Employers are looking for individuals who can express themselves clearly and concisely in writing and who have a command of the conventions of the English language. A bachelor's degree is not currently the best guarantee that an individual possesses this skill set, but a certificate would be.

This same approach could be extended to college majors themselves and content mastery within them. For example, an economics major could receive a certificate in econometric modeling or cost-benefit analyses. Sociology majors could receive certificates in quantitative analysis techniques, survey instrument development, and database analysis. The granting of the certificate would require additional assessment beyond what commonly occurs in courses and would occur after a sequence of courses focused in one skill area had been completed. For the more occupationally aligned degrees, such as business, the opportunity to offer certificates would be a natural fit with their course structure and the content being taught. In addition to having a major and minor, business students might receive a series of certificates for specific business-related skills, such as marketing research, business plan development, or entrepreneurship. This is a practice that has some history in schools of this type, and it will be relatively easy to build on and expand the use of certificates. What will be new will be the quality and challenge level of the assessments used to demonstrate mastery necessary to earn the certificates.

Competency Models and Student Ownership of Learning A competency assessment framework will be far more challenging for many students because they will need to own their learning to a much greater degree than they do currently in order to succeed. Far too many students today do not feel very accountable or responsible for their own learning. Right now, many US students in secondary and postsecondary schools struggle with the ability to take ownership of their learning.

> Far too many students today do not feel very accountable or responsible for their own learning.

At the heart of the problem are conflicting worldviews between traditional instruction and competency models and how each conceives of the degree of responsibility students need to take for their learning. Teachers control the access to learning in traditional secondary school instructional models. However, the student is able to shift some of the responsibility for learning back onto the teacher by refusing to do more than the minimum that is asked. A competency approach gives students the ability to exert much more control over their own learning. In a competency model, instructors are responsible to provide students with necessary instruction and support to succeed, but ultimately students bear primary responsibility for their own success. This necessitates greater involvement by students in learning.

The challenge inherent in the new Common Core standards for college and career readiness is that the standards are more cognitively complex and cannot be fully mastered without deeper cognitive engagement, which requires significantly more student ownership of learning. This added engagement is unlikely to occur in environments where teachers fully control learning and students are simply complying with dictates.

For students to learn the Common Core through a competency approach, teachers will need to create learning environments where students will succeed to the degree to which they demonstrate strong self-management skills, including the ability to organize their time, keep track of assignments, make sure they access required material, prepare to study, devote sufficient time to completing assignments, and seek help when they need it. While these behaviors are not greatly different from what effective students do in general, they are somewhat less important in highly structured, sequential learning environments where teachers exert close management over instruction and student engagement. Getting students to produce work that demonstrates their competency, not just their compliance, will challenge teachers to let loose and will challenge students to take the reins.

Neither will be entirely comfortable doing so, and a period of uneven transition will have to ensue. In the end, students will reach higher levels of learning as they demonstrate their competency on learning standards that ask them to engage fully and push themselves closer to their limits.

Competency Models and Online Learning The discussion of certificates, also called badges by some, leads naturally to a consideration of online learning in postsecondary education. Why is this a natural connection? Because competency models lend themselves to multiple delivery modes in addition to face-to-face instruction, particularly online models. If the key requirement is to demonstrate competency, then the way the knowledge and skills are acquired is less important. Students need not sit in a class for an entire academic term if they can complete a challenging assessment sooner than that and earn their competency designation for that class.

Online learning has been held out as a potential solution to some of the problems that higher education faces now. Somehow, it seems, most degrees will be shifted overnight to an online format, thereby dramatically reducing cost and time while increasing access and convenience. The recent advent of massive online open courses, known by the awkward acronym of MOOCs, has led to an almost giddy, euphoric view of the potential online learning possesses to make postsecondary learning available across the globe to everyone at almost no cost to anyone. However, indications exist that growth in online courses in college is slowing somewhat and students are expressing some dissatisfaction with them. It may be necessary to rein in the hyperbole until some key issues are resolved.

One of these issues is the role of competencies and the ability to assess them online. In short, not everything taught in every course can be assessed well online, particularly if the competencies are complex. What this means is that the assessment methods used by online courses will need to improve. Students in the future might not be assessed just on the knowledge taught in each individual class. Some assessment might be designed to measure more complex cognitive strategies developed across courses. Right now, online assessment works best when it measures explicit knowledge, where right and wrong answers prevail. When a subject requires more complex cognitive capabilities, a more complex assessment strategy is required.

For online courses to assess more complex aspects of student learning without raising the cost of these courses too much will require more attention to effective ways to grade more complex work products, such as research papers. Current solutions bank on advances in artificial intelligence scoring engines. Other methods may emerge as well that allow for the large-scale scoring of more complex student work. If this occurs, expect to see a wider range of online courses, including those that teach more intellectually demanding topics and assess more student thinking and not just basic content knowledge.

A Blurring of the Line between High School and College

As a practical matter, receiving college credit or competencies in high school is going to become increasingly important. Significant increases in the number of college credits earned in high school can be predicted if for no other reason than that it helps keep down the cost of college. In addition, research has demonstrated that students who have a college-like experience while still in high school are likely to do better when they get to college. The net effect will be to blur the sharp dividing line now in place between high school and college.

The methods for offering credit to high school students are relatively well known:

- Advanced Placement (AP) or International Baccalaureate (IB) examinations where students may receive college credit for scores above a level designated by the college
- Concurrent enrollment courses taught at the high school where students receive both high school and college credit for the course
- Early attendance in college courses on a college campus by high school students
- Online college courses taken for college credit only
- Early enrollment in college through high school programs that allow students to earn an associate's degree while completing a high school diploma

Some states have set the requirement that all students take at least one college course before graduating from high school, though few high schools manage these programs in a systematic fashion that integrates them well with secondary-level courses. The jump from a regular high school course to any of the college-level courses is often abrupt, limiting the number of students who succeed in college courses while in high school or take full advantage of postsecondary options.

One of the changes that can be predicted to occur in high schools is the growth not only of programs that allow secondary students to obtain college credit, but the development of a continuum from high school course to college course. Instead of having to make the leap all at once, students will be able to try out college or at least have some college-like experiences more gradually and with greater support. The key to this will be careful calibration of the progression of middle and high school courses so that college-like expectations are integrated into the course sequence from middle school on, with increasing approximations of a college challenge level.

High schools will likely develop closer partnerships with local colleges to create more seamless transition programs for their students. These partnerships will use more data on student performance in college. They will lead to more concurrent enrollment courses being offered at the high school campus by properly trained and certified high school instructors. Enrollment in AP courses and students taking AP exams can be expected to continue to increase as well, although perhaps not quite at the rate of the past decade and a half. The program has the advantage of consisting of thirty-three different subject areas, thereby offering something of potential interest to almost every high school student. Of course, not all of these courses can be offered on any single high school campus, but the growing availability of online AP courses will widen student access to all students seeking an AP option.

For students not ready for a college-level challenge, high schools will likely offer more college readiness seminars to help a wider range of students gain greater awareness of the expectations they will face as they go on to college and what they can do to prepare now. These seminars will include visits from recent graduates who have made a successful transition to college, as well as presentations from local college faculty.

Students in these seminars will prepare mock college applications and review college course catalogues to understand general education requirements and to learn about the demands of the major they hope to pursue. They will sign up with online services that help students organize their materials to apply to college and explore institutions of potential interest to them.

This type of seminar is already mandatory for every student at some high schools. When a high school has many students who would be first in family to attend college, the only way they can learn about the postsecondary expectations they will encounter is through their high school. Increasingly, high schools will take on this role as the population of first-generation college attendees continues to swell. The college readiness seminar is yet another example of how the line between a high school and a college education will begin to blur, and the two will overlap more.

The Future of the Common Core State Standards and Consortia Assessments

The potential changes in higher education explored so far in this chapter do not depend on the existence of the Common Core State Standards or the consortia assessments. The Common Core and its attendant assessments can certainly promote and encourage better connections between high schools and colleges, and they should lead to improvements in student readiness for postsecondary studies. They can help to establish a clearer benchmark for college and career readiness, one that colleges and universities can use as their point of reference for specifying necessary competencies, making decisions on placement, and ultimately determining applicants' potential for success in college and in their chosen program of study or major.

For the Common Core State Standards and consortia assessments to have an effect on K–12 and postsecondary education, they will first need to survive. Some organization will need to own them. The methods by which they will evolve, adapt, and improve over time will need to be specified in detail and put into practice. Recall that educational governance in the United States is still highly decentralized and localized and that although the federal government has demonstrated heightened influence over the past decade, current breezes are blowing in the direction of less rather than more federal involvement in education policy. This suggests the next chapter in the story of the Common Core and consortia assessments will lie outside federal control and in the hands of whatever group takes ownership of the Common Core.

The US Department of Education's 2009 Race to the Top competition, in which states competed for major amounts of federal funds if they agreed to pursue certain reforms, was a major influence on many states' decision to adopt the Common Core State Standards. This type of massive, competitive expenditure of funds is not likely to be repeated anytime soon, however. While the 2012 district-level version of Race to the Top may be repeated, the $4.35 billion for Race to the Top and the $350 million devoted to the two consortia of states that developed Common Core assessments are strictly one-time monies. The Department of Education will support implementation of its vision of standards-based reform focused on college and career readiness. However, its leadership role on Common Core implementation is likely to be limited to technical assistance activities. Department staff do retain control over the consortia through 2015, but they will need to be considering their exit strategy sooner rather than later.

Who Will Support Implementation?

States, in partnership with national organizations, will be called on to provide the leadership to implement the standards and keep the assessments moving forward. As noted in chapter 7, the Council of Chief State School Officers, the group representing most of the state chief education officers, along with the National Governors Association, were the original developers of the standards, with significant support from groups such as the Bill & Melinda Gates Foundation and Achieve. These groups will likely continue to play a decisive role in the future of the Common Core State Standards. However, the range of organizations with a stake in the standards and assessments is growing, as the following sections illustrate.

 The range of organizations with a stake in the standards and assessments is growing.

The range of organizations with a stake in the standards and assessments is growing. *The Business Community* Several major corporations, under the banner of the US Business Roundtable, took up the cause of the Common Core State Standards and mounted major ad campaigns and produced material to promote heightened emphasis of the need to improve mathematics and science performance in particular. While corporate support for the standards is not viewed positively by all, these organizations do provide a major pillar that lends legitimacy to the standards, particularly in the eyes of some policymakers and elements of the general public. Corporate support is likely to create a degree of automatic backlash among those who are suspicious of the motives of corporations and with educators who are uneasy about public education being yoked to the needs of profit-seeking institutions generally and major multinational corporations specifically. On balance, however, support from the business community is likely to lead to a broader acceptance of the Common Core State Standards.

Philanthropic Foundations Many philanthropic foundations beyond the Bill & Melinda Gates Foundation are supporting implementation in significant ways. The Hewlett Foundation and the Carnegie Corporation of New York are two prominent examples. After twenty or more years of supporting projects designed to raise standards, Common Core State Standards solve some problems for national foundations that believe expectations for students should be higher and consistent across all states. The Common Core and its assessments offer some foundations a natural focal point where their efforts can be targeted for maximum effect. Implementation is such a massive issue that foundations have a natural need to collaborate if they support the Common Core in the first place. The boards of directors of many foundations truly believe in the Common Core State Standards and are enthusiastic about their potential to improve the US educational system dramatically, a goal to which many of the foundations subscribe.

Professional Associations of Educators National education groups, including the professional organizations for principals, superintendents, and curriculum developers, among many others, have gotten fully behind implementation of the Common Core State Standards. These groups view implementation as likely, and many now feature the Common Core and consortia assessments at their national meetings and in their communications to members. The two national teachers' unions, the National Education Association and the American Federation of Teachers, have lent their formal support to the Common Core State Standards, although some state and local affiliates are on the fence, particularly on issues related to the use of student achievement data from the consortia assessments for teacher evaluation purposes.

Educational Vendors and Their Customers Vendors are already offering a wide array of products and solutions designed to help all students learn the standards and perform well on the assessments, even as the assessments continue to be finalized and field-trialed. The Common Core State Standards solve a major problem for purveyors of a wide range of products and services that have heretofore had to be customized to the needs of each state. Vendors are now free to develop and produce a base product that is consistent across all adopting states and then work on any specific enhancements or adaptations with individual states. This is far more cost-effective than the old model. Having invested heavily in products that can be marketed nationally, vendors will have a tremendous vested interest in seeing the Common Core State Standards remain in place.

Vendors exert effects at other levels in the system as well. Once they have made a significant investment in the Common Core State Standards and consortia assessments, they will be highly motivated to lobby to maintain them. Vendors have more resources to devote to such activities and are not as constrained as educators from attempting to influence public policy by means of lobbying efforts. They also can offer deals and otherwise make it financially attractive for schools and states to stay the course on the standards and assessments.

The activities of vendors create another set of forces and constituents favoring continued implementation of the standards and assessments. School leaders who are now purchasing textbooks, curriculum, and training to align their schools' instructional programs to the Common Core State Standards will not take lightly any significant movement away from the standards once all the materials have been paid for and trainings conducted. At the least, they would raise their voices to demand resources and support if they were asked to take on any replacement for the Common Core State Standards and consortia assessments. They would caution against changing so soon after such a massive initiative. They would point out the myriad practical effects of abandoning the Common Core State Standards after such a significant investment in time, energy, and resources had been made.

Support from corporations, foundations, educational professionals, and vendors will potentially help get the standards and assessments over a critical hump. Right now, they have no permanent home and no organizational structure to maintain them and manage their evolution, including the programs of research and improvement that they will soon need. The standards and assessments require separate support systems, but they will have to be kept closely connected by whoever ends up owning each or all of the three pieces—the standards and each of the consortia assessments.

The Wild Cards Affecting Implementation

The wild cards at the state level affecting implementation are governors and legislatures. Many politicians define themselves as much by what they oppose as by what they support. It is hard to imagine the Common Core State Standards and consortia assessments not coming under fire as new administrations are seated in many states. They did not vote on or agree to the requirements associated with either the standards or the assessments. More ominous, the Common Core in particular can be portrayed as having been foisted on states by the federal government through Race to the Top, not the best rationale currently to adopt or support a program.

Implementation will be affected by how quickly the standards and assessments become an integral and normal part of schooling. Once this happens, the political calculus of changing or replacing them begins to change. Full implementation needs to happen before an issue arises in a state where some word in some standard is challenged, some question on a consortium assessment is called out as inappropriate, or anything else, real or imagined, results in a blanket condemnation of and general attack on the standards and assessments. Once implementation reaches a tipping point, it will become nearly impossible to dislodge the standards and assessments with ease. However, reaching such a point will probably take several years in most states. In the interim, the potential for politicians to seize on the standards and assessments as issues is very great.

Schools are very conservative in this respect. While it's difficult to get new practices implemented, it's far more difficult to remove them once they're fully in place. As new curriculum is adopted, training occurs, lessons are changed, test preparation practices are adopted, new lessons become more familiar, parents start to understand the standards, various performance metrics creep into state accountability and school improvement systems, and the standards become fully internalized and incorporated into the mental maps teachers use to organize and conduct teaching and learning. As a practical matter, it would be difficult to come up with a drastically different set of content standards in English and in mathematics, meaning that most replacement systems would in any event be variations on the Common Core State Standards. While all these factors may not deter some politicians, it will become increasingly difficult as time passes to make the case that the standards are somehow fatally flawed in and of themselves, independent of how and why they were adopted initially.

Consortia Assessment Implementation and Other National Exams

The consortia assessments are a somewhat different story. It's a lot easier to change assessments than to change standards, although just as painful and messy. For example, many states have changed assessments multiple times while their standards have remained more or less the same. The Common Core State Standards can conceivably be assessed in numerous ways. The fact that two completely separate assessment systems have been developed to do so illustrates this point dramatically. Having done so opens the door to any of a range of additional assessments of the Common Core, and at least one national testing company has already taken advantage of this fact. One of the most difficult results to achieve will be keeping the two consortia of states intact and in agreement on the content of the precise assessment each state uses under the rubric of PARCC or Smarter Balanced. When will a state have changed what it does so much that its approach is no longer comparable to other consortia members? Under what circumstances or criteria will a consortium member no longer be a consortium member?

Issues will arise as student scores from the pilot administrations of the assessments are released, but the issues will intensify when the first full administrations take place in 2015. Educators, many of whom will have sworn allegiance to the Common Core State Standards and their states' assessment consortium, can be expected nevertheless to raise a litany of issues and concerns regarding the shortcomings of the consortia assessment their state uses, particularly in states where the results feed into high-stakes accountability determinations.

Policymakers in some states will want more information; others will want less. Some will want the consortia assessment to be the centerpiece of their state accountability system; others will not. Some will find the philosophy behind the consortium of which they are a member to be fully consistent with their states' educational values; others will find they are no longer in full agreement with the philosophy. Holding the consortia together will be truly challenging.

One possible result is the identification by states of a subset of standards on which student performance would have to be compared across states within a consortium. All members of the consortium would have to agree to test this minimum—what I am labeling the "core of the Core." A number of states are already moving toward the system of assessments model outlined in chapter 10 and will want to use the consortia assessments in different ways from fellow consortia members for whom the test is a primary or solitary measure of Common Core mastery. One likely scenario is for groups of states within a consortium to begin to drift away toward models that better reflect their educational and political culture, values, and priorities while at the same time remaining committed to comparing student performance on the "core of the Core."

Role of the ACT and the SAT Under this scenario, national college admissions exams such as the ACT and SAT would continue to have a role to play because they would continue to allow comparisons across all states. A surprising number of states, eight as of this writing, have adopted the requirement that all students be given the opportunity to take either the ACT or SAT even as they also move to implement the consortia assessment or have another state test. Many states seem to be withholding judgment on the viability of the Common Core State Standards and consortia assessments as eventual supplements to or replacements for national college admissions tests, and they are hedging their bets in the meantime. If the ACT and College Board adapt their traditional tests to be more in line with the Common Core, which each seems poised to do, they may be able to make a case that their exams yield equally useful information on college and career readiness and that their scores are more comparable across states than the consortia assessments, particularly if states begin to modify these to suit their own needs.

Intentionally or not, these admissions exams may be viewed as alternatives to the consortia assessments at the secondary school level, although the consortia assessments will have the advantage of more testing time to collect a greater amount of information because they are more longitudinal than ACT's EPAS or College Board's Pathways, which are administered once in middle school and twice in high school. The consortia begin collecting data at third grade, which gives them an advantage in schools that want to align instructional programs across levels and build around learning progressions. However, ACT released Aspire in 2013, which spans grades 3 to 11 and, the company claims, is fully aligned with the Common Core. If nothing else, the consortia assessments have spurred testing companies to make rapid upgrades in their tests and explore options for providing more information on how student scores reflect Common Core knowledge and skills.

A great deal of attention gets paid by the media to colleges and universities that have become less enamored with ACT and SAT. It appears that colleges will be reluctant to jump ship wholesale until and unless the consortia assessments remain stable and consistent across states long enough to be found to be at least as predictive of college success as traditional measures. Some states may simply mandate that a consortium exam take the place of the national admissions exams, but it seems unlikely that this will occur anytime soon in more than a handful of states, in part because the consortia are downplaying the possibility of using results from their tests for college admissions decisions, preferring to limit their use to remediation determinations, at least initially.

Role of the National Assessment of Educational Progress The National Assessment of Educational Progress (NAEP) could also be used to compare the college and career readiness level across states as it is now used to compare reading, math, and science skills. Administered in fourth, eighth, and twelfth grades, it is probably the best exam in the United States currently for making comparisons nationally in English language arts, mathematics, and science. The National Assessment Governing Board, the organization charged with managing and updating NAEP, is undertaking a series of multiyear, large-scale studies and projects to review and redesign the NAEP Frameworks, the statements of knowledge, skills, and abilities used to determine what will be tested on NAEP in each of the subject areas NAEP tests. This process will no doubt result in English language arts and mathematics frameworks that are more closely aligned with the Common Core State Standards than are current NAEP frameworks.

The National Assessment Governing Board is also undertaking a series of studies to determine if the twelfth-grade NAEP can be used as a measure of college and job preparedness. If findings from this research determine that NAEP is a viable measure of preparedness, which is functionally the same as readiness, the test will not displace the consortia assessments, but its results will be added to the mix when trying to determine at the state level how well prepared students within a state are for college.

The NAEP exams use a technique known as matrix sampling, whereby individual students each take one of several forms of the exam, each form covering a different part of the NAEP Framework in the subject area being tested. This allows NAEP to test a wider range of content in terms of topics and cognitive complexity. Because students are tested on only a portion of a framework, test items can be more complex and take more time to complete. One student might have a form with a lot of multiple-choice items, while another student may have items requiring constructed responses. By using large numbers of students and not reporting student-level scores, and not reporting school or district-level scores either (except for districts participating in a special program), NAEP can assess a far wider range of knowledge and skill, conceivably at a deeper level of cognitive challenge.

This means that in the final analysis, NAEP may be a potential indirect measure of the Common Core State Standards for states but not for individual districts, schools, classrooms, or students. The problems will come about if NAEP scores and those from the consortia assessments differ dramatically in the picture of college readiness they paint in a state. This has been the case for the past twenty years when state tests were compared to NAEP and generally reported far more students meeting standards than did NAEP, and it will bode poorly for the consortia if their alignment with NAEP is low without some clear explanation of why this is the case. Clearly the Smarter Balanced and PARCC assessments have an important role to play. They will provide unique and valuable information locally, at the state level, and nationally about students' knowledge of the Common Core State Standards. The precise means by which these two assessments will be managed and how they will evolve is another matter that leads us to ask the same question about the Common Core State Standards.

Owning and Improving the Common Core

The Common Core State Standards are already three years old at the time of the publication of this book. Most standards undergo some form of review every five years. If the Common Core State Standards were to be reviewed on such a cycle, planning for a review would have to begin about now. The review would likely be completed just as the results from the first administration of consortia assessments were being released. This timing would create challenges because teachers would rightly argue that they were just getting their instruction well aligned with the tests as the standards were about to be revised. The fact that most first reviews end up refining rather than changing the makeup of a set of standards dramatically is of little consolation. Educators will likely view any change in the Common Core with a degree of trepidation and concern because they will just be getting fully accustomed to the standards.

So when should the standards be reviewed, and by whom? The initial problem is that the future of the ownership of the Common Core State Standards is not entirely clear. They reside currently with the Council of Chief State School Officers and the National Governors Association but probably should not remain there permanently for a variety of reasons, most important of which is that neither organization is designed to host or revise standards. They are membership organizations for which a whole host of potential conflicts could begin to arise if some of their members favored handling the standards one way while others pushed for different ways.

Recently released voluntary national science standards will face the same problems regarding ownership and revision. Will it make the most sense to place all of the standards under the aegis of one governing structure and organization? Does it make sense to house them in an existing organization or create a new one just for this purpose?

It is perhaps not wise to speculate too much further on the specifics of how best to handle ownership of the standards because work groups are examining this issue in depth as this is written, and the ownership question may be resolved by the time this book is published or soon after. What can be done here now is to consider the review process in more detail along with some of the larger issues that will need to be addressed in any review, regardless of where the standards are housed.

 It is perhaps not wise to speculate too much further on the specifics of how best to handle ownership of the standards.

Reviewing and Revising the Common Core

Ignoring for the moment who might control the Common Core State Standards and therefore organize and conduct a review of them, what might result from such a review? Are any areas particularly strong candidates for revision? Do any need to be deleted? Any major omissions? The analysis I present here will not necessarily reflect what a majority of educators or the sponsors of the Common Core might say. It is a personal view that derives from previous research I have conducted on college and career readiness, content analyses of the Common Core State Standards, insight gained during my role as cochair of the Validation Committee for the Common Core State Standards, and my role as a principal consultant and advisor to the Innovation Lab Network, a group of states looking beyond the consortia assessments. Here is what I see as necessary. I venture no opinion on how likely it is that any of this will come to pass.

Address the Relative Importance of Each Mathematics Standard Although the mathematics standards seek to develop math skills students can use in all subjects, they were written, reviewed, and debated with significant influence by mathematicians. While this makes perfect sense, it also led to inclusion of a wide range of mathematics. The standards number about two hundred in total and are written in a way that often combines multiple skills in a single standard. They clearly represent a higher level of mathematical proficiency than is reached by all but the most demanding state standards.

One of the tensions in the development of mathematics standards generally is how to address the strong math demands of technical fields while still acknowledging that most occupations and degrees have less rigorous mathematics requirements. Students should surely be given the opportunity to learn challenging mathematics. The question, though, is what level of performance should be expected of all students. Any review of the mathematics standards would need to begin by establishing a stronger validity argument for each standard. The following questions should be asked:

- Is the standard absolutely fundamental?
- How does knowing it contribute to student readiness for college and careers?
- With which postsecondary programs of study does it connect?
- How broad is its real-world use and value?

It would make more sense to me to organize the mathematics standards into a hierarchy of need and value. No standards would have to be eliminated, because dropping even one standard at this point has the potential to create a firestorm of protest by those who would take this to be a lowering or diluting of the mathematics standards as a whole. Creating a structure for the standards can give states, schools, teachers, and, most important, students some greater guidance on which topics have the strongest and most immediate significance and value for their futures. Some states have called these "power standards," but I am conceiving of this structure not to be just for designating some standards as more important than others. The goal would be to identify the standards that have the strongest connection to college and career readiness in its broadest construction. As I've noted previously, the ultimate goal would be for students themselves to identify the standards of most immediate need to them to pursue their goals and achieve their aspirations while always having the opportunity to learn the full Common Core in math. Helping them do so would lead ultimately to their taking more ownership of their learning and being more motivated to learn more of the math standards at a higher level.

Some may view this as being inconsistent with the notion of a common core in the first place, but the Common Core State Standards in mathematics are going to represent a significant leap for many students. Schools will need practical strategies for raising the bar for students accustomed to doing the minimum asked of them. Some empirically supported insight into the relative importance of the standards seems like a reasonable starting point to establish before eliminating any without knowing which are truly important. For most students, it will be possible and perhaps necessary ultimately to afford them a modicum of flexibility on the combination of standards they master to be deemed college and career ready. Identifying the most foundational and relevant ones helps establish a clear framework that establishes what all students must do before being allowed to compensate for weaknesses in some areas with strengths in other areas.

Create a New Data Analysis and Interpretation Standard In order to help students develop analytical research skills that can be applied across subject areas, I would place much more direct emphasis on data analysis and interpretation, not just in the statistics standards but throughout the standards. Perhaps a specific data analysis and interpretation standard could become the ninth Standard for Mathematical Practice.

Most young people will be exposed in their daily lives to a tremendous amount of information they will be expected to comprehend in some fashion. Charts, graphs, tables, and other forms of data representation abound and are found in daily life in many settings inside and outside school and the workplace. I would argue for much stronger and explicit valuing of this type of data analysis and interpretation as a foundational mathematical skill.

Create an Explicit Technology Standard The use of technology as a tool is touched on briefly in both English language arts and mathematics, but it is not sufficiently well developed as a set of skills. Its importance as a learning tool needs to be specified to a greater degree. Many of the mathematics standards imply the use of a calculator or a variety of computer programs. Reading and writing both are becoming more technology intensive and integrated. Research requires a high level of fluency with a variety of technological tools. The skills needed to use these technologies should be explicit, not implicit as they are now, or the gap between technology haves and have-nots will continue to grow. Schools need to be encouraged even more strongly to integrate technology more fully and on a daily basis into the teaching and learning process. A Common Core standard devoted to technology as a learning tool would help promote this goal.

Elevate Speaking and Listening This is more an assessment than a standards issue, but it does have implications for how the standards are taught. As I've noted, speaking and listening are far more prominent and important in daily life and particularly on entry into a career pathway than are English and mathematics, and yet they will play a secondary role in the consortia assessments, at least initially. Elevating speaking and listening in importance through more direct, contextualized assessment of a wider range of the speaking and listening standards and by having a separate speaking and listening score will help keep the Common Core State Standards in step with the real needs of students and the expectations they will face as they move into the workplace and society in general.

Identify Key Learning Skills, Strategies, and Techniques Finally, the standards do not enumerate the learning skills, strategies, and techniques that students absolutely must master if they are to become self-directed, lifelong learners able to perform consistently well on the consortia assessments. These have been referred to as "noncognitive" skills, when nothing could be further from the truth. They require high levels of cognition for students to apply them successfully. They are better described as metacognitive learning strategies. Examples cited throughout this book include these:

- Being able to organize one's time
- Knowing how to study for a test, work with others on a project, and be able to persist when things don't come easily
- Realizing that effort is more important than aptitude
- Being aware of the quality of one's work and what it takes to produce quality work

- Having goals and aspirations and then demonstrating the behaviors necessary to achieve those goals

These characteristics and many others like them are at least as important as specific content knowledge in explaining the success, or lack thereof, of students who possess at least a foundational set of academic skills. Students at the higher end of the academic distribution aren't automatically smarter, but they almost always possess far more of the metacognitive learning strategies than do students at the lower end of the distribution.

In a nation fully committed, at least in principle, to closing the achievement gap between different ethnic, racial, and income groups of students, it seems incomprehensible that no one has been willing to consider the importance of developing the learning strategies of lower-achieving students as a means to close this gap. Even schools that devote tremendous resources to extra instructional time and academic support for students almost completely overlook the need to equip all students with a set of learning tools that allows them to master and retain content more efficiently and effectively.

The Common Core State Standards will never be complete until they address this issue. Specifying the content knowledge that everyone should have and assuming this will lead to equality of educational outcomes is problematic when some students have far more of the tools, techniques, and strategies it takes to learn the standards than do others. The general unwillingness to talk about what schools should be doing to enable all students to be effective learners results in the perpetuation of the learning gap.

The Overall Outlook

The likelihood at this point is high that the Common Core State Standards will be around for a while in one form or another. They quite comprehensively and completely describe the English language skills and mathematical content that all students should be aspiring to master to be college and career ready across a wide range of possible postsecondary programs of study. They support the creation of competency learning models, and they can help forge a tighter bond between secondary and postsecondary education. Even if some states abandon them, those states will find themselves influenced by the content of the Common Core. While the standards will need some tuning and issues of their ownership need to be resolved, the energy and effort that states and, increasingly, school districts are devoting to implementation are pushing them ever closer to the tipping point at which they will become an integral part of the US education system. Many challenges remain, to be sure, but the outlook for the Common Core State Standards is guardedly positive at the moment, and their role as a means to gauge college and career readiness in English language arts and mathematics also seems highly promising. While the future is nothing if not unpredictable, the Common Core State Standards are shaping up to be a vehicle for framing college and career readiness expectations for all students and a part of the educational future of the United States for some time to come.

ⓐ Awareness and Action Steps

- Explore further the idea that readiness has a component that relates to student aspirations and interests. What types of program models might allow students to explore interests without having to make an irrevocable choice about career?
- For an example of an entirely competency-based college degree program, visit the website of Western Governors University (http://bit.ly/1aq5KrU).
- For a look at the potentially disruptive effect of competency-based learning on postsecondary education, see the Center for American Progress's policy brief on this topic: "A 'Disruptive' Look at Competency-Based Education: How the Innovative Use of Technology Will Transform the College Experience" (http://bit.ly/11wiOFx).
- For an example of a fully developed and field-tested proficiency-based college admissions program, see Oregon's Proficiency-based Admission Standards System (PASS) (http://bit.ly/12bDTE5).
- For more on the notion of badges, see Jobs for the Future's white paper, "Portable, Stackable Credentials: A New Education Model for Industry-Specific Career Pathway" (http://bit.ly/11m557G).
- For more ideas on how to award college credit to high school students by offering quality college courses in high school, see the National Alliance of Concurrent Enrollment Partnerships (http://bit.ly/17WeTJz).
- For an overview on the notion of a senior seminar to get students more college ready, see the Senior Seminar Handbook description and materials at at:http://bit.ly/1bSG3y9.
- Review "Education to Employment," the McKinsey report that provides case studies and examples of how to prepare students for this critical transition (http://bit.ly/12TxbKC).

CONCLUSION

CHANGING DEMOGRAPHICS, NEW INSTRUCTIONAL CHALLENGES

It takes a long time to change educational institutions. Many steps are necessary to accomplish something as significant as implementing common standards and assessments. It is even more complex and challenging to bring high schools and colleges into closer alignment around a shared definition of readiness and then to use a wider range of indicators to determine readiness. Adding to the challenge is the fact that the world doesn't stand still. At the same time that schools are attempting to implement the Common Core State Standards and consortia assessments, myriad reforms and policy initiatives are being formulated by states and pushed out to be implemented in high schools and, increasingly, colleges.

The Common Core State Standards will not transform education in and of themselves. Twenty years of investment and effort by states to develop and implement standards that lead to improved student performance have yielded decidedly mixed results. Neither will assessments dramatically improve student achievement on their own, even if they are standards based, although stronger alignment between standards and assessments will increase the effects (and effectiveness) of both. New curriculum alone will not do the job, even when combined with standards and assessments.

The final ingredient essential to the educational transformation envisioned by the authors of the Common Core State Standards is high-quality instruction, a factor that has not been discussed very directly in this book but is implied in many places. The formula for improving US education, then, consists of these components:

- Standards that specify key learnings
- Assessments that measure important aspects of learning
- Increased student involvement in and ownership of learning, and
- High-quality instruction combined with quality curriculum

Put all these pieces in place, and substantially improved student performance will result. Students are unlikely to produce the types of demanding academic performances envisioned in the standards simply because they are presented with new standards, new assessments, and new curriculum materials. They need teachers who can lead and support their ownership of interesting and relevant learning activities at an achievable challenge level.

 The final ingredient essential to the educational transformation envisioned by the authors of the Common Core State Standards is high-quality instruction.

One predictable trend that will continue simultaneously with Common Core State Standards implementation is the shift in the demographics of students attending school in the United States. The change in the composition of high school graduating classes illustrates this shift dramatically. Estimates are that the number of high school graduates peaked in 2011 and will decline for several years before gradually increasing again to a new high in 2025. At the same time, the makeup of these graduates will continue to become more racially, ethnically, and economically diverse, a trend that has continued uninterrupted for the past two decades. White non-Hispanic students will constitute half of graduates in 2024. At that point, students of Hispanic origin will comprise about 30 percent of all graduates. Black non-Hispanic students will constitute just over 10 percent of graduates, with Asian/Pacific Islanders making up 9 percent and American Indian/Alaskan Native representing the remaining 1 percent. From that point in time on, white students become a minority of all graduates. The high school graduation cohort of the future will be composed entirely of minorities; no one group will be a majority.

What this means is that US schools will be implementing new and higher standards and attempting to get more students to achieve at a level needed to be college and career ready at the same time that the makeup of each successive class becomes more diverse, not only racially and ethnically but in terms of the number of low-income students. Many of these students have historically been more challenging to educate for a variety of reasons, some related to the organization and nature of schooling itself. The Common Core State Standards will not, in and of themselves, result in this more diverse and varied student body choosing to fully engage with the challenge of higher academic achievement the standards imply. The Common Core State Standards, fully implemented, will give students a greater opportunity to learn more of the key content in English language arts and mathematics that they will need to go on to success in college and careers. Classrooms will have to change dramatically if more students are to take advantage of the opportunity of the Common Core State Standards. This means more than just aligning content to the standards. Each class will need to offer high-quality, engaging learning opportunities that are assessed by a range of methods that provide information to students that motivates them to improve and that enable teachers to build on student interests and aspirations.

The challenge, as laid out in this book, is to get these students more actively involved in thinking about and planning their own futures and then take more ownership of their learning—in essence, taking more control over their lives. Many of these students will need to make very personal connections with the material they are learning. Compliance-based learning behaviors will not be sufficient for them to succeed in college or the workplace. This all needs to occur in school and classroom settings that provide students with new tools to take control of learning and that support them in making the transition to being empowered learners.

Rethinking education in ways that create much stronger connections between what students are learning and why they are learning it will not be easy. It will be a shift for teaching to focus on and incorporate students' interests and for schools to help their students explore broadly and deeply the college and career options available to them. Isolated pockets of success can already be found, and most schools seem committed to taking on in earnest the hard work of making instruction challenging and engaging, relevant and important, and of organizing schooling so that students can

 Rethinking education in ways that create much stronger connections between what students are learning and why they are learning it will not be easy.

succeed if they always give their best effort and seek help and support when they need it.

This book began by emphasizing the importance of involving students actively in their learning and of linking that learning to their goals and aspirations. This exceedingly difficult task may be the missing link to getting more students to meet the challenges of the Common Core State Standards. It also holds the key to preparing them for college, careers, and life in a dynamic, ever-changing global economy and society. When students get involved in their education and dedicated to their own success, teaching becomes a lot more rewarding, which can create a positively reinforcing cycle: more deeply engaged kids, more deeply committed teachers.

Implementation of the Common Core State Standards is much more than replacing an old set of standards with a new set and figuring out what's on a new test. It is the process of getting all students to want to take charge of their futures, adjusting instruction so that it engages students and connects challenging content with their interests and aspirations, and having postsecondary education be a plausible and important focal point for those futures. It is a challenge that I think many educators will find exciting and invigorating.

I began this book by noting that all teachers want students to learn. I close by restating this fundamental and often overlooked truism. The Common Core State Standards and new systems of assessment, coupled with increased deeper learning and greater student engagement can, if properly implemented and supported, help teachers reach this fundamental and foundational goal and, as a result, improve the chances that all students will be able to lead productive, successful lives.

APPENDIX

A NINE-PART READINESS SYSTEM

Bringing about the changes described in this book will require new tools for high schools and colleges to work on their own and collaboratively to increase the college and career readiness of all students. As has been noted, the US educational system was not designed to align well between K–12 and postsecondary education. This creates an extra burden on both systems to find ways to bring policies and practices into closer alignment so that more students can make a successful transition from high school to post–high school studies.

Many of the resources available to educators wishing to help students improve their prospects for postsecondary success focus on performance on tests, particularly admissions tests. Other systems help students make choices about which college to apply to or how to secure financial aid. Some are designed to increase student chances of acceptance to elite universities. College readiness is conceived of, for the most part, as acceptance into a particular program and not the ability to succeed subsequent to admission.

This is where the College Career Readiness System (CCRS) is different. Developed by the staff at the Educational Policy Improvement Center (EPIC) over the past decade, it addresses the multiple factors that affect readiness. Some of these relate to students, some to teachers, some to course design, some to postsecondary expectations, and some to relations and connections between high schools and postsecondary institutions and faculty. Each of the tools that make up the CCRS was developed based on research on how to improve college and career readiness and on the needs of schools in each of these key areas. These tools and techniques have been strategically selected and developed based on their ability to bring about the key changes schools need to make to get more students ready for college and careers.

Taken as a whole, the CCRS is designed to help schools design their overall programs so that they do a better job of making students college ready while also providing students with more information on their college readiness. To do this, the CCRS is organized in three categories: Calibrate, Create, Connect. These three categories are designed to enable schools to calibrate their practices based on a wider range of data on student readiness, create classes and courses of study that are well aligned with college and career readiness and success, and connect with postsecondary institutions in a way that results in more students making the transition to college successfully. What follows is a brief description of the tools and techniques that comprise the CCRS.

Calibrate

Calibrate means finding out more about how ready students are for college by gathering information on all of the four keys to college and career readiness explained in chapters 3 and 4 . The Calibrate dimension of the CCRS is composed of three elements: ThinkReady, CampusReady, and I'mReady.

ThinkReady

ThinkReady is a system of classroom-based performance tasks that develop in students key cognitive strategies that reflect what EPIC's research has found to be important for success in entry-level college courses. The key cognitive strategies are

- Problem formulation: Formulate hypotheses or theses before proceeding further, and develop strategies to complete the task.
- Research: Identify appropriate sources and collect information sufficient to address the problem.
- Interpretation: Analyze information using appropriate methods and evaluate results against rules and evidence criteria.
- Communication: Organize the response before writing or constructing, and construct according to the formats and rules of the discipline and with the audience in mind.
- Precision and accuracy: Monitor and correct mistakes throughout; then confirm the accuracy of all aspects of the final product.

ThinkReady tasks are scored using a guide that determines student performance on each of the key cognitive strategies along a novice-expert continuum. Tasks are developed at four benchmark levels, reflecting material normally taught in the sixth, eighth, tenth, and twelfth grades and then scored against criteria ranging from novice to expert. Students receive a designation of their performance at one of seven levels: emerging novice, novice, accomplished novice, emerging strategic thinker, strategic thinker, accomplished strategic thinker, and emerging expert. Tasks are administered at the beginning and end of the school year to gauge progress in the development of strategic thinking skills. School districts receive reports that display all student scores at the component level (figure A.1). Results over time show longitudinal progress toward becoming a strategic thinker, the level at which a student is college and career ready (figure A.2).

CampusReady

CampusReady is a self-report instrument that students, teachers, counselors, and administrators complete that contains a series of items for each of the four keys to college and career readiness. This online instrument takes about a class period to complete and is comprehensive in nature. The response patterns can be used to create a schoolwide action plan to improve college and career readiness. Individual students who complete CampusReady receive a diagnostic report of their readiness in each of the four keys to college and career readiness, along with recommendations for areas of potential improvement and resources to help them improve (figures A.3 and A.4). The schoolwide recommendations also are accompanied by links to recommended resources.

FIGURE A.1 DISTRICT AGGREGATE REPORT FROM THINKREADY

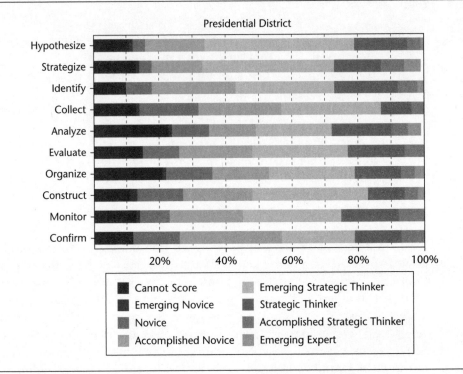

FIGURE A.2 STUDENT LONGITUDINAL REPORT FROM THINKREADY

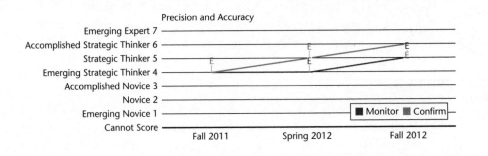

I'mReady

I'mReady is still in development. When completed, it will offer models for potential comprehensive profiles that combine information from a range of data sources to produce a more complete picture of student readiness for college and careers. The unique contribution of I'mReady is its

FIGURE A.3 STUDENT ASPIRATIONS REPORT FROM CAMPUSREADY

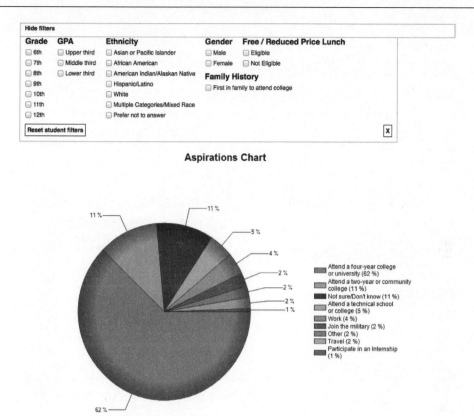

Aspirations Chart

ability to integrate information from diverse sources such as ThinkReady, CampusReady, high school grades, courses taken, admission tests such as the PSAT/SAT or EXPLORE/PLAN/ACT, Advanced Placement, International Baccalaureate, concurrent enrollment courses, and state tests, including the two consortia assessments of the Common Core State Standards. This profile is updated frequently with new information so that it yields a regular reading on the degree to which and the areas in which students are on course to be college and career ready. I'mReady also generates recommendations and maps out an action plan students can pursue to improve their readiness.

Create

Activities in the Create pillar enable schools to redesign or adjust their program of study so that courses are better aligned with one another, the

FIGURE A.4 MY COLLEGE READINESS DASHBOARD REPORT FROM CAMPUSREADY

My College Readiness Dashboard

CampusReady assesses the Four Keys to College and Career Readiness, a nationally recognized model developed by Dr. David Conley and the Educational Policy Improvement Center (EPIC) that identifies the knowledge, skills, and strategies that students need to be successful in college and the workplace. These are grouped into four areas that are critical to college readiness—Key Cognitive Strategies, Key Content Knowledge, Key Learning Skills and Techniques, and Key Transition Knowledge and Skills.

A report summarizing your school's college and career readiness is shown below. You can access more detailed reports to determine how your school compares to best practices by following the links provided below each of the Four Keys listed on this page.

The Four Keys to College and Career Readiness

Key Cognitive Strategies
The Key Cognitive Strategies are the patterns of intellectual behavior that lead to the development of s ills and capabilities necessary for higher order thinking.

View Report
View Item Level Data

Key Content Knowledge
Key Content Knowledge includes not only foundational knowledge but also the attitudes toward the core subjects that students need in order to value learning, be motivated, and expend the necessary effort to succeed.

View Report
View Item Level Data

Key Learning Skills and Techniques
Key Learning Skills and Techniques include the attitudes and behaviors that students need to succeed in college and the workplace.

View Report
View Item Level Data

**Key Transition Knowledge and Skills
(College Knowledge)**
Key Transition Knowledge and Skills include the privileged knowledge and skills that are necessary to apply to and enroll in college and to navigate the college environment.

View Report
View Item Level Data

Participation
By participating in CampusReady, you are already on the way to supporting college readiness! By meeting the participation criteria, you ensure that your results are representative of your school.

View Report

How does my school measure up?[*]

The overall ratings on the graph below summarize your school's performance for each of the four keys and your participation. Responses are provided and reported on a 5-point Likert scale.

Achieving

Key Transition Knowledge and Skills
Key Content Knowledge
Implementing
Key Learning Skills and Techniques
Key Cognitive Strategies

Developing

Participation   Emerging

Initiating

Indeterminate

Common Core State Standards, and college and career readiness. This is an area that is often overlooked by schools seeking to improve student college and career readiness in favor of programs such as financial aid night or college visitation day. Student-oriented programs are important, but to ensure that students develop the foundational knowledge and skills that will prepare them for postsecondary education, schools need to look closely at their instructional programs, a task that is both complex and challenging. The Create dimension of the CCRS is composed of three elements: CourseCreate, CourseAlign, and CoursePathways.

CourseCreate

CourseCreate is a tool that can be used to take the first step in aligning programs across levels: the development of high-quality syllabi for all courses.

No school can even begin to determine how well aligned its instructional program is internally or externally without clear specification of what is being taught in each course. CourseCreate is an online tool that employs a wizard-like process in which each teacher in a school is guided through a step-by-step process to build a syllabus that contains detailed information about the standards that are taught in the course, how those standards are taught and assessed, the prerequisite knowledge and skills necessary for success in the course, and the subsequent courses for which students who do well in the course will be prepared. In addition, the wizard prompts teachers to complete sections in which they elaborate on their expectations, course goals, activities, and attendance and behavior policies. Common boilerplate language can be inserted into fields for which schools wish to have consistent language in all syllabi.

CourseAlign

CourseAlign is a tool that allows comparison of the standards that are taught in each course to determine any overlap or omissions. Once all courses have high-quality syllabi that show which standards are taught, CourseAlign allows each course to be compared to the standards to which it should be aligned. It is then possible to make decisions about where various standards should be taught, particularly when areas of overlap and omission are identified. In this way, a school can ensure that all courses are properly aligned to one another so that all courses of the same title address the same standards and that all courses in a sequence across grade level teach standards in a way that is consistent with the learning progression of the subject area.

CoursePathway

CoursePathway is a tool to determine whether each student in the school is being afforded the opportunity to learn all of the standards necessary for college and career readiness. This tool generates a pathway analysis of each student's planned program (figure A.5). Because the syllabus for each course already lists the standards to be taught in the course, the pathway analysis aggregates all the standards students encounter in all of the courses on their transcript (and their planned program) and then yields a report that indicates if the student is on track to have the opportunity to learn all the necessary standards.

This type of tool is particularly useful to make sure students are not going to be tested on material they have not had the opportunity to learn.

FIGURE A.5 COURSE PATHWAY ANALYSIS REPORT FROM COURSEPATHWAY

CoursePathway™

Pathway Analysis

Standards

● All Components Submitted ✔ Submitted

◐ One or More Components Submitted

Common Core English Language Arts 11-12

COMMON CORE ENGLISH LANGUAGE ARTS 11-12 STANDARDS	PATHWAY CONFIRMED	ENGLISH 11 COURSE CREATE	MATH 101 RUTHERFORD BEE	ENGLISH 12 RUTHERFORD BEE
1. Cite strong and thorough textual evidence to support analysis of what the text says explicitly as well as inferences drawn from the text, in...	●	●		●
2. Determine two or more themes or central ideas of a text and analyze their development over the course of the text, including how they intera...	◐	◐		
3. Analyze the impact of the author's choices regarding how to develop and relate elements of a story or drama (e.g., where a story is set, how...	●			●
4. Determine the meaning of words and phrases as they are used in the text, including figurative and connotative meanings; analyze the impact o...	●			●
5. Analyze how an author's choices concerning how to structure specific parts of a text (e.g., the choice of where to begin or end a story, the...				
6. Analyze a case in which grasping point of view requires distinguishing what is directly stated in a text from what is really meant (e.g., sa...	●			●
7. Analyze multiple interpretations of a story, drama, or poem (e.g., recorded or live production of a play or recorded novel or poetry), evalu...	●	●		

Given that the test can't be changed to suit the student, the best alternative is to make sure the student at least has a chance to learn material on which he or she will be tested. The pathway analysis is the best way to handle what can quickly become an overwhelmingly complex process of trying to find out which students have been able to learn which standards.

Connect

The Connect pillar consists of activities and processes designed to build stronger linkages between secondary and postsecondary education for the purpose of understanding expectations and aligning programs. Connect activities are designed to address the fundamental disconnect between high school and colleges by providing specific tools and techniques that help high schools understand better the expectations of postsecondary institutions while also creating opportunities for secondary and postsecondary faculty to collaborate directly and indirectly in order to learn from one another and calibrate expectations for students more closely and tightly. The Connect dimension of the CCRS is composed of three elements: ReadinessConnect, ReadinessBridge, and ReadinessPartner.

ReadinessConnect

ReadinessConnect is a series of carefully developed, highly detailed model entry-level college courses organized in a way that allows secondary faculty to review them to understand better what their students will encounter once they enter college. These reference courses were developed by collecting and then synthesizing syllabi and other course documents from general education entry-level college courses at a wide range of postsecondary institutions. After the materials were synthesized, college faculty reviewed them and filled in any gaps so that the resulting reference course contains all the information necessary to understand the goals and purposes of the class, the key material taught, assignments, assessments, available help and support, and the roles learners are expected to take in demonstrating ownership over their learning. Reference courses are a good resource for internal conversations within a high school about how well current courses match up with postsecondary expectations at the entry level.

ReadinessBridge

ReadinessBridge is a novel means to develop alignment at the local level between the last course in a sequence taken by high school students and the first course they will encounter in that subject in college. The idea is to align the content, assessments, and expectations between the exit-level high school course and the entry-level college course by adapting syllabi at each level. The means to do this is a design conference in which high school and college faculty meet and compare syllabi. The result is to identify overlap in content coverage and then try to determine who should be teaching which content, along with identifying content, where it makes sense to introduce the topic in high school and then review it in college.

This paired-courses approach also creates opportunities for faculty to compare the degree to which they expect students to work independently, how they support students in need of help, and how they handle behavioral issues and other challenges. In the process, faculty often learn from one another and share and exchange tips and techniques. In places where these design workshops have been held locally, many faculty make connections that last beyond the paired-courses design process and lead to classroom visitations and exchanges between local high schools and colleges. The fact that this is a local approach to alignment makes it all the more powerful because everyone involved sees the immediate need and potential payoff.

ReadinessPartner

ReadinessPartner is a workshop format in which faculty from local high schools and colleges come together to build action plans to improve alignment and increase the number of students going on to successful postsecondary studies. Readiness Partner may be the first or the final step in the Connect process. In some localities, it makes the most sense for high school faculty to begin by looking at reference courses and considering how best to align syllabi before having a more general planning meeting focused on overall alignment. In other places, the reverse order is more effective: beginning with an orientation meeting in which faculty agree to a general plan of action, one that might include ReadinessConnect and ReadinessBridge or may involve any of a range of other activities, such as using the college- and career-ready level of the Common Core State Standards as a starting place for discussions of content coverage and performance expectations.

These workshops let high school and college instructors share specific observations about work quality and more general expectations for students in their classes. This can lead to changes in instruction and expectations at both levels. One interesting activity that has been incorporated into ReadinessPartner workshops is the sharing of student work, generally written products. This can be done either with blinded or nonblinded work. Blinded sharing is the process of combining the work from both levels into one set and having faculty from each level evaluate the work without reference to which level at which the work was produced. After reviewing the work, the level of each piece is revealed, and faculty have the opportunity to see the differences between a high school–level and college-level piece of work. In the nonblinded method, faculty simply exchange papers, read them, and discuss what they are trying to accomplish through the assignment and any challenges they face getting students to achieve at the desired level.

CCRS ThinkReady

ThinkReady measures the key cognitive strategies through engaging performance tasks that teachers conduct within existing lesson plans and that align with their curricular requirements. An example of a science task follows.

Plugged In: Analyzing Teen Media Use

Overview

Task Level Benchmark III

Time Frame Plan about two weeks for students to complete the task. Schedule in-class times for students to complete their research and word process their essays. Other work may be in or out of class, at teacher discretion.

Standards Addressed Standards for Scientific Practice (Framework for KÑ12 Science Education. Public Draft released in July 2011)

   ETS2.B: Influence of Engineering, Technology and Science on Society and the Natural World. How do science, engineering, and the technologies that result from them affect the ways that people live? How do they affect the natural world?

Grade 12 End Points

- Modern civilization depends on technological systems, including those related to agriculture, health, water, energy, transportation, manufacturing, construction, and communications.
- Widespread adoption of technological innovations often depends on market forces or other societal demands, but it may also be subject to evaluation by scientists and engineers and to eventual government regulation.
- Analysis of costs, environmental impacts, and risks, as well as of expected benefits, are critical aspects of decisions and technology use.

Prerequisite Knowledge and Skills Use the following list of assumed knowledge and skills to determine the appropriateness of this task for your students, in order to make it a fair assessment.

- Make predictions.
- Conduct independent research using appropriate sources.
- Summarize research results in written form.

Description

   New technologies can have enormous impacts on society. For example, today's youth are used to constantly accessing technology and may not even realize the number of hours that they spend plugged in to technology.

   This STEM task begins with students making predictions about their own use of Internet, mobile, and broadcast technologies, keeping individual logs for a week. After comparing their personal results to class members' results, they will research national and international trends in the use of technology. Finally, as students make predictions about long-term changes to technology, they will develop a proposal for new product that will address one or more issues related to technology use in the future.

Instructions for the Teacher

Preparation About using this task with your students: Though classroom differentiation is instructionally sound, ThinkReady tasks must be delivered as written in order to maintain their integrity as performance assessments. *If a task is modified, it should be considered a formative assessment for classroom use only, and student work samples that are obtained from modified tasks should not be graded or submitted in the ThinkReady system.*

Make a copy for each student of the Student Task Information and the scoring guides at the appropriate benchmark. You may distribute all pages of the Student Task Information at the start of the task or provide pages individually as students are ready for them.

Provide access to computers, the Internet, and a printer for students' research. If available, provide access to computers with word processing software for students to record their work, as appropriate, and to create their policy paper.

Students may benefit from access to some subscription-based resources, depending on their individual projects. Potentially useful sources could include publications such as *Education Week*, *Chronicle of Higher Education*, *Science News*, and MIT's *Technology Review*, as well as the *New York Times* and research journals, such as those published by the National Academies, the IEEE, AAAI, and ISTE.

Become familiar with sources of information on teens' use of mobile and online technologies in the United States and abroad and the potential impacts of these trends on such issues as teen health, employment practices, educational innovation, and the development of products.

Credible sources of information regarding U.S. teens' use of connected technologies can be found online and include the Pew Internet and American Life reports, Project Tomorrow's Speak Up surveys, and the Horizon Report's predictions about technology use in K–12 and higher education over the next five years.

Information about student use of connected technologies internationally may be difficult to find. One good source is UNESCO, which convened a "Mobile Learning Week" in late 2011 and has produced a series of working papers that examine the topic by region (Latin America, Asia, Europe, and so on).

Administering the Task Students will produce two different products to submit for ThinkReady tasks. The first part of the task has students label each component of the key cognitive strategies (such as Hypothesize) from the *directions*. These sections include explanations and reflections about what students are thinking and doing.

Once this preliminary work is done, students use appropriate information produced for each component to create the final product(s) that the original task instructions require.

Distribute the Student Task Information pages. Have students complete the name and course information on the cover page. Explain that students will submit all their work attached to this page, and they should *ONLY* write their names *on blank backs* of all other pages they submit. (Before they submit their work, you will facilitate a check by students to remove their names from pages as needed.)

Use this script and then have students read "The Task": "How do communications technologies affect the way people live? This is a huge question that is made more complex because communications technologies are changing rapidly. New gadgets, channels, applications, and communities are introduced and discarded almost overnight. As part of this task, you will be conducting a scientific inquiry that begins with predicting and observing your own behavior, then researching trends in the United States and elsewhere."

Clarify features of the real-life context that may be unfamiliar to some students, such as types and variety of communications technologies and social media, pointing out that "older" technologies, such as televisions and landline phones, are technologies that may be included in their research.

Continue using this script: "Based on your research and data, you will develop a proposal for a new technological product. Zero in on a particular pattern, trend, question, or impact of technology that you could study further. Propose a solution that will resolve one or more of these issues."

Distribute the scoring guides. Introduce or review the structure of the guides. Facilitate discussion of how students can use the scoring guides while working through the task. If students are new to using the guides, consider discussing the guides for one key cognitive strategy at a time as students approach each part of the task. You may facilitate understanding of the guides in several ways (for example, by holding a class discussion, by having students write the expectations in their own words, or by considering expectations at performance levels *above* and *below* the level of this task).

Continue, using this script: "Make sure you record all the thinking, justifications, and explanations for the work you do."

Let students know when they will work on the task and about how much time you expect they will need. Include due dates for parts of the task, if you wish. If students will use computers or other task-specific materials, provide instructions on accessing them.

Student Work Methods Students should work independently throughout this task.

Remind students to review the performance expectations in the scoring guides as they work.

Do not provide prompts beyond those in the task. You may paraphrase instructions or ask questions to elicit student understanding in order *to help students understand what they are being asked to do.* Similarly, you may paraphrase the scoring guides or ask questions of students to clarify performance expectations. By avoiding overprompting or excessive scaffolding, you will ensure the task is a true assessment of students' current abilities.

In order to give students feedback on their rough draft, you may provide feedback yourself, engage students in a peer review process, and/or ask them to do a self-review. When providing student feedback, it is appropriate to quote or paraphrase the scoring guides. It is not appropriate to give direct instructions on how to "fix" the work. You should be giving hints, not correcting students' work. If students will provide peer review, explain these guidelines to them.

Remind students to keep all drafts and their feedback for submission upon completion of the assessment.

Once students receive feedback on drafts they produce, have them use the *Assessing Your Work* sheet to reflect on the completeness and quality of their work before revising final versions for submission. Explain that they should score their work and defend their scores for each component using scoring guide language.

To collect students' work, use this script: "Collect each section of your work and organize it in the order presented in the directions—by key cognitive strategy. After that, attach your drafts, including the final draft. Remember that your name should only appear on the cover page and on blank backs of other pages. Your name should not be visible on pages that show your work."

Provide time for students to black out their names where necessary.

Facilitate Reflection After students have submitted their work, hold a class discussion to facilitate reflection on the experience. Was this task like any others students have completed? How might they use what they have learned on other science assignments? In other situations?

Include discussion of methods, conclusions, and implications to help students gain more understanding of using the key cognitive strategies to complete complex tasks. The intent is to develop students' insight into the nature and complexity of extended assignments. This is also an opportunity to clear up any misconceptions that may have occurred.

Vocabulary
- Adolescents
- Design proposal

Extensions Students could research the process of taking a proposal from idea to market. With parental permission, a student may even consider placing a proposal on kickstarter.com or a similar venue to try to make his or her idea a reality.

Student Task Information

Benchmark III: Science

Name _____

Course _____

If you put your name on pages submitted with this cover page, your name should be on blank backs of pages ONLY.

The Task

Plugged In As you consider potential career paths, there are many possibilities within the field of media technology that may interest you. Given the rapid pace of development in this field, many of the next decade's professions probably haven't even been invented yet! This task asks you to conduct research and make predictions about long-term changes to media technology. Then you will have the opportunity to put forward your own ideas for possible inventions that could meet the needs of future generations.

You will begin by making predictions about your own use of technology, which could include researching information on the Internet, using mobile devices, watching television, or playing video games. How many hours do you think you use these and/or other media technologies each day? Then you will need to log your daily use (for school and work, entertainment, and socializing) over the course of a week. How did your actual technology use compare to your predictions? Discuss your personal results with some of your classmates to see how your results compare.

In order to find out if you and your friends' use of media technology is similar to habits of other adolescents, research data on teens' use of technology in the United States and at least one other country. Compare the information you find with your previous results and identify trends.

You may not realize that many of today's technological products are a direct result of the habits that our society developed in the past. Based on your studies of teens' media technology use, design a product that you think will meet the needs of youth in the future.

- What problem is your new product designed to solve?
- How does your research on the use of technology back up your product proposal?

Final Product Write up your findings on your own technology use over the course of a week, as well as your classmates' use, that of your peers in the United States, and in one other country of your choice. Identify trends and make predictions about how you think technology is likely to change and adapt. Then use all of this information to design a new product that will be useful to teens in the future.

Directions This task involves completing a final product as outlined in The Task above. You will also create a ThinkReady Portfolio. This portfolio is a record of all of your work for this project. You will demonstrate how well you solve problems, research information, and communicate your ideas.

Save all of your work as you complete the sections. Organize your ThinkReady Portfolio in the order presented in the directions below (by key cognitive strategy). At the end of the entire task, you will submit all of your work attached to the cover page.

Problem Formulation   *This Section Due*:_____

Solving problems often involves considering more than one possible solution. First, you need to make sure you understand what the task is asking you to do. Then, take time to make a plan for your work.

Hypothesize In this section, you will think about the task and choose a topic for your research.

- Label this section of your project *Hypothesize*.
- *Write a hypothesis that contains a cause-and-effect or thesis statement.* Explain your thinking at this point.
- *Be sure that your hypothesis or thesis is written so that it might be able to solve the problem in the task.*
- *Be sure that your hypothesis or thesis makes sense and is complete.*

Strategize In this section, you will explain your plan to gather information and your steps to complete the project.

- Label this section of your project *Strategize*.
- List the steps you will take to successfully complete this project. Be sure that these strategies work with the science subject area.
- Be sure that your strategy or strategies address the problem in the task.

Tip: Remember that your first plan is only a place to start. It may change as you work on the task.

Research   *This Section Due*:_____

When you begin a task, be sure to consider all your options for finding information. The Internet is a good place to gather information, but not always the best place.

Identify In this section, you will explain your plan for finding information.

- Label this section of your project *Identify.*
- *Decide on a method for searching for information that you think will work with the problem outlined in the task.* Record your plans for collecting data and information.
- *Be sure that all the sources you might use are related to the problem.*
- *Be sure that you have chosen enough sources to address your hypothesis or thesis.*

Collect In this section, you will collect and record your information in an organized way. Make sure you record it in a way that will let you analyze it later. As you collect your sources, you should be deciding if the evidence is valid and reliable and which sources are most useful for your project.

- Label this section of your project *Collect.*
- *Collect your sources using a system or plan.* Take notes from your sources.
- *Be sure that you collect enough information to address your hypothesis or thesis.* Attach your source information (author, date of publication, and so on). Also attach the notes you took as you read your sources. (Do not attach the actual documents you find.)

   Tip: Now that you have researched the task and gathered data, think back to your initial prediction. Has your thinking changed? If so, record your new thinking and add your ideas to your *Hypothesize* section.

Interpretation   *This Section Due*:_____

After you gather information, you need to decide how reliable it is. Now is the time to start making some conclusions.

Analyze In this section, you will analyze your evidence by organizing your notes and ideas strategically to recognize patterns and relationships.

- Label this section of your project *Analyze.*
- Organize your notes by grouping information and identifying patterns. *Be sure that your methods will work well with the problem outlined in the task.*
- *You may use an analysis method you remember using or one you develop to complete this section.*
- *Check that your analysis helps you support or challenge your hypothesis or thesis.*

Evaluate In this section, you will use the information you organized during your analysis to identify trends, draw conclusions, and create arguments.

- Label this section of your project *Evaluate*.
- Identify trends, conclusions, and arguments from your analysis. These may be written in narrative, bullet, or other form.
- *Select findings that you think will help you complete the task.*
- *Put your findings together in a way that you think will address your hypothesis or thesis.*
- *Be sure that you have enough findings to support or challenge your hypothesis or thesis. Describe any changes in your thinking and your reasons for them.*

    Tip: Review your progress. How are you doing? Do you need to collect additional information?

Communication   *This Section Due:*_____

Your task is to write a policy paper on a natural disaster. Your paper will address the problem and make a recommendation for avoiding or lessening the impact on humans and the environment.

To communicate your conclusions clearly, you will first need to create a rough draft so that you can get feedback from others.

Monitor As you begin to work on your draft, look at the section called *Monitor* on the following page. There you will find directions on how to check your work and how to make your final product the best it can be.

Organize In this section, you will produce your first draft.

- Label this section of your project *Organize*.
- Produce a written draft that demonstrates a logical progression of ideas and supports your thesis or argument. Make sure an outside reader would be able to identify all the components of a draft: an introduction, supporting evidence, and a conclusion that summarizes the most important points.
- *Use a logical organizational structure to create your final work product. Make sure your work product is organized the same way throughout the product.*
- *As you create your final work product, use formats and conventions that fit with science.*
- Follow your teacher's directions to participate in a teacher-, peer-, or self-review process. Attach all your drafts and the feedback you receive.

Construct In this section, you will revise your draft for the intended audience and purpose.

- Label this section of your project *Construct*.
- Read the original task again to make sure you remember what you are supposed to produce.
- *Be sure that you use the results from Problem Formulation, Research, and Interpretation in your final product.*
- *Make sure that each of your drafts gets better with each version. Double-check that you have considered all the feedback you received.*
- Attach all drafts, clearly showing where you revised your work (based on teacher-, peer-, or self-review) between drafts.

Precision and Accuracy   *Final Product(s) Due:*_____

Part of making the best final product means taking the time to check your work. You should check your drafts at every step of the process, but now is your chance to really make your final work product the best it can be.

Monitor In this section, you will make and carry out a plan for editing your work.

- Label this section of your project *Monitor*.
- *Be sure that your work is precise and follows the rules and conventions for social studies.* Describe the methods (such as spell check, reading aloud, or asking a friend) you will use for checking your work as you write your drafts.
- *Properly record or document your references.*

Confirm In this section, you will edit and confirm all elements of your work.

- *Check for technical and grammatical accuracy.* Be sure that you have used language, terms, and formats appropriate for social studies.
- *Double check that you have followed all the task directions.*
- Attach your final draft. Follow all given instructions for deadlines, length, and formatting.

    Follow these steps to prepare your work for submission.

- Collect all of your work.
- Organize it in the order presented in the directions above (by key cognitive strategy).
- Review all of the sections of your ThinkReady Portfolio to be sure they are complete, legible, and your best work.
- Check that your name appears on the cover page *ONLY*. Remove your name from other sheets.

    Submit your work attached to the cover page.

Assessing Your Work   *This Section Due:*_____

Use the scoring guides to score your work and justify your score.

Key Cognitive Strategy	Component	Score	Reasons for Score
Problem Formulation	Hypothesize		
	Strategize		
Research	Identify		
	Collect		
Interpret	Analyze		
	Evaluate		
Communicate	Organize		
	Construct		
Precision/Accuracy	Monitor		
	Confirm		

INDEX